Understanding the Local Media

university college
for the creative arts
at canterbury, epsom, farnham
maidstone and rochester

Farnham, Falkner Road, Farnham, Surrey, GU9 7DS 01252 892709
Return on or before the last date stamped below. Fines will be charged on overdue books.

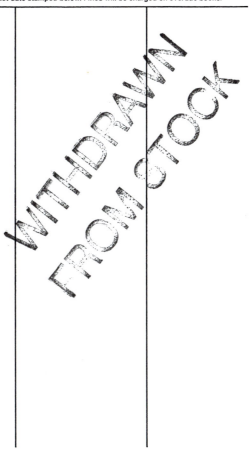

Understanding the Local Media

Meryl Aldridge

 Open University Press

Open University Press
McGraw-Hill Education
McGraw-Hill House
Shoppenhangers Road
Maidenhead
Berkshire
England
SL6 2QL

email: enquiries@openup.co.uk
world wide web: www.openup.co.uk

and Two Penn Plaza, New York, NY 1012–2289, USA

First published 2007

A catalogue record of this book is available from the British Library

ISBN-13: 978-0-33-522172-1 (pb) 978-0-33-522713-8 (hb)
ISBN-10: 0-33-522172-6 (pb) 0-33-522173-4 (hb)

Library of Congress Cataloging-in-Publication Data
CIP data has been applied for

Typeset by BookEns Ltd, Royston, Herts.
Printed and bound in Poland EU by OZGraf S.A.
www.polskabook.pl

The *McGraw·Hill* Companies

Contents

Introduction

Local media: popular, important – and ignored

Today holding an academic post in a UK university is little different from working for any other big employer – with one notable exception. In all disciplines everyone, whatever their seniority or experience, operates on a virtual global stage. Travelling to international conferences and national job mobility are the norm. Perhaps it is, therefore, not surprising that academics in general show little interest in local and regional newspapers and broadcasting, but it is much more surprising that the same is true of those whose central scholarly interest is the media. Yet the non-national press is a very large and exceptionally profitable industrial sector, consumed in one way or another by most members of the public. On television, regional bulletins are the most watched news genre, and local radio stations have a large following.

I first discovered the fascination of the news media as an undergraduate, when I edited the student newspaper. My first two jobs were in research on urban issues. The legacy of the latter as well as the former emerges more than once in this book, as do many other aspects of my life and career. That is one of the pleasures of writing books, as opposed to journal articles: the authorial voice can be used openly.

Early in my career I discovered that my preferred method of teaching and learning is to move from the practical to the theoretical. This and the familiar, but still durable, advice that one should 'write about what one knows', explains why the book is full of specific examples. My hope is that they will demonstrate the niceties of regulation and the imperatives of profit and loss in practice: how the media we consume come to be as they are. Being so specific of course has its price. Readers may inwardly exclaim that their local paper or their regional television news is not at all like that. In that case I hope that the outcome will be much more interest in and work on local media. They are important to us as citizens; there is so much to be explored; and the raw material is right in front of us.

The plan of the book

Globalization has become a daily reality for ordinary people, whether through the appearance and disappearance of employment opportunities, the goods on their supermarket shelf or their choice of holiday destination. Chapter 1 argues that, nevertheless, for most people, most of the time, their immediate locality is very important. Here social change and political decisions become real; it is in actual localities that people function as citizens. A local public sphere is therefore vital to democracy, however far short of the conditions for Habermas's 'ideal speech' it falls. From this follows the thread that runs through the rest of the book: to what extent can the local media in the contemporary UK contribute to this 'space'?

Chapter 2 explains the organizational and financial architecture of the regional press. Still profitable, still popular, how is the industry dealing with the proliferation of competing media platforms and convergence of technologies? The editorial strategies developed to accommodate these pressures in the context of wider social and economic change is considered in Chapter 3, which concludes with a case study of Birmingham and its newspapers. Faced with an increasing diversity, what techniques are used to 'imagine' the community? Does attempting to address everyone push human interest topics into the foreground at the expense of information and debate?

Chapter 4 reviews the rapidly changing regulatory framework for regional broadcasting. The British Broadcasting Corporation (BBC) is being cast as the main player, but it is questionable whether it can devote extensive additional resources to news-gathering, given that its status and funding is legitimated by its nationwide responsibilities. Regional news on television is very popular with audiences, but they are not wholly satisfied with it. Chapter 5 argues that current analogue television regions and a 'family audience' together produce an interpretive frame in which the affective and subjective is bound to edge out content useful to the public as citizens. Only the BBC provides an adequate local radio news service, but its potential is limited by the target audience. The nations of the UK, the subject of Chapter 6, vividly demonstrate that every aspect of media, ownership, regulation and content is highly politicized. A case study of S4C illustrates both the importance of, and difficulties in sustaining, public service broadcasting. Chapter 7 opens with a review of the vital place that local media still occupy in journalism's mythology. Many regional journalists take special pride in their work, despite deteriorated conditions, inadequate pay levels, and increasing concerns about whether the work-force, whether in print or broadcast, is properly diverse in all its meanings. Finally, Chapter 8 considers the future of both publicly funded and commercial regional media as new communications technologies drive potentially dramatic changes in audience behaviour and sources of revenue. It concludes that, if inclusive citizenship is to be sustained, blogs, citizen journalism and community media are, as yet, no substitute for conventional media forms.

Acknowledgements

A book that depends so much upon real examples could not have been written if relatives and friends had not been willing to help me collect the raw materials of newspapers and video recordings. My thanks go to Alan Cornell, Claire Horrocks, Mike Lachowicz and Roger Tanner. Academic colleagues were equally generous in supplying ideas, information and assistance, even when it was a 'cold call'. David Ayrton, Sue Bryman, Graham Crow, Christian Karner, Jeremy Lane, John Richardson, Tim Strangleman, James Thomas, Dave Ward, Debbie Wilson and Kevin Williams all contributed in various ways. Olwen Lachowicz assembled the database of women editors referred to in Chapter 7. The case study of Birmingham, the discussion of media in Northern Ireland, and the chapter on working as a journalist in regional media all draw heavily on interview data. I am particularly grateful to John Brewer, Steve Dyson, Mike Hughes, and my necessarily anonymous journalist informants in English regional daily and weekly papers, for taking time from very pressured working lives in order to talk to me.

Working with Chris Cudmore at Open University Press has been enjoyable at every stage. He has been encouraging, constructive, decisive and – not least in a tight writing schedule – swift to reply to questions.

One academic has managed to turn his sociological gaze very productively from the global to the local. Alan Aldridge applied, as he always has, just the mixture of interest in the topic, high standards of style and expression, and sympathetic but incisive criticism of structure and concepts that every author needs. This book is dedicated to him.

1 Why local media matter

Life is global; living is local

Media of mass communication are one of the main drivers of globalization and have become a key organizing factor in the everyday lives of people in the developed world. Yet mass media have existed for less than 150 years. Towards the end of the nineteenth century the combination of increasing literacy, advances in printing technology, and railway transport created the conditions for producing and distributing large numbers of newspapers and magazines designed for an audience of ordinary people, rather than only the wealthy, educated few. The UK's first 'popular' national daily newspaper, the *Daily Mail* was launched in 1896 (Engel 1996: pt 2) and *My Weekly*, the first magazine 'specifically for working class women' in 1910 (Braithwaite 1995: 26). Cinema films followed early in the twentieth century, and radio began to reach a mass public in the 1920s. Television technology existed from the 1930s but its development was interrupted by the Second World War of 1939–45. Although broadcasting resumed soon after the war, in the UK owning a television did not become commonplace until the mid-1950s.

Being a member of an audience is a shared experience with the potential, as Benedict Anderson ([1983] 1991) classically observed, to create 'an imagined community' even when, for instance, a newspaper is being consumed individually at a time of the reader's own choosing. Anderson's central thesis was that the search for a market under 'print capitalism' led to the standardization of language and enabled the 'mass simultaneous ceremonies' (Anderson [1983] 1991: 35) that helped to consolidate the modern nation state. Dayan and Katz (1992) have pursued this theme in the contemporary world, speaking of the 'high holy days of television'. These take a variety of forms. Every year the BBC televises the State Opening of Parliament, but how many people now watch this symbolically important assertion of national sovereignty? The BBC also televises the FA

(soccer) Cup Final to a rather larger audience, as does ITV1 (the main terrestrial commercial channel). This annual match is also seen to have
nation-affirming cultural significance. For this reason, like several other
major sporting events, it is 'listed', meaning that the exclusive rights cannot
be sold to subscription-only channels; it must be available for broadcast on
free-to-air channels. (For the current list, see DCMS 2005a.)

It is in the nature of rituals that they are planned, but television can
also invest the unplanned event with enduring iconic status, a key aspect
of the reflexiveness of contemporary 'promotional culture' (Wernick 1991)
understood by publicists, protesters and terrorists everywhere. The 'imagined community' for such events can transcend the national, as it also does
for seemingly less serious media content like television drama and comedy
series. Issues of ideology and morality are, of course, just as central to fictional media genres as they are to those positioned as factual, like news and
current affairs programming. *Desperate Housewives*, as well as being an
everyday tale of gender, marriage, family life and the problems of parent-
ing, is also about the grandest of Grand Narratives: the struggle between
good and evil. It is hardly surprising, then, that both public controversy
and academic research has tended to focus on, for instance, the domination
of media platforms and content by transnational corporations; the potential impact of images of Western world living standards and personal behaviour on audiences when programmes like *Desperate Housewives* are sold for
broadcast elsewhere; and the increased possibilities for the creation of
worldwide networks of like-minded people.

Fascination with this potential for mass media to create non-place communities dates back more than 40 years. For Marshall McLuhan (1962), as
a Canadian, the concept of the 'global village' had particular resonance: it
has been argued that Canada was made possible by communications media
(Vipond 1989). At that time, however, at a global level the 'village'
metaphor did not really work, because communication between most 'residents' was both expensive and difficult in practical terms. Moreover, as
Thompson (1995: 84) has pointed out, the characteristic of this first round
of mass-media development has been that the relationship between sender
and receiver is both a monologue and one-to-many. Whether the text that
is sent (for example, the radio programme or cinema film) has the same
meaning for every recipient is a highly contested matter, and audiences are
of course capable of debating the text among themselves and of rejecting it.
What they cannot do is change it. The exceptional case is the telephone,
which enables dialogue, but normally on a one-to-one basis.

Now those of us with access to the necessary knowledge and material
resources are in a fundamentally transformed situation: truly interactive
media have arrived. Many-to-many communication is now possible. Cheap
computing and the photocopier made publishing available to the lay

public, but distribution remained the problem to which the Internet is the solution. Even those for whom a constructing web site or (we)blog is beyond their capacity can address an audience using only an email distribution list and a digital camera – and the audience can reply.

Globalization has not, however, just brought the possibility of real-time social interaction without co-presence – in other words much more of a real 'global village'. Another dimension is transportation and thus 'increased international mobility of persons and capital and exchange of goods' (Marcuse 2002: 133). Regardless of age, many people on moderate incomes now regularly travel long distances for pleasure. Forty years ago, migrating to Australia to fill skills shortages, as many young Britons did on 'assisted passages' as '£10 poms', took six weeks by ship. As it now takes 21 hours by air, visiting the friends and family who migrated then has become relatively affordable and achievable. (Doing so will probably also illustrate Marcuse's point about exchange of goods as many of the clothes in your suitcase get much closer to their point of origin in east Asia.)

Commentators on globalization often point out that voluntary migration and transnational spheres of influence are hardly new, whether one is referring to those parts of the UK occupied by the Vikings, or those who travelled to spread and consolidate the message of their religion, or the Scottish Renaissance, or the customary 'Grand Tour' of Europe by members of England's monied classes. The obvious reply is that at least some of these experiences are no longer the preserve of an elite, even if they remain barred to most people in some countries and some people in every country. Taken together with the possibilities for 'many-to-many' communication discussed above we have a situation without historic precedent, which has naturally further reinforced the importance of 'the global' as a focus of political and academic attention.

For anyone involved in UK higher education, this preoccupation with the world beyond the local is anchored in daily experience: the gap year; the web-based materials; the transnational publishers; the growing proportion of students from other countries; the proliferation of international exchanges and conferences; and, driving much of this, the attempt to make the whole institution – or at least some departments – 'world class'. The academy and academics are forced not only to think global but act global too. But this is not true for most people, most of the time. Long-haul holidays are simply episodes. Commuting across borders for work may be easier, but is still commuting. Being constantly on the move without a single 'home' is still exceptional, the preserve of the very wealthy whose exceptionalism attracts disproportionate attention.

For the majority, then, life is local. Asserting this is, however, not at all the same as assuming that the self-contained community can exist in the contemporary UK. The search for the functioning 'community' was a core activity in British sociology as it expanded in the 1950s and 1960s, reflecting both the rapid social change of the immediate post-Second World War era and the historic links with social anthropology. (For a review of this tradition and its successors, see Crow 2002.) In a classic article, Margaret Stacey reviewed progress so far, observing presciently 'what system of social relations has any boundary except a global one?' (1969: 136). The core of her article is a set of 31 propositions extracted from the very rich literature which, Stacey intended, would enable a more theoretically clear-sighted approach to future locality based studies. Ironically the paper is now often, inaccurately, seen as the epitaph for a research tradition. Prefiguring our current preoccupation with the global, in the 1970s studies of locality moved to a higher level of generality, for instance how investment and disinvestment patterns under capitalism have produced the industrial ecology of the UK. (For a discussion of this 'turn' see Day and Murdoch 1993.) Stacey's central point still stands, however: that social institutions operate within localities and that in most cases there will be connections between them, although of course 'in any locality some of the social processes that we will want to consider will take us outside the locality' (1969: 145). Today one might argue that it is not so much connections between institutions as their lack that shapes people's lives and opportunities. For example, deciding to concentrate acute hospital services in order to maximize the efficient use of highly specialized units may leave small towns in the same region without their limited, but useful and well-loved general hospital. How serious this is for the population will depend upon their access to transport, another complex intersection of wider social processes and of policy decisions taken at a distance in time and space.

In the same way that it is important not to slip from locality to community, people's behaviour must not be confused with their sentiments. Because of the shift of scholarly perspective described above, much of the recent research on ordinary daily activities in ordinary places has been commissioned for commercial purposes. In a meta-analysis of official statistics and market research, the Future Foundation concluded that the mean maximum distance within which the routine activities of daily life take place is 14 miles (2000: 20). Average travel to work was 8.1 miles. A later market research report gave the average distance for grocery shopping as 3.8 miles – but 57 per cent of respondents shopped within two miles (Newspaper Society 2004: 21, 27). As the Future Foundation discussion points out (2000: 20) typical distances travelled vary with age, gender and income level. The 'territory' of older people, women and people in lower-income groups tends to be smaller.

The immediate locality is also the arena for many important social relationships. Using data from a study of contact with kin (Grundy et al. 1999), the Future Foundation reports that 'half of us live within half an hour's drive of the place where we spent most of our childhood' and provide their own average figure of 12.6 miles to respondents' mother's home. Fewer than 20 per cent of their respondents said that 'less than half' or 'hardly any' of their friends lived 'in the same area' (Future Foundation 2000: 20–1). According to the Newspaper Society survey (2004: 77–8) the mean distance travelled for all forms of leisure activity was under 12 miles, of which the most frequently named (by 72 per cent of respondents) was 'eating out' for which the average distance travelled was 7.4 miles. Asked about how far they would be willing to travel to work, 64 per cent said up to 20 miles, of whom two-thirds said no more than 10 miles.

Respondents to these surveys also demonstrated ties to their current home area in relation to their behaviour over time. Forty-eight per cent had lived in their present home for more than 10 years – and 62 per cent had previously lived within 5 miles. Twenty-three per cent had moved a mile or less (Newspaper Society 2004: 67).

The distinction between behaviour and sentiments is vital: it is possible to have a strong stake in a locality without any affective attachment to it or being part of a social network, however defined. 'Different social groups have different stakes in a place, and their interests vary from the more obviously material (which itself varies from the more straightfor-wardly "economic" to that of ontological security) to the more cultural and aesthetic' (Urry 1990: 189). Orientations may be entirely individualistic and instrumental: 'Home ownership is a crucial factor, giving homeowners a highly tangible economic stake in the well-being of their local area' (Future Foundation 2000: 18). Residents' responses to issues like hospital closure can be equally focused on their own needs or those of their immediate family, as with education. 'Schooling is crucial, and of ever-growing impor-tance in the sense that children are starting school earlier and leaving ever later' (Future Foundation 2000: 18). Hargreaves and Thomas's research illus-trates that much of people's desire for news of the locality is driven by these practical and material concerns. 'Housing is a problem for us. It is difficult to get a flat. We need to know what is going on in this area' (lower-income group man in a 16–24 age group from outer London); 'My girlfriend is about to have a baby, so I'm concerned about reports about the local hos-pital' (upper income group man in a 16–24 age group from another part of outer London); 'We need to know about crime – there's a lot of problems with drugs in this area' (lower-income group man over 45 years from Cardiff) (Hargreaves and Thomas 2002: 65).

All these studies of 'lifestyle' were commissioned by media organiza-tions. The Newspaper Society is the trade association and lobby group for regional and local newspapers in the UK, all of which depend upon selling various categories of advertising to survive, as we shall see in later chapters. Reasonably enough, their primary concern is patterns of present, and likely future patterns of consumption. For their practical purposes people are simply a bundle of spending choices. At an ideological level, too, the theme of choice and flexibility is prominent in a follow-on report by the Future Foundation (2003): the ideal consumer is flexible, not bogged down in habit and tradition; open to new experiences but not unpredictably volatile. People in the UK are, they assert in the 'Executive Summary', 'active creators of their own regions through the places, people and activities that they choose to engage with. The boundary of their "self-created region" corresponds with the shape of their regular lives – and it evolves in accordance with their changing circumstances and needs' (Future Foundation 2003: 7). Despite this emphasis on the pragmatism and rationality of social actors, however, much of the report is concerned with links between region and identity that go well beyond ways of spending money.

Locality, identity and attachment

Respondents in the *My UK* research were asked about their sense of attachment to a range of territories, all subjectively defined: the local neighbourhood; the city/town/village; the region (Future Foundation 2003: 11). Those expressing 'strong attachment' ranged from 26 per cent to 30 per cent, while those describing their attachment as 'moderate' ranged from 25 per cent to 27 per cent. Some respondents had strong feelings about more than one level of locality but 'the region had slightly less resonance in people's minds' (Future Foundation 2003: 11). Over half of respondents defined it entirely subjectively, in terms of the 'reach' of their regular activities, while 22 per cent replied that they did not have 'a strong sense of how far my region extends'. Only 15 per cent used 'the boundaries that have been set by government and local authorities' (Future Foundation 2003: 18) reflecting the complexity of UK administrative boundaries, particularly in England. Successive local government reorganizations have produced confusion. Moreover, there is no 'fit' between local government boundaries and those used by central government agencies or, for example, privatized utilities such as water and rail transport. Indeed, some of the respondents who referred to the externally defined region were complaining about it: 'We've been passed round from pillar to post. One year we're in Northamptonshire, next year we're in Cambridgeshire' (Future Foundation 2003: 16). Peterborough, the city in question, is a particularly vivid example of problems with recognized regional identity. Residents were able to receive television from three commercial television regions (Central, Anglia and Yorkshire) while their BBC local news was coming from Nottingham, 50 miles away. This is particularly significant as, when asked (from a preset list) which factors contribute to a region's identity, only regional industry, named by 69 per cent, rated higher than regional news-papers, television and radio. In many cases 'regional industry' means deeply rooted traditions in extractive industries (coal-mining or deep-sea fishing) or heavy manufacturing (for example, shipbuilding) or light manufacturing (building cars or making garments) and is now more a matter of collective memory than actuality. Since the late 1970s the restructuring of the UK economy in response to the economic manifestations of globalization has almost eradicated most of these.

Lack of clear, shared definitions does not, however, prevent people from being attached to their region of residence. Overall, 55 per cent of the Future Foundation's respondents said that they wanted to continue living in the same local area and 'a further 16 per cent say that they want to con-tinue living in the same region but in a different area' (Future Foundation 2003: 14). The wish to stay in the same area ranged from 73 per cent in the North East to 47 per cent in the West Midlands. Unsurprisingly, the desire to remain in the area increases with age, but it is not determined by being of local origin. 'Forty-eight per cent of those who had grown up elsewhere said that they wanted to remain in the area where they now lived, while a further 14 per cent said that they wanted to live in a different area within the same region' (Future Foundation 2003: 15).

Moving home to an area of choice is a freedom available only to those in possession of material and social capital. Poverty brings an attachment to the immediate locality which is not voluntary, even if it has its compen-sations. 'People in this area don't make a connection with the rest of Edinburgh . . . Most have no reason to go outside the area. They've no money to spend up the town' reported a community worker in Atkinson and Kintrea's study (2004: 442) of deprived areas of Edinburgh and Glasgow. Lack of local jobs and of the skills needed for jobs further afield meant that '"getting on" meant "getting out"' (Atkinson and Kintrea 2004: 445) but, given that the housing was rented from the local authority, this was not necessarily possible. And anyway 'people want to stay here as well, if you've been brought up here for example . . . people would probably tell you that [another deprived area in which the Housing Officer interviewee grew up is] a tip as well, but I quite like it you know. Just cos I'm used to it' (Atkinson and Kintrea 2004: 446).

When times are difficult, however, the locality can be the arena for multiple forms of 'getting by' based on long-standing social networks, as has been demonstrated in areas as diverse as the Isle of Sheppey, an isolated area of east Kent (Pahl 1984), and rural Wales: 'in the face of volatile com-modity markets and uncertain state support, farm families draw on the key resources of land and labour . . . Working patterns can be adapted to meet prevailing conditions (Day and Murdoch 1993: 107). Nor is this kind of locality based mutual aid limited to family networks. Harris's (1987) study,

Redundancy and Recession in South Wales, captures the impact of the radical reduction of UK steel-making capacity on the workforce of industrial south-west Wales. Steel and coal, with their associated service industries had been the twin pivots not only of the region's economy but of its distinctive cultural life since the Industrial Revolution. Writing of the mass job losses in the 1980s, Harris points out that this was only the latest in a long history of such events, notably in the recession of the 1930s when hardship was extreme and produced what he describes as a 'diaspora', even though the 'unwillingness of the Welsh to change the locality of their residence is proverbial' (1987: 13). Accordingly, at the time of his research in 1980, it 'had been assumed that a significant proportion would leave the area for work in more prosperous areas. In the event . . . [it] was under 6 per cent' (Harris 1987: 15). Later on in the study, however, this seeming irrationality and lack of enterprise is shown to have an entirely rational basis. While the redundant men were not formally employed, local contacts provide the vital means of supporting themselves and their family: informal, undeclared work. For this, discretion is vital. 'I only take work through people I know I can trust, tidy boys. You could cut their hands off and they would not tell . . .' (Harris 1987: 131). This male network of pubs and clubs also enabled redundant workers to find formal employment, although often it was dirty, unskilled work and for only short periods (Harris 1987: 132). For women, too, 'Entering paid work was found to be largely the result of exploiting informally acquired knowledge of suitable work opportunities' (Harris 1987: 139).

The disruption of employment patterns is not the only reason that practical, materially based and affective ties to a locality can intersect. Having the skills that enable geographic mobility can, in the context of reasonable prosperity, allow people to make choices based on kinship, friendship and more intangible beliefs about 'quality of life'. Devine et al.'s (2003) study of Manchester and the wider North West region of England specifically addresses the employment mobility of well-qualified and relatively young professional people. Their 'case study' approach (2003: 497) targeted business and financial services (for example, advertising and corporate finance), the quintessential 'leading-edge' sectors of the economy.

All 59 of their respondents were graduates. Six had never left the region, having been brought up in the North West, been to university and then found their first and any subsequent jobs there. 'None of these "immobile" young professionals envisaged moving in search of better career prospects in the future . . . the career advantages of London were considered "marginal" and especially when the close proximity of family and friends was taken into account' (Devine et al. 2003: 499). The same considerations applied to the 27 (the largest group) who had family ties to the region and had returned, after having been to university and/or taken a job elsewhere. Thirteen interviewees had come to the region to attend university and had stayed (ten cases) or returned after a spell working elsewhere (three cases). Devine and her colleagues conclude that 'quality of life' had been a major driver in their respondents' choice of living and working away from London. 'It was for this reason that so many of our young interviewees – rather to our surprise – did not live in rejuvenated Manchester and its trendy suburbs. Rather they lived in semi-rural and rural localities, close to family, friends, train stations and motorways' (Devine et al. 2003: 507).

The stake of these young professionals in their area of residence was presumably potentially the stronger for its being a matter of relatively free choice. It is clear from this study, however, that even for those who might be expected to be the most instrumental in their attachment to their locality, it can have a deeper, more central place in the sense of self. As both Crow (2002) and Day and Murdoch (1993) point out, many classic 'community studies' centred on the cleavages between long-standing residents and newcomers. Such distinctions persist, even in the face of economic restructuring and the almost compulsory viewing of alternative ways of life brought by mass media. Describing life in the Ithon Valley in mid-Wales, Day and Murdoch (1993: 100) write 'a native of Llanbadarn told that although he now lived in Llandewi, six miles from his birthplace, he did not "know" it well and would like to return to where he really belonged'. More recently still, Crow et al.'s (2001) work on the Isle of Wight found that respondents of all ages and backgrounds recognized the distinction between those who originated on the island and those who did not as a key organizing principle of daily life.

'If you come across caulkheads they'd soon tell you' according to a middle-aged male respondent (2001: 34) who, presumably, was an 'overner' that is, not from the island. 'Caulkhead' implies having only the wadding used to seal the gaps between ships' timbers between your ears; those who qualify tended to talk of themselves rather as 'real Islanders'. Crow et al. (2002) also illustrate how extensive local links can be – although this does not, of course, necessarily mean that such links are strong or even positive. Of their 40 respondents, when asked how many people in their street they could name, excluding relatives, 13 said between 11 and 20 and a further 13 said 21 to 50. The mean number of friends in the street was five, while the majority of respondents had at least one of their 'best friends' living in the same street. From the point of view of attachment to the area, it is unimportant whether the friendship or the proximity came first, nor does it matter if there is some kind of social 'network', that is, that to a greater or lesser extent any individual's contacts are known to each other. And while the Isle of Wight might be said to be an extreme case in terms of contemporary self-containedness, we have already seen the same patterns of proximity in the Future Foundation's national data.

There is little doubt that for many people, their stake in their area of residence is based not only on issues of convenience but goes well beyond behaviour into the realm of sentiments. We should not, therefore, be surprised that there is a well-established appetite for local news.

Local news: an unsatisfied hunger?

Hargreaves and Thomas describe local news as the 'missing link . . . we do not have sufficient research into changing consumption patterns of local news to draw firm conclusions' (2002: 62) so here, too, commercial market research is an essential source.

According to their trade organization (www.newspapersoc.org.uk > Facts and Figures > Regional Press Overview) in 2005 40 million adults in the UK read a regional or local newspaper. At 83.6 per cent this represented a greater proportion of the population than reads a national newspaper (69.6 per cent). Moreover the figure is rising. (It should be noted, however, that these data do not distinguish between paid-for and free newspapers.) On television, the regional news is 'appointment viewing', 'seen as a vital service and something in which all expressed a high degree of interest' by 82 per cent of respondents in research carried out for the Independent Television Commision (ITC) and Broadcasting Standards Council (BSC); 'most viewers felt that regional television helps keep regional identities alive' (Sancho 2002: 4–8). Aspiration and laying claim to being a good citizen may be at work here, however. Hargreaves and Thomas (2002: 33–4) reproduce audience research figures which show a steady downward trend in the viewing of regional bulletins in the period 1994 to 2002 for London, the Midlands, and the North West of England. Although the decline was as steady for the BBC as for Independent Television (ITV), the BBC had overtaken ITV and the gap was widening.

Asked about their main sources of local news, 45 per cent of Hargreaves and Thomas's informants (2002: 64) named television, 39 per cent newspapers and 12 per cent radio. Television was used most by those aged 16 to 34 years, while older people relied almost as much on local newspapers. This is potentially problematic because, as Hargreaves and Thomas point out:

> most television news does not even attempt to focus at the truly local scale: the geographical areas served are, for the most part, much too large for this to be possible . . . Newspapers, which can serve quite small localities by the use of multiple editions, have a tenuous hold on young readers and a very weak position among the black and Asian population.
>
> (Hargreaves and Thomas 2002: 64)

Media organizations are also concerned with the level of trust placed in them by the public. Research outcomes tend to be contradictory, no doubt reflecting differences in survey methodology, in turn related to the particular preoccupations of the sponsor. The *Press Gazette* of 24 September 2004 announced 'Regional press topples BBC in trust survey', based on research commissioned by the Newspaper Society. This survey showed that 20 per cent of respondents named 'any regional newspaper' as 'particularly trustworthy', ahead of the BBC at 19 per cent and national daily newspapers at 11 per cent. However, a YouGov poll published in the *Press Gazette* on 21 January 2005 reported the BBC (even when its channels were not aggregated) with the highest number of mentions when interviewees were asked to 'name a news provider they trust'. Regional newspapers were mentioned as often as ITV (national) news, which was less often than most of the national daily newspapers, but well above ITV regional news.

Whether or not the audience places a high degree of trust in them, two things are clear about the consumption of regional news media in the UK: they are very popular in terms of viewing and reading, yet consumers are not wholly content with their news sources. Sancho (2002: 5) reports: 'Those living in England were ... likely to think that their television stations were not local enough, particularly if they lived on the fringe of an ITV region.' This is confirmed by Hargreaves and Thomas (2002: 63) who found that while 83 per cent regarded themselves as 'well served' (by all media) for news about their locality, only 27 per cent regarded themselves as 'very well served' which compared badly with the 54 per cent who felt very well served about national news and 49 per cent about international news. Moreover 'the almost one in five who feel "not well served" with local news are concentrated among ethnic minorities'. Satisfaction also varied by region, with lowest satisfaction in London and highest in Northern Ireland and the North East. Both are 'areas with relatively strong newspapers and local radio' (Hargreaves and Thomas 2002: 64) and, as we have already seen, in the case of the North East, a strongly held sense of the region.

For Hargreaves and Thomas, that 'people feel least well-informed about their localities' compared with national and international matters (2002: 6) is sufficiently important to be one of three 'problem areas' highlighted in their summary and recommendations. Why are they so concerned? It is because this lack of relevant local information and debate 'could help explain why so many people find so much [in] politics meaningless or difficult to engage with because they are not able to judge its effects in their own communities' (Hargreaves and Thomas 2002: 6). Day and Murdoch ground this in the daily life of rural Wales:

> the people of the Ithon Valley must respond to the fundamental pressures bearing on them from beyond the immediate locality . . .

apart from immigration, and its impact on housing, perhaps the most important influences derive from the various forms of state intervention ... from the subsidies and grants on which local farmers depend so heavily, through the employment creating and concentrating activities of rural development agencies to the drive for the centralization and 'cost-effectiveness' in the supply of services.

(Day and Murdoch 1993: 107)

To which of course can be added public sector policies on education or transport links, those of wholly or partly private sector-supplied services such as post offices, banks, shops, access to broadband and many others. How these are determined and their cumulative impact on localities and their residents is constitutive of politics and demands 'space' in civil society for informed debate.

Democracy, debate and the public sphere

Providing public information and an arena for its discussion is not simply something that *involves* news media; it is what they *are*. 'People must have access to reliable reports, portrayals, analyses, discussions, debates and so forth about current affairs' (Dahlgren 2000: 321). The quality of that information and its accessibility are therefore fundamentally political issues. Anthony Sampson's (1996) polemic 'The crisis at the heart of our media' is often referred to as initiating a debate about the 'tabloidization' of the UK news media, but it was not simply a diatribe about too much news of C-list celebrities or the proliferation of self-absorbed opinion columns. Sampson was concerned with what he saw as the 'vacating' of the 'high ground of serious reporting, investigating and foreign coverage . . . The world is disappearing out of sight' (Sampson 1996: 45).

Although some have dismissed this type of lament as both elitist and empirically inaccurate (for summaries and comment see McNair 2000; Aldridge 2001a), fierce controversy continues. Within academic media studies a number of research studies, including McLachlan and Golding (1998), Barnett et al. (2000) and Hargreaves and Thomas (2002), have debated the relationship between the quality of news and the style of its presentation. For instance that 'tabloid' has much deeper cultural resonance than simply being a size of paper was proved yet again by reaction to *The Times*'s move to what it preferred to call 'compact' format. Adopting tabloid size was seen as symbolizing abandonment of its long-standing claim to be the UK's national 'newspaper of record'. Meanwhile *The Guardian*, uniquely in the UK so far, was adopting the Berliner size familiar in mainland Europe, thus signalling the paper's self-positioning as modern and internationalist.

Hargreaves and Thomas's research, discussed earlier in the chapter, vividly demonstrates not only the perceived importance of the issue but its complex interconnections with core questions of media policy. Like Sancho's (2002) report, it was commissioned by the ITC as it tried to define (and defend) to what extent commercial television should have 'public service broadcasting' responsibilities. As we shall see in later chapters, this frustratingly fugitive concept is highly politically charged. Essentially it means forcing for-profit media businesses to undertake potentially unprofitable activities, crucially the provision of a minimum quantity and quality of news, precisely because effective democracy demands good quality public information. But being informed, or even consulted, is not sufficient: 'Participatory democracy requires a citizenry that is both informed and has a continuing opportunity *to be heard* in the market place of ideas' (Melody 1996: 18; emphasis added). Accordingly 'a critical feature of movements toward democracy has been the creation of a "public sphere" meaning all the places and forums where issues of importance to a political community are debated and discussed' (Herman and McChesney 1997: 3).

Jürgen Habermas's *The Structural Transformation of the Public Sphere*, first published in 1962, was not translated into English until 1989. Habermas's central concern was, and is, 'radical democracy', that matters of importance to citizens should be decided by the citizens themselves under conditions where all have the same right to speak and be heard. These conditions of 'emancipation', he had concluded, were no longer likely to come about by a class-based revolution but through the impetus to communicate and to be autonomous shared by all humanity. In his later work, (principally *The Theory of Communicative Action* ([1981] 1986; [1981] 1987), Habermas has become more concerned with trying to define the conditions necessary for arguments to be truly rational, those of 'ideal speech'. For example, what are the boundaries of legitimate claims to expertise? Recent commentators have tended to reify this change of emphasis as Habermas's 'linguistic turn' but there is no real discontinuity with his earlier focus on the kind of social and institutional arrangements necessary for 'rational critical debate'.

As is now well known, in *The Structural Transformation of the Public Sphere*, Habermas argued that the specific historic circumstances of early eighteenth-century Britain produced social spaces in which an independent bourgeois public opinion could form and challenge the established structures and privileges of the state – then only partially separate from the royal court – and the church. Given the material conditions of the time, these 'spaces' were real locales: coffee houses, salons and face-to-face debating societies. There is no doubt that Habermas saw these concrete but transitory circumstances as simply a useful approximation of the 'social imaginary' of the public sphere (McLaughlin 2004: 160) but the very specificity of his worked example has, inevitably, provided a multiplicity of lines of criticism. Historians have argued that he ignored the extent and effectiveness of working-class movements, while feminists (notably Fraser 1992) have challenged him at several levels. First, that most of the participants in these arenas were male because, second, the 'public opinion' being formed by reasoned argument was not 'public' in the sense of pertaining to 'the public', but 'public' as opposed to the 'private' or domestic world, within which judgements based on the emotions should be confined. The rights of self-determination being sought did not extend to women or children. (If they had, the laws on, for example, marriage and divorce would have been under challenge.) Finally, many feminists have argued that 'reason' is socially constructed as a binary relationship with 'emotion', thus reflexively defining women as incapable of rational argument, a half-hidden motif in the tabloidization debate (Aldridge 2001a). Latterly, much of the debate on the public sphere, and of Habermas's response to his critics (see, for example, Habermas 1992), has centred on there being not one, but a multiplicity of public spheres – and that it is precisely the contest between them that has the potential to generate as authentic a 'public opinion' as is possible in large-scale society.

There is, however, one framing assumption which has, until recently, been shared by all scholars debating the principles and practices of the public sphere: that the matters under discussion have axiomatically concerned national culture, institutions and governance, because durable civil rights must be secured under the law. As Dahlgren (2000: 324) puts it: 'Historically, modern democracy evolved with the formation of the nation-state, and the concept of "citizen" was firmly anchored in this entity . . . Despite the march of globalization, the power of nationalism in the modern world scarcely needs reiteration.' Those questioning this level of analysis argue that, rather, globalization is a challenge to the rights of ordinary people that should be met by the transnational 'publics' that modern communications have made possible. Curran (2002: 233–4), for example, asserts that 'liberal thought about the democratic role of the media has been rejuvenated' by Habermas, and he goes on to give an approving summary of his more recent thinking on the public sphere: 'Yet despite its manifest improvements, this version still offers a largely nation-centred understanding of democracy which ignores the impact of globalization.' Similarly, McLaughlin describes *The Structural Transformation of the Public Sphere* as 'this groundbreaking contribution to democratic political theory' and vigorously refutes the idea that 'as some scholars would have it . . . the very notion of a public sphere is hopelessly old-fashioned in a context where the Internet has become the exemplar of public space . . . public sphere theory is capable of reasserting its relevance, but only if it ceases to ignore the impact of globalization processes' (McLaughlin 2004: 157) as a prelude to arguing for the importance of transnational feminist networks.

Few in the 'cottage industry' of 'problematizing the public sphere' (McLaughlin 2004: 162–3) appear to have paid sustained attention to publics operating at the sub-national level. In *Between Facts and Norms* Habermas ([1992] 1996) emphasizes organized groups, rather than individuals, as the drivers of effective public debate while Keane (1998, cited in McGuigan 2005) speaks in general terms of 'micro-public spheres'. However, as McLaughlin (2004: 160) sharply points out, there is a tendency for public sphere theorists to 'speak of socially situated agents without carefully describing their social situations'. One of these social situations is locality.

Many of the voluntary groupings so central to grass-roots democracy are organized on a geographic basis. For example the National Federation of Women's Institutes exists 'to educate women to enable them to provide an effective role in the community'. The federation campaigns vigorously and effectively on a national level and about global issues: in late 2005 one of its projects was joining with 18 other organizations to 'Stop Climate Chaos'(www.womens-institute.co.uk/climate.shtml). At the same time, in Nottinghamshire there were 129 WIs with 4000 members 'located in the large number of . . . farming and former colliery villages throughout the county. The character of these communities is as diverse as the members of our WIs' (www.womens-institute.org.uk/notts/). These individual institutes also work at the local level, with a range of perspectives and priorities related to the very different social fabrics which their contrasting social and industrial history have produced.

The National Federation of Women's Institutes was founded in 1915. It hardly needs saying that more transient groups are often formed around locality based issues, particularly aspects of the environment – 'no' to the proposed waste disposal plant at Newhaven, East Sussex; 'no' to more house-building on the River Trent floodplain – or are formed in response to the local impact of national policies, themselves related to global shifts: 'no' to refugees at our disused military site, RAF Newton or, conversely, coalitions of secular and religious organizations formed to support refugees.

Habermas himself provides an implicit reference to the potential importance of locality, writing, in *Between Facts and Norms*, of 'the public sphere as a communication structure rooted in the lifeworld through the associational network of civil society' ([1992]1996: 359). He amplifies the point thus:

> The political public sphere can fulfill its function of perceiving and thematizing encompassing social problems only insofar as it develops out of the communication taking place among *those who are*

potentially affected. It is carried by a public recruited from the entire citizenry. But in the diverse voices of this public, one hears the echo of private experiences that are caused throughout society by the externalities (and internal disturbances) of various functional systems . . . Systemic deficiencies are experienced in the context of individual life histories; such burdens accumulate in the lifeworld. The latter has the appropriate antennae, for in its horizon are inter-meshed the private histories of the 'clients' of functional systems that might be failing in their delivery of services . . . The communication channels of the public sphere are linked to private spheres – to the thick networks of interaction found in families and circles of friends as well as to the looser contacts with neighbours, work colleagues, acquaintances and so on . . .

(Habermas [1992]1996: 365–6; original emphasis)

Here Habermas is drawing on the distinction he makes in *The Theory of Communicative Action Vol. 2* ([1981] 1987) between 'system' and 'lifeworld'. This is deployed very effectively by Friedland in his argument that 'a strong version of democracy that is deliberative and participatory' (2001: 359) must start at the community level and that, in contemporary society, this requires effective means of communication. For Friedland, simply uncovering the existence of social networks is not enough:

personal communities, however important for individuals, do not, per se, sustain the kinds of social relations necessary to support the common endeavors traditionally associated with community: the maintenance of public and civic life, strong forms of association, and the trust and reciprocity that make solidarity possible.

(Friedland 2001: 366)

To bring about change at the system level (for example, the economy and the polity itself) people need to respond collectively via communicative action. This, by definition, takes place in the lifeworld where culture, society and personality combine so that 'social life as a whole is reproduced and from which new knowledge, identities and solidarities emerge' (Friedland 2001: 370). In Habermas's terms it is communities in a concrete and everyday sense which lie at the 'seam' of system and lifeworld because 'when system effects reach downwards into local communities, the seam between system [and] lifeworld becomes visible, and *this level of the system becomes a structure that is capable of being thematized and acted on*' (Friedland 2001: 374; emphasis added).

We have already seen how important locality remains to people's sense of identity and to their day-to-day opportunities and sense of well-being.

When grand global changes cascade down, the impact is in real places and, as we have also seen, the interaction between these processes produces outcomes which, if not wholly unique to particular localities, are extremely diverse. Fighting the proposal for a refuse incinerator at Newhaven may be helped considerably by contact with similar groups elsewhere, but in the final analysis their circumstances cannot be identical. In short, local issues need a local public sphere for which, today, local communications media are essential.

Before moving on to considering what in the UK we mean by 'local communications media' it is important to remind ourselves that getting caught up in the public sphere 'cottage industry', as McLaughlin has so nicely put it, can result in setting the bar too high for any media organization, whether for-profit or publicly funded – or even for most of our communicative action as citizens – to meet the performance standard. In an early and still influential commentary on the *Structural Transformation of the Public Sphere*, Garnham ([1986] 1990: 109) says: 'the concept of the public sphere and the principles it embodies represent an Ideal Type against which we can judge existing social arrangements, an which we can attempt to embody in concrete institutions in the light of the reigning historical circumstances'.

The ecology of UK news media

Communications media are so intermeshed with globalization that it is easy to forget that they are highly culturally specific in the way that they are produced and consumed. How the news media industry is organized, how it is regulated and how the different media address their audience cannot be explained simply by the combination of today's technology, the current state of the economy and whether focus group research seems to indicate that newscasters are more credible if they dress formally. Geography and history are also central to the 'ecology' of news media, both when comparing countries and in understanding how media within a country position themselves in relation to one another. What long-standing UK residents take for granted may be the exception.

A vivid example of this 'exceptionalism' is the national newspaper market. Ten newspapers, all but the *Financial Times* with Sunday sister papers, are distributed throughout Great Britain and Northern Ireland. There are papers for upper-, middle- and lower-income groups; papers that have long-standing political allegiance or are famous for the perceived impact of changes in their allegiance; papers addressed particularly to women or men; profitable papers and papers that seem to defy the laws of economics and capitalism. Despite a steady decline in newspaper sales that goes back decades, the British are still among the heaviest consumers of newspapers in the world. Would one not expect the same to be true of the French, whose passion for literature and for political argument is part of their national self-identity? In fact the French are notoriously reluctant readers of newspapers (Charon 2003: 97–104). *Le Monde*, the biggest selling of the 13 distributed nationally has roughly one tenth of the sales of *The Sun* of London. (For France see www.ojd.com.fr; for the UK see monthly figures published in *Press Gazette* hard copy version.) Several of the French papers are very specialized in that they, for example, cover only sport or are affiliated to a political party. Only one of the non-specialist titles (*le Parisien/Audjourd'hui en France*) is addressed to a socially diverse audience; the rest essentially represent the economic, political and cultural elite talking to itself. In France the newspapers that most people read are regional, like *Ouest France*, the biggest selling, or *La Voix du Nord*. In 2004–05 the latter declared average daily sales of 303,621 copies. One September 2005 St Omer edition, for example, consisted of 28 pages, of which two were world news, one was national (that is, French) news, four national and international sport, 13 news of the immediate locality, including sport, and the rest listings, advertisements and so on. The news of the locality was organized by community, many of them villages, and in this Tuesday edition the community news was dominated by weddings from the previous weekend – with pictures. In other words, the newspapers which most French people read are what a UK resident would describe as 'local' papers. This is because of the dominance of the *département* or region in French political, administrative and cultural life – not least gastronomy. In turn this relates to the governance of a very large country with a relatively small and dispersed population, until recently much of it rural. By contrast the UK is small, with a relatively large population which has been predominately urban-dwelling since the mid-1800s, all of which provided a national mass market for newspapers once the technology to produce and distribute them became available.

The same dominance of regional newspapers over national exists in North America, for a similar complex of reasons. Canada is a vast country with, according to the 2001 Census (www.12.statcan.ca/english/census01), a population of 30.08 million people. Most of them live within 125 miles (200 km) of the border with the USA, particularly in the Quebec City/Montreal/Toronto triangle on the eastern seaboard, and along to the 49th parallel. Distributing a truly national daily press to such a population was impossible before the development of the modem. Conrad Black's launch of The *National Post* in 1998 was underpinned by his acquiring a chain of provincial papers, transmitting copy electronically from Toronto for printing locally, and then using their local distribution networks (Aldridge 2001b). Until Black's very expensive and only partly successful venture the nearest to a 'national' newspaper in Canada was the Toronto-based anglophone *Globe and Mail*. (Quebec has its own set of francophone papers addressed to different market sectors but these are necessarily regional.) Canadians therefore had to rely on their regional papers carrying national and international news as well as news of more local origin or relevance. Conversely the *Globe and Mail* has always contained news of the Toronto region in a style much more reminiscent of the way that *The Birmingham Post* includes coverage of Birmingham business and Birmingham people than the UK national dailies' relationship with London.

Another illustration of the cultural specificity of news media is the media category of serious weekly news magazines in both France and North America: for example *l'Express* and *le Nouvel Observateur* in France; *Time* and *Newsweek* in the USA; and *McLean's* in Canada. These occupy the 'space' left vacant by a relatively underdeveloped national press. Not only is there no current equivalent in the UK but there never has been. The often quoted *Picture Post* and similar publications were indeed picture-led; titles such as *New Statesman* and *The Spectator* in all their incarnations are part of a comment and opinion-led genre.

Being a big country also has an impact on the structure of radio and television news. Canada has five time zones; the USA has four. Despite this, the importance of communications for Canadian nation-building led to the establishment of a strongly regulated and partly publicly funded broadcasting system (Ferguson 1994). Alongside this determined effort to create the 'imaginary community', however, a much more dispersed television and radio system has developed, as it has to an even greater extent in the market-led US broadcasting system.

By contrast, in the UK, on top of the geography and demography that have produced a genuinely national press was superimposed the political circumstances in the period between 1920 and 1950 when first radio and then television became publicly available. The BBC was initially founded to meet the needs of early radio manufacturers. That 'content is king' is not a twenty-first century discovery. John (later Lord) Reith, the first Director General, was the quintessential representative of an era when the paternal imposition of cultural values passed without question. The BBC became a publicly funded and highly centralized corporation administered very much in the style of the civil service (or the empire) rather than a for-profit enterprise. When television was developing in the late 1940s and 1950s this mode of operation came even more naturally. Not only had wartime conditions produced cross-party coalition politics, but the post-Second World War Labour government was committed to social and economic planning, in the interests of socialist redistribution but also necessarily to deal with the severe shortages of everything from coal to food to furniture that lasted until the early 1950s. Regulated and centralized news media were, one might say, exceptionally unexceptionable.

Commercially funded television was established in the UK in the mid-1950s, licensed on a basis of regional franchises. As we have already seen, only some of these regions related to any lived reality for their populations and, as time has gone on, their significance in terms of locally produced output or content with specific regional relevance has been steadily eroded. Whether the vestigial regional responsibilities still imposed by the Office of Communications (Ofcom) add up to a worthwhile regional news service on either commercial radio or television – let alone being a potential contribution to a vibrant local public sphere – will be a central issue in Chapter 4.

Much of the discussion so far has been about the complex interdependence of new communications technology and globalization. Paradoxically, digitalization is now providing the basis for more localized news output. One manifestation of this is the proliferation of locally badged free morning papers, for example the *Metro* franchise. These, however, are essentially the exploitation of the content already generated for both the regional and national papers belonging to the conglomerate that holds the franchise. (In Nottingham, for instance, this is Daily Mail and General Trust (DMGT) who own both the Nottingham *Evening Post* and the national *Daily Mail* and *Mail on Sunday*.) Truly 'new' news and, potentially, news framed around the scales of locality that have meaning for the audience is in prospect from at least three different directions. More for-profit and not-for-profit radio licences are being granted – although of course many of the stations will not be broadcasting any news. 'Community television' is beginning to be established, with the potential for local output produced by local people. Most significantly, the BBC is likely to become a more dominant provider of local news. Already its Internet-based 'Where I Live' regional news is organized by county in England, and several sub-regions in Scotland and Wales; 'ultra-local' television regions enabled by digital broadcasting have also been piloted. Both are driven by the BBC's publicly funded public service broadcasting responsibilities; both developments are alarming owners of local and regional newspapers, who fear that their audience will now get all their news electronically – much of it on-demand, 24 hours a day – and buy or sell through Internet sites too.

'Ecology' is a powerful metaphor for the relationships between media. As the account so far has shown, how a particular medium has developed in a particular country depends not only on the terrain, the technology, the size and distribution of the audience, and the political and cultural environment but its position in relation to other media. So far, however, little has been said about content – why all these factors produce some metaphoric 'plants' rather than others. To take only one example: it is often said media are full of bad news. Is this true of a typical local weekly paper in the UK, or of the early evening regional news on ITV? If not, surely it cannot be that life is going on in two existential dimensions? What factors explain this difference? This will be the central theme of subsequent chapters, but with explanation will come critique. If we value democracy, news must be more than a list of events enlivened by gossip, however interactive. Can the contemporary ecology of UK local news provide anything that might justifiably be said to be a local public sphere?

2 Regional and local newspapers: just another retailer?

What are 'regional and local newspapers'?

According to their trade association, the Newspaper Society, the regional press is 'the backbone of the British media' and 'the largest print advertising medium in the UK'. In 2005 '83.6 per cent of British adults read a regional newspaper compared with 69.6 per cent reading a national newspaper'. A large claim for a large market: in August 2006 there were 1301 newspapers included in the Society's database. (See www.newspapersoc.org.uk for up-to-date figures on this and many other aspects of the industry.)

This often overlooked media sector is not only large, but also complex. Titles can be categorized along **four dimensions**: whether they are paid for or free; their cycle of publication; the geographic base of their audience; and how they are distributed.

Paid for or free?

Of the total above, 631 titles were **paid for** by readers, while 670 were **free**. The Newspaper Society readership figures quoted do not fully distinguish between the two categories. 'Free newspaper' has been almost a term of abuse, synonymous with such limited news content and lack of editorial independence from advertisers as to make the term 'newspaper' contestable. Since the late 1990s, however, this category has suddenly become so much more layered and controversial that it will be the subject of separate discussion later in the chapter.

When is the paper published?

In terms of **frequency of publication**, 1191 titles were **weekly**, including 22 **Sunday** papers, and 110 **daily**. Like so much else about this volatile sector, the customary distinction between **morning** and **evening** papers is rapidly breaking down as most 'evening' papers become better described as mid-morning to mid-afternoon papers and some have repositioned themselves as morning titles. Moreover Tindle Newspapers runs a series of **monthly** publications with a 'diary' theme which do not figure in the Newspaper Society statistics.

What is meant by 'regional' and 'local' newspapers?

The Newspaper Society refers to its domain as the 'regional' press but, as noted in Chapter 1, the UK is notable for lacking a regional level of government. Nineteen newspapers might be said to be '**regional**' in the everyday sense, all of them mornings. They fall into two subsets. First, those that address all or part of the constituent **nations** of the UK. The Cardiff-based *Western Mail*, for example, promotes itself as the 'national newspaper of Wales' but has long been criticized in north Wales as biased to the south, economically, politically and culturally. The market is more complicated in Scotland, where titles like *The Scotsman* (Edinburgh) are classified as national papers but are challenged not only by powerful 'regional' titles (for instance, *The Press and Journal*, Aberdeen) but Scottish editions of the London-based national press. In Northern Ireland there is an unusually large number of titles in relation to the size of the population because of the deep-seated cleavages along political and religious lines. These papers for the nations will be discussed in more detail in Chapter 6.

Second, there is a small group of **paid-for morning** newspapers targeted at **English regions** or very large cities: for example *The Northern Echo* (Darlington); *The Birmingham Post*; the *Western Morning News* (Plymouth) and the *Eastern Daily Press* (Norwich). Why do some regions continue to support a morning title in head-on competition with the national press while they have disappeared elsewhere? The common factor seems to be an unusual level of self-containment either in terms of regional identity (as in Darlington), sometimes bolstered by geography (Norwich) or, historically at least, a densely interdependent local economy (Birmingham).

The particularities of the **London** newspaper landscape will be discussed in Chapter 3.

Daily **evening** papers are nearly all **city**-based, often with multiple editions covering the surrounding area. Thus the Nottingham *Evening Post* covers much of Nottinghamshire. **Weekly** papers are usually **small town**-based, for instance the Nottinghamshire *Mansfield Chad* and *Newark Advertiser*, or the *Kent Messenger*, based in Maidstone. While closest to the everyday term '**local** paper' many of these, too, have several locality based editions and a wider 'reach' than their title implies.

For simplicity's sake this and the remaining chapters on the press will use the term 'regional' to refer to other than the London-based 'national press', but readers should keep in mind their range, from the *Liverpool Echo* (average daily sale 117,976 for the first half of 2006) to papers like the

Kincardineshire Observer (1113 weekly for the same period). It should also be noted that the words 'free' or 'advertiser' in titles are often of very long standing and do not indicate a no-cost-to-the-reader paper.

How does the paper reach the readers?

When regional papers were all paid-fors, getting the paper to the customer was mostly by one of two means: an arrangement for **home delivery**, or **purchase** from a shop or street seller, either on a regular or casual basis. **Postal subscription** is still offered by some papers. As we shall see later in the chapter, the novel Big Idea behind free newspapers was that they would be **delivered unsolicited** to every household in an area. More recent free papers, like the *Metro* series and the 'Lite' versions of the London *Evening Standard* and *Manchester Evening News* are usually distributed by a combination of **on-street agents** and dump bins for the public to **pick them up**. Some free papers, for example the highly successful *Kent on Sunday*, can only be collected in this way, with bins in non-traditional venues like garden centres as well as (surprisingly) alongside paid-fors in some newsagents. (There is also an industry category of 'pick ups', meaning advertising-only publications with no editorial content. From the legislative point of view these are not 'newspapers' – see Department of Trade and Industry 2004: para. 3.11.)

Regulating the regional press

Whether paid for or free, daily or weekly, regional newspapers are regulated by the same industry-funded voluntary scheme as national newspapers and other printed media in the UK: the Press Complaints Commission (PCC) (www.pcc.org.uk). The Commission was set up in 1991 as a direct consequence of public and political disgust at several high-profile invasions of privacy involving, for example, well-liked celebrities who were seriously ill. (For a fuller account see Aldridge 2004; Frost 2006; Pinker 2006; and www.pcc.org.uk, which also provides up-to-date details of its structure, powers and procedures, and an archive of complaints and their outcome.)

The regulatory regime is based on a code of practice (www.pcc.org.uk > Code of Practice), which is the responsibility of the Code Committee, consisting of (at late 2006) 14 senior figures involved in the management and editing of print media (see www.pcc.org.uk > Who's Who). The PCC makes much of the fact that it is, compared with attempts to gain redress through the courts, 'free, quick and easy' (www.pcc.org.uk > About the PCC). In part this very 'light touch' is a consequence of its lack of power to impose financial sanctions on offending publications. The most severe penalty is to publish the PCC's adjudication 'with due prominence'. In practice few complaints get to that stage: most of those that fall within the Commission's remit are resolved by conciliation resulting in 'an informal apology, published letter or voluntary correction' (Pinker 2006: 119). Only the most serious or those where editors are convinced of their position go to formal adjudication. The PCC has many critics (see, for example, Culture, Media and Sport Committee 2003) who claim, for instance, that it relies too much on newspaper industry appeasement and schmoozing. As a result it is not as feared by media organizations as it should be.

According to the Commission's *Annual Report* for 2004 (www.pcc.org.uk > Annual Reports) 'the majority of the Commission's workload was not devoted to national papers (either broadsheet or tabloid): 49% of its investigated complaints related to . . . regional titles, compared to 44% which related to nationals'. As Frost says (2006: 272) 'a key element in the continuing popularity of local papers is their ability to record and celebrate community life'. Inevitably, he goes on, many of the complaints against them are triggered by the 'age-old concerns' of birth, marriage and death. Thus the number of complaints relating to children and innocent relatives, and to intrusion in general, is *proportionately* greater than it is for national titles, while complaints about harassment and misrepresentation do not figure at all (Frost 2006: 271).

What the PCC fails to point out is that the 44 per cent figure relates to only 20 national weekday and Sunday titles, while there are 1301 regional newspapers (www.newspapersoc.org.uk > Facts and Figures > Regional Press Structure) – 65 times as many. This seemingly greater virtue on the part of editors in the regions and their staff is partly driven by commercial realism: when you are so close to your audience giving offence loses sales. Beyond this, though, as we shall see in Chapter 7, the relationship with readers is a major satisfaction of the job for local journalists. The real regulator of the regional press is the public.

The driving logic of advertising

It is a contemporary truism that more media formats means more competition for the audience and a perpetual search for additional forms of revenue. The pressures on regional newspapers are particularly intense. Like all newspaper markets, it is 'mature' – a euphemism for shrinking – while news, the defining product, is ephemeral. Unlike, say, cinema film, there is no profitable after-life on video, DVD (digital versatile disc) or television. As a result, the principal sources of revenue remain direct payment by consumers (much of which is on the unpredictable basis of daily decisions, not even monthly subscription) and the sale of advertising.

Regional newspapers do, however, retain one key advantage when promoting themselves to would-be advertisers: the audience is defined on the basis of the locality. As we saw in Chapter 1, most everyday consumption takes place within a relatively small area and long-distance commuting is unusual outside London and the largest metropolitan areas. Encroachments from the Internet (about which more later) have led to the Newspaper Society quietly shelving its long-standing claim to have the monopoly of local information, but newspapers are still the usual outlet for recruiting from local labour markets, and for advertising local services and products. This is terrain on which neither local radio nor television have ever seriously competed: 'regional newspaper groups . . . make 80 per cent of their revenue from advertising, of which two-thirds is classified' (*The Guardian* 3 October 2005). The **classified** advertisements are those sections listing, for example, jobs, housing for sale and rent, cars, leisure and entertainment, statutory notices (for instance, of planning applications) and, not least, BMD – births, marriages and deaths. Many city daily papers have specialized supplements, according to the day of the week. **Display** advertising describes those that appear on the news pages or 'run of paper'. Typical examples of the latter in a September 2005 edition of the Nottingham *Evening Post* were a local car dealer advertising a new model and a national fashion retailer announcing a new branch in the city.

Whatever the precise format or placing of the advertisement, the cost will be based on a combination of its size and prominence and the number of people who will potentially see it. Sections of the population which typically have more disposable income (that is, some combination of higher earnings and fewer fixed commitments like a mortgage and fuel bills) are particularly attractive to advertisers. Consequently the Joint Industry Committee for Regional Press Research (JICREG) data, reproduced by the Newspaper Society to woo advertisers, include information on income group and age. What is of interest to advertisers is **readership**, but this is very hard to track, so the basis of advertising rates is either **sales** or, in the case of free papers, the **number distributed** either to households or individuals. Clearly these numbers are crucial, so various forms of **audit** have been established. Free weekly papers, like the Nottingham *Recorder* series, often publish their VFD (Verified Free Distribution) figures on the front page. Paid-for papers tend to be more coy about their 'ABCs' (Audit Bureau of Circulation) returns because for most papers, most of the time, they show a decline.

Just how critical these figures are was demonstrated by a Newspaper Society news release in September 2005, announcing that 'The regional press has taken another step forward in increasing the transparency and comparability of sales figures' (Newspaper Society 2005b). Why was this necessary, given that these figures are produced by independent audit organizations? Behind it lay the saga – in which the national press was equally implicated – of 'bulk sales'. These are copies sold, in bulk and at a very nominal price to, for example, train operators to give to passengers. While one goal was raising the profile of the paper, the real motive has been to offset declining sales. Advertisers set greater store by 'active purchase', presumably because it implies that the paper will be read more thoroughly and with closer attention. At least some of the mid-2000s' decline in newspaper sales figures has been caused by an industry-wide agreement to distinguish between full-price sales and others – including schemes like discounts to students.

Desperate measures in the viciously competitive newspaper market-place have not been limited to well-understood and formerly tolerated devices like bulks, discounting, and including various 'special editions' in sales figures. When Trinity Mirror bought the Birmingham Post and Mail group in 1999 they discovered that 'the number of *Evening Mails* actually printed was maybe 25 per cent below the figure entered into the books'. Moreover 'It is inconceivable that what went on . . . was peculiar to Birmingham' (Hastilow 2000).

Free newspapers: the sleeper awakes?

If advertising is the principal revenue stream of a newspaper and you are able to charge relatively high rates because of the close 'fit' between your readership and the advertisers, why incur the expense of collecting a cover price, particularly if it involves intermediaries like newsagents? This equation (worked out long ago by many student newspapers) was made easier to balance by the arrival of new technologies in the 1970s and 1980s. Both printing and the inputting of text and graphics no longer require very specialized skills. Not only did the printing process itself become cheaper, but it enabled would-be publishers to employ a less well-organized and thus lower paid workforce. With minimal editorial content, assembled from freely available sources like commercial and public sector press releases and second-hand from other news media, the cost of employing journalists could also be reduced. Entice advertisers away from the existing, probably rather sleepy, local weekly and the possibility of a good profit is obvious, particularly during a period of greatly increased consumer spending. According to Franklin's history of this era (2006: 153–5), between 1977 and 1986 the number of titles increased from 201 to 882, at a rate which peaked at 52 per cent in 1981.

This phase of free newspaper publishing was relatively short-lived. First, existing publishers grasped the logic too and launched their own free titles. Then they took over the original freesheets, many of which had been published by small proprietors. Finally, the economic recession of 1989–93 discouraged the launch of new publications (Franklin 2006). By the early 2000s most free weekly newspapers belonged to a large publisher, often the one producing the local paid-for paper. Thus the *Leicester Mail* series belongs to Northcliffe Newspapers, part of DMGT, owners of the local evening daily, the *Leicester Mercury*. With this arrangement the free paper is able to draw on the news-gathering resources of the parent group, but the non-advertisement content is usually very limited, much of it in that grey area of 'advertorial': text produced to provide a sympathetic editorial environment for an advertisement feature.

Franklin (2006) attacks the 'consumer-led' nature of freesheet 'news' content, typically focused on bland descriptive items about crime, leisure and sport. Policy, politics and even business are avoided. That this is a deliberate strategy, not a regrettable side effect of keeping costs down, became very clear during a Competition Commission investigation into the proposed sale of a set of English Midlands titles by Trinity Mirror to Johnston Press (Competition Commission 2002). In their evidence both publishers argued that while paid-for papers are sold specifically on their news content, free papers need merely a digest (Competition Commision 2002: para. 6.134), consisting of descriptive items – just enough to cause the householder to pick it up and read it (Competition Commission 2002: para. 6.30). One series of seven papers had seven reporters to cover the seven towns and shared an editor, 'so the depth of reporting is quite shallow' (Competition Commission 2002: para. 6.33). Another paper shared its editor with the local paid-for, would use 'general' and 'human interest' stories from the news-gathering pool, and would tend to favour the use of group photos (Competition Commission 2002: para. 6.135). In other words, the free newspaper is often 'deliberately positioned at the bottom of the market because publishers have established paid-for titles and don't want to rock the boat' (Bourke 2003: 16). Moreover it can be used to generate additional advertising revenue by offering packages covering the paid-for paper and several local editions of the free title.

This version of the advertising/editorial content equation is not universally accepted, however. There are some notably successful free newspapers with substantial editorial content. Some are owned by big publishers, for instance the *Milton Keynes Citizen* (Johnston Press) and, in a growing number of cases, used to be paid for. More typically they have been set up by individual entrepreneurs. For several years *Bedfordshire on Sunday* (the first of a series of similar titles in the English South Midlands) was well known for its robust investigative style and explicitly not 'being nice to everyone' (Slattery 2000), even the police and local politicians. The policy of the (unrelated) *Kent on Sunday* has also been to take advantage of the longer lead-times of weekly papers to produce substantial news and feature material – much of it generated by 'former editors and executives who have tired of the world of big business publishing and its "endless stream of redundancies"' (Lagan 2004) – and to market it on the basis of editorial autonomy, rather than intimacy with advertisers. What all these papers have in common, however, is their location in the affluent south-eastern corner of the UK. That, and their being actively acquired by being 'picked up', is bound to be an important element in their financial logic when negotiating with advertisers.

These titles are worthy of comment precisely because they are exceptions. For over 20 years free papers were, as the exchanges before the Competition Commission (2002) so clearly demonstrate, useful commercially but not seen as a challenge to other media as a source of news. 'They have lined cat litter trays across the nation' writes Bourke (2003). No longer. In the mid-1990s a Swedish-based firm launched a *daily morning* free newspaper in Newcastle-upon-Tyne (Ponsford 2004a). It failed, but only because UK national newspaper publishers immediately grasped the potential threat. Associated Newspapers (part of DMGT) launched a competitor *Metro* title, which has since been rolled out across major urban areas on a franchise basis. In Manchester, for instance, it is operated by Guardian Media Group, which also owns the *Manchester Evening News*. By 2006 the total *Metro* circulation in the UK was 1.1 million (*The Guardian* 13 March 2006). While they are badged and distributed on a regional basis, *Metro*s are not, however, regional papers. A typical East Midlands edition (3 October 2005) contained no news of the locality, not even on the sports pages. Its regional distinctiveness lay in the listings and classified advertisements: pages 31 to 38 of 48.

If *Metro*s are not regional papers and there is, as Chapter 1 argued, a public appetite for local news, why has this development been so significant for the regional newspaper industry? Why did the two biggest selling 'evening' newspapers, the London *Evening Standard* and the *Manchester Evening News*, launch free 'lite' editions alongside their paid-fors? To understand this response, we need to consider the intersection of the changing ecology of news and changes in readers' circumstances, tastes and habits or, more accurately, contemporary newspaper industry discourse about their readers.

Vanishing readers: bored with newspapers, or just too busy?

Newspaper reading is declining in all countries, in all sectors of the market and particularly, so it is thought, among younger people. Some explanations verge on the apocalyptic: 'The assumption that the "general reader" should take an interest in a wide span of subjects is evaporating' writes Blackhurst (2005: 58–9) who concludes, on the basis of the 37 per cent voting rate among 18 to 24-year-olds in the 2005 UK General Election, that 'it's obvious that civic motivation is disappearing fast'. This preoccupation with the behaviour of young people is typical not only of media organizations but of all sellers of goods and services as they try to encourage commercially favourable patterns of future consumption and to foster brand loyalty. Is Blackhurst just another in a long series of pessimists or have social conditions changed decisively in ways that are adverse to newspaper consumption?

Within the overall framework of a shrinking market, city evening paper sales have for a long time been declining at a faster rate than that of weekly papers. The new conventional wisdom among newspaper publishers is that they are 'competing for people's time', as Trinity Mirror said in evidence to the Competition Commission (2002: para. 6.18). This may be true in a literal sense, but is often enveloped in a rhetoric of 'choice', particularly in relation to competing leisure activities. While this interpretation is consonant with the commercial interests of newspapers, typically of 'trade talk' it fails to distinguish between attitudes and circumstances and to apply a sufficiently nuanced analysis of how they interact.

Many of the problems of regional daily papers are driven by changing social structure. Traditionally the 'evening paper' was either home-delivered or habitually collected on the way home. This pattern of consumption was closely associated with a workforce based in large factories and offices who kept regular (if sometimes long) hours and travelled a relatively short distance to their job on foot or by public transport. 'Flexible' hours, shrunken workforces and constantly changing shift patterns, coupled with commuting by car, have disrupted these habits. The new city of Milton Keynes captures the trends perfectly. According to the editor of the *Milton Keynes Citizen*: 'A lot of people, when they relocated . . . left their newspaper buying habits behind them. Added to that is the fact is that there isn't a traditional commuting route when people can pick up a paper.' The solution, she argues, is a home-delivered free paper that aims for editorial credibility alongside its guaranteed market penetration (Bourke 2003: 16).

Another challenge to newspaper consumption rituals has been the decline of the 'male breadwinner' form of household, in which reading the evening paper while the evening meal was prepared was regarded as deserved relaxation for the principal wage earner. Now households are more varied in form; most women are full-time 'housewives' only for a very short period while their children are infants – or not at all – and most fathers are willingly involved in childcare and (some) household management. The very fact that sales of local paid-for weekly papers, and regional Sunday papers in particular, are declining at a slower rate suggests that simply having the time to sit down and read the paper is an issue. According to the editorial director of the *Kent Messenger* series: 'There is still a real thirst for local news and [people] are prepared at the weekend to set aside time to catch up on that local news' (Ponsford 2003).

As in other media sectors, newspapers continue anxiously to extrapolate future trends in consumption from the behaviour of the youngest adult age cohort. Yet for most people early adulthood is the life stage when leisure activities can be given priority, as newspapers themselves acknowledge through both the listings and editorial content of titles like the *Metro*s and similar frees. Both are aimed specifically at younger people in general, in the metropolitan areas at young commuters, and particularly at young women, because they do not typically buy newspapers. As we saw in Chapter 1, however, concern with the locality is closely linked to life stage: when people have children, education policy is suddenly real and its local impact important; as they age their interest in health care inevitably grows. Some of the gloom about younger people and newspapers could be misplaced because wanting local news is something you grow into.

On that basis, perhaps the *Metro*/free strategy should be understood as a rational two-way bet: it may establish a newspaper reading habit but, if not, at least these additional readers have been profitably sold to advertisers. The potential risk is that these titles are feeding the very social trend that they are trying to contain: 'The unmentionable fact stalking newsrooms throughout the world is that hardly anyone under 25 is interested in paying for their news' asserts Blackhurst (2005: 53) as he catalogues the proliferating sources of free (to the end user) news, for example, multiplying radio and television channels; online sources, notably *The Guardian*'s site, which has eclipsed those of other 'quality' national newspapers in the UK precisely because it has resisted moving to a subscription basis; other, more specialized, Internet sites; and, the trigger for his polemic, the *Metro*/free phenomenon. As we shall see in Chapter 3, further free papers have appeared in London and the Swedish company that failed with the original *Metro* in the UK has succeeded elsewhere: editions in 38 cities worldwide and a readership of 13 million by mid-2004 (Ponsford 2004a).

Not only are these sources free, many are 'ambient': available 24 hours a day and almost anywhere, at home, when commuting, on your personal computer (PC) at work, in public spaces and on your mobile phone, if you choose. No wonder the often quoted 'smearing ink on dead trees' image appears to persuade that regional newspapers are simply one manifestation of a dying technology. Further, because news is free and ubiquitous, the aura and theatricality of newspapers is redundant, Blackhurst believes, 'Online we snack on small mouthsful of information . . . Constant grazing makes us lose our respect for mere words (2005: 58). In this world the title of the series for French big-city commuters, *Vingt Minutes* (Twenty Minutes), implies a heavy read!

But Blackhurst's argument also has its weaknesses. First, he relies on US-derived data for his statements about young people and newspapers. As we saw in Chapter 1, the UK still has a relatively strong newspaper reading tradition, underpinned by a truly national press. Second, the media he catalogues are delivering national and international news. (In the case of the *Metros* and similar titles one might argue that much of the 'news' is of a kind of non-place transnational celebosphere.) If, as the evidence suggests, most people become more anchored in their locality of residence as they move through the life course, from where are they going to get relevant news? Few of these new media forms have any commercial interest in providing truly local news and consequently are unlikely to set up the infrastructure to generate such content. Commercial radio in the UK does not provide it, while commercial television is pulling back from it as quickly as the regulator will allow, leaving 'space' that is unlikely to be comprehensively filled by developments in 'community television'. (See Chapters 4, 5 and 8 for further discussion of all these trends.) Blackhurst may well be right that the Internet is a threat to regional newspapers, but not for the reasons he gives. In the UK the immediate problem is not the promiscuity of the audience, but the simultaneous expansion of the BBC's web-based local news and the migration of some categories of advertising to specialized web sites.

Taking readers; diverting revenues

The challenge to regional newspapers from electronic media other than radio, long expected, has been slow to materialize. Local commercial television delivered via cable only reached a viable level of market penetration in a few locations, and then because of particular local circumstances, for instance the cultural and commercial needs of Leicester's large population of south Asian origin. For terrestrial television, analogue technology restricted the number of discrete regions. Consequently, they have been so geographically extensive that only news with generalized appeal can be included, leading to the kind of audience dissatisfactions recounted in Chapter 1. Now all this has changed. Digital technology has allowed the BBC to propose 'ultra-local' television/broadband coverage, a development that alarmed the Newspaper Society sufficiently for it to mount a campaign, including the submission of a lengthy report to the Department of Media, Culture and Sport (DCMS) because, it claims, 'The BBC risks distorting the key growth trajectory for the regional newspaper industry over the next five to 10 years' (Newspaper Society 2005a).

In fact the BBC was opening up a second front: the BBC 'Where I Live' web pages (www.bbc.co.uk) had for some time included extensive local coverage organized by county in England (the television regions often span several counties) and by sub-region in Wales and Scotland. Apart from travel, weather and community information, these not only included substantial breaking news content but were extending into 'what's on' listings and other kinds of 'lifestyle' material upon which regional newspapers increasingly depend. Complaints from newspapers and commercial rivals about the apparently unchecked expansion of BBC Online into, for example, pure entertainment such as fantasy football, led to the DCMS's commissioning of the Graf Report (DCMS 2004). The central thrust of Graf's recommendations was that the BBC should focus on its core public purposes: the provision of information and education. News, however, was specifically identified as a priority (DCMS 2004: para. 2.1), so the impact on 'Where I Live' sites has been limited, consisting mainly of the addition of links to other online news sources. In truth much of the BBC's web-based local news has consisted of short descriptive – often frankly dull and probably source-led – accounts of events. It may be that even the BBC will not have the resources, relative to its overall budget and priorities, to generate a large volume of detailed and lively news content on either of these electronic platforms. Nor does it have the freedom to campaign or be deliberately controversial.

The Internet challenge to newspapers in terms of their editorial content could be less than they fear but, according to agitated trade talk, its potential impact on advertising revenue could be catastrophic. As access to the net has become more widespread, especially among the all-important younger and relatively wealthier sections of the population, dedicated advertising sites have become commercially viable. Some of the most lucrative categories of classified advertising are being targeted. For instance, the launch of the free-to-users NHSjobs.com site was cited as one cause of a 30 per cent decline in advertising sales at *Nursing Times* (*The Guardian* 28 September 2005). The same is happening with motor vehicles and with property sales, which demonstrate the logic particularly vividly. Advertising property online is not only cheaper to the advertiser, but cheap to the customer, as well as providing much more information in the form of several colour pictures and the ability to search by categories like price and area. In mid-2005, one of the UK's largest estate agents claimed that already people bought a newspaper only to get an idea of the effectiveness of competing agents, not to search for the property itself (*Press Gazette* 3 June 2005).

Given that loss of classified advertising means not only lost revenue but a potential loss of sales, industry alarm at the spectre of a irreversible downward financial spiral is easy to understand, particularly in the light of sales figures for 'evening' dailies January–June 2006 headlined as 'Worst results in memory' in the trade press (*Press Gazette* 8 September 2006). It is, though, important not to lose sight of advertising's vulnerability to the general economic cycle. At Johnston Press, for example, a bad year in 2005 was mostly attributed to a decline in manufacturing industry, leading to reduced recruitment advertising and also to reduced consumer spending on items like cars (http://businessguardian.co.uk/story/0,,1666586,00.html).

Profits *versus* plurality?

Sales of paid-for dailies and weeklies are on a permanent downward curve; there seem to be few opportunities for further free paper launches; the BBC is offering localized news on radio and its web site, and may provide equally fine-grain television news; advertising is highly sensitive to the wider economic situation; and this core source of revenue is also being attacked by the rapid expansion of dedicated online sites. A detached observer might well conclude that the regional press is an industrial sector faced with so many threats that investment in it would be a mistake. Yet while most of the movement in ownership of the regional press is now consolidation rather than new firms entering, as yet there has been no large-scale disinvestment: why?

The explanation is straightforward: the regional press is still relatively profitable. In mid-2005 Johnston Press had profit margins of 30 per cent and Trinity Mirror of 28 per cent (*Press Gazette* 1 July 2005). Given the declining demand for the product, much of this has been achieved by the potential for **economies of scope and of scale**, the driving force behind a process of amalgamation into fewer, larger groups that has radically altered the pattern of ownership. In the decade up to 2004 'scores of groups, many with famous names and long pedigrees vanished ... In their place have grown giant chains' (Greenslade 2004b). By July 2006 the 20 largest regional press publishers accounted for '88.5 per cent of all regional press titles and 96.6 per cent of total weekly circulation' (www.newspaper-soc.org.uk). Four groups dominated: Trinity Mirror; Newsquest; Northcliffe and Johnston Press. Between them they owned 846 of the 1162 titles owned by the 'top 20', with a weekly circulation of 40.3 million copies. Outside the 'top 20' were a further 151 companies, of which 38 published only one title.

Three of the four largest companies are UK based: Northcliffe (part of Daily Mail and General Trust) and Trinity Mirror have extensive holdings in other media sectors, while Johnston operates only in regional media, which makes its profitability even more noteworthy. Newsquest, however, has been owned since 1999 by Gannett, 'the USA's largest newspaper group in terms of circulation' (www.newsquest.co.uk/stateside). When Gannett bought into UK newspapers it was assumed that the company saw possibilities for greater profitability through cost savings (Reeves and Blyth 1999). Being a new entrant to the market it could make this initial acquisition without being subject to UK competition law. According to Greenslade (2004b) it is government intervention, rather than the state of the industry that has curtailed the process of amalgamation.

Vetting company mergers is the responsibility of the Office of Fair Trading (OFT) operating under the Enterprise Act 2002. A key aspect of the act was to remove responsibility for this from government ministers (DTI 2004: 5). Instead the 'vast majority' of proposed deals would be decided by the OFT, who may refer them for further investigation by the Competition Commission 'to determine whether it has resulted or may be expected to result in a substantial lessening of competition' (www.dti.gov.uk/ccp/topics2/mergers). Media ownership, however, in the UK as in most other countries, is believed to have the potential to raise such important questions that it requires special consideration. Thus the 'transfer of a newspaper or newspaper assets which concentrates in the hands of one newspaper proprietor, newspapers with an average paid-for circulation of 500 000 or more copies per day' must be approved by the Secretary of State on the basis, in most circumstances, of a report from the Competition Commission. Similarly, the Communications Act 2003 (pt 5, ch. 2 – see www.opsi.gov.uk/acts/acts2003) amended the Enterprise Act so that the Secretary of State can 'intervene' to allow investigation where changes to the ownership of newspaper or broadcasting enterprises are proposed, even where the change does not raise competition issues (DTI 2004: 7, para. 1.2). In such cases the final decision remains with the Secretary of State – but he or she cannot dispute OFT decisions about competition issues if they are also involved in the transaction being scrutinized. Where the holding of broadcasting licences is concerned, the Secretary of State will seek advice from Ofcom. (This aspect of the regulatory regime will be explored in more detail in Chapter 4.) Advice on newspaper-only cases will be provided by the Competition Commission.

The reason for these departures from the general policy goal of reducing market intervention, pursued by successive UK governments, is that there are larger issues at stake. Media mergers are one of only two categories where 'public interest' criteria must be applied. The other is national security. 'Market forces alone, even regulated by competition law, cannot necessarily provide the marketplace of ideas that enables democracy to prosper' (DTI 2004: para. 2.6). The aim is a 'sufficient plurality of media ownership' for which local newspapers are singled out for comment because they may be 'of key significance for their local communities, which if small may not be able to support a great diversity of newspaper titles' (DTI 2004: para. 3.5). On this basis even relatively small transactions might be significant in terms of the 'accurate presentation of the news or free expression of opinion', terms which are expanded upon later in the document. In para.7.7 it is argued that 'It would be a concern for any one person to control too much of the media because of their ability to influence opinions and *control the agenda*' (emphasis added), but this almost sociological view of media power is introduced only in relation to broadcasting and cross-media mergers. For newspapers, the only quoted case in which real political and cultural 'plurality' was at issue was a 1989 decision involving Belfast-based newspapers with contrasting religio-political affiliations (DTI 2004: para. 5.13).

Following a spate of closures in the 1960s (see Jackson 1971: ch. 2), regional papers with substantial editorial content, in which 'opinion' might be expressed, now compete directly in very few areas. In practice the operational definitions of 'accurate presentation' and 'free expression' seem to have centred more on the moral character of the parties concerned. Involvement with the semi-pornographic *Sport* newspaper led to David Sullivan being prevented from taking over the Bristol *Evening Post* (DTI 2004: para. 5.6), while the 2002 investigation of the proposed Trinity Mirror/Johnston deal, discussed above, took up an allegation that Johnston had interfered with the independence of one of their editors. As we shall in the next section, in regional newspapers, as in every other newspaper sector, only editors who are willing to work within company policy will be appointed. 'Interference' is therefore unlikely to be necessary, rendering this justification for intervention in the 'public interest' little more than symbolic.

Contemporary actuality is that the only competition in local papers is between directly delivered free papers, as in the Trinity Mirror/Johnston case. With a hint of irony the report of the investigation reveals (Competition Commission 2002) that one of the main arguments deployed by the two companies was that the newspapers in question were so devoid of news, let alone comment or opinion, that there was no risk to either accuracy or free expression! In that case, the most vigorous disputes about 'plurality' related to the potential monopoly control of advertising that might follow if the deal went through. This, too, has a recognized 'public interest' dimension within the regulatory regime. (See Competition Commission 2002: summary.)

Trinity Mirror and Johnston argued that all local free papers, whether in competition with another or not, face many competitors for advertising: leafleting; advertising-only publications like *Loot*; and, even then, the potential of the Internet. Counter-arguing, the Institute of Practitioners in Advertising, among others, asserted on the basis of previous experience that a single paper would enable the owners both to raise advertising rates and (further) to reduce editorial content (Competition Commission 2002: paras 7.68–7.78). Given that advertising is the pivot upon which the newspaper industry turns, it would seem unlikely that strategies to maximize it can be forgone, particularly by publicly quoted companies whose primary duty is to their shareholders, rather than to either their direct customers or the public in general. At September 2005 the evening daily papers in Nottingham, Derby and Leicester were all owned by Northcliffe, who also owned a home-delivered free title in all three cities. In Nottingham it faced competition from the independently owned Topper Newspapers Limited; in Derby from a Trinity Mirror publication. In Leicester there was no competing title: the advertising rates per column centimetre of the *Leicester Mail* series were twice those of the Nottingham and Derby Northcliffe papers (www.nsdatabase.co.uk).

Making regional newspapers pay: the underlying principles

To keep making profits in a declining industry requires active, even aggressive, management. For those working in the industry the process can be alienating: 'We could be producing baked beans for all it matters' according to a reporter at a DMGT paper (*Press Gazette* 5 August 2005). But, as we have seen, that media output is *not* simply analogous to other mass production is recognized by statute. Industry debates about what **content** strategy to adopt in order to fulfil the social purposes of regional newspapers and still make them pay will be the subject of Chapter 3.

As Doyle (2002) points out, media production is very like the 'research and development' stage in other industries. **Initial costs**, that is producing the drama series or the first copy of the newspaper, are very high indeed because the process involves sophisticated technical equipment and, more significant still, is very labour intensive. Before a profit can be made, these costs have to be recovered by selling the product as often as possible at as high a price as possible. Here electronic and printed media part company. Good quality cinema film or television programming is eye-wateringly expensive, but does not get 'used up' as it is consumed. Some classic films, for example, have had a 'life' of several decades and are still appearing in new formats. Television, and now the Internet, have the additional advantage of costing almost nothing to distribute, once the 'platform' of ground station, cabling or satellite is in place. The **marginal cost** of increasing the number of consumers is thus low. This relationship between production and distribution suggests a strategy of **economies of scale**: increasing the number of buyers as far as possible.

Newspapers, by contrast, are less expensive to produce but by their nature have a 'shelf-life' shorter than many foods and require a very complex logistical operation to distribute them while still 'fresh'. Regional newspapers are thus faced with very demanding time limits, but also restrictions on the size of their potential audience precisely because they deal in locality. For this section of media, unlike the BBC with *The Blue Planet*, the global marketplace is not a possibility. Economies of scale must therefore be achieved not by producing yet more copies of, say, the *Merthyr Express*, but by **cutting costs**: using equipment and staff to produce several similar products. This has been the rationale for **horizontal expansion** such as the formation of regional clusters of newspapers so that they can, for example, share a printing plant and, as we shall see, some human resources too. Faced with incursions from online rivals, **diagonal expansion** into radio, television and web sites is also developing rapidly.

Compared with electronic visual media, the chain of newspaper production and distribution is relatively straightforward – but it is very time sensitive. Like other sectors of the media industry it is, as Doyle (2002) points out, vulnerable to 'bottlenecks' in, or delays to, the production cycle. Newspaper groups try to guard against this by **vertical integration** both to guarantee the flow of content and to keep costs under their own control. The majority of content is still, therefore, produced in-house by directly employed staff on, where possible, wholly owned presses. One of the barriers to small entrepreneurs starting up is that they must negotiate with a printer, which loses the element of surprise so important in an industry where big players regularly head off challenges by producing 'spoilers'.

Despite the perishability of news, newspapers can apply some **economies of scope**: producing a range of products (Doyle 2002: 14) by 'reformatting' or 'repurposing', for example using material collected for the paid-for paper in its free sister title or the web site, or mutual exchange of news and, particularly, features and comment, around a regional group or between regional and national titles. This is the motor of the *Metro* series.

Making newspapers pay: what it means in practice

Since the early 1990s regional newspapers have been in constant flux, both in their pattern of ownership and in their internal structures and policies. As operated and experienced day to day, many of the strategies discussed below have multiple, overlapping objectives and outcomes. For the sake of clarity, however, they are pulled apart into four clusters.

Rationalization of assets

Acquiring newspapers with a view to setting up regional groupings would have had few advantages if there had not been the potential for rationalization of assets. One of the most compelling of these had been opened up by the technology for transmitting content electronically, making '**remote printing**' possible. Printing presses are so expensive that they are a 'once in a 20-year outlay'. Once replaced they are not only cheaper and more flexible to run but enable the use of colour, which 'not only provid[es] a competitive edge in terms of entertaining the reader – it vastly increases ad. revenues' (Ponsford 2004b). When Northcliffe acquired the Nottingham *Evening Post* it quickly moved printing to Derby, 15 miles away, where it also prints copies of DMGT's national newspapers, the *Daily Mail* and *Mail on Sunday*.

The move generated another typical benefit of this kind of rationalization: **realization of property assets**. The old *Post* building, housing both the printing hall and the editorial and marketing departments, was a local landmark in the middle of Nottingham. Once a new editorial/marketing building on the edge of the city centre was completed, the old site was quickly sold and redeveloped. It is now a cinema, club and restaurant complex. When the *Post* was in the centre of town, members of the public were constantly in and out, placing small ads, ordering copies of photos and reading back numbers. The *Evening Post* offices are now much less visible, accessible and familiar. The future may be online, but for many readers of the paper it is not now and will never be. One cannot help wondering to what extent the decline in the sales of city evening papers has been hastened by a loss of literal visibility and thus identification with 'our' paper, whether loved or hated.

Clustering papers also allows the **centralization of 'back office' functions**. One element of these is newspaper-specific activities like selling advertisements to the public and to agencies buying on behalf of clients. The other is the kind of administrative infrastructure common to all organizations, whether public or for-profit: for example, human resources management, accounting and marketing. At the Johnston-owned regional morning *Yorkshire Post* 'The accounts department was more or less abolished . . . Centralisation of everything from audit fees to annual insurance has led to two floors of the Leeds [landmark HQ] building being vacated' (*The Guardian* 14 June 2005). While the job loss that makes this kind of exercise financially worthwhile is hard on individuals, the process itself is relatively uncontroversial. Many newspaper groups have, however, been attempting to apply similar **rationalization to some editorial functions**.

At the less contested end of the scale, the digitalization of photography has so transformed the taking, transmitting and storing of photographs that **merging picture desks** seems inevitable, as Archant has done in Norwich between the *Evening News* and their successful regional morning *Eastern Daily Press* (Plunkett 2004).

Commenting on this trend, former editor Alison Hastings (2003) questions its effect on staff motivation and the quality of the final product, a criticism that has been made much more stridently in relation to **centralized subbing** where one set of staff serves a group of papers. Sub-editing is the stage of production at which raw content is fitted into the paper, both literally in terms of its layout (length, sub-headings, headline, position on the page) and stylistically. Not only do sub-editors correct spelling and grammar, their role includes rewriting stories to increase their impact, or to match them better to the paper's customary style of address to its audience. In some papers most of this is now done by reporting staff, but many in the trade argue that, far from being an obsolete stage in the production process, 'subbing' remains a vital specialized skill. As Hastings observes: 'staff feel that their rôle has been devalued over recent years . . . the jobs most difficult to fill on many regional papers are those of a down-table [that is, middle-ranking] sub – someone fast, reliable, accurate and cre-ative' (Hastings 2003). Another former editor, arguing against this policy as part of the Trinity Mirror 'Biggest and Best' management strategy, in place between 2001 and 2005, writes 'The new central subbing unit was supposed to be a centre of excellence, using the best subs to produce the best-looking papers . . . But the papers which came out were appalling . . . littered with errors and riddled with inconsistencies. No-one seemed to understand the areas or the different editions' (Gransby 2002: 19).

This commentator no doubt felt particularly aggrieved as he had been caught up in a another aspect of 'Biggest and Best': **rationalizing the role of editor.** 'Editors would no longer be needed. There would be an editor-in-chief (an admin. role in effect) and a production editor with several subs. New "content" editors would be based at each district office' (Gransby 2002: 19). These papers, it should be noted, were not free titles with minimal editorial content, but paid-for weeklies in particularly affluent areas around London. Three years later the same process was continuing with 'Editors surplus to requirements at two Scottish regional papers' (*Press Gazette* 29 April 2005). Among free papers, editors overseeing several papers is, as we saw from the Competition Commission (2002) hearings, already standard practice.

Financial pressure from elsewhere in the group impelled these radical moves by Trinity Mirror. Life at DMGT/Northcliffe had been more tranquil, until 'the newspaper equivalent of the Grim Reaper that goes under the name of "Johnston's [profit] margins" came looming over the horizon' writes Lowe (2005: 12). Several of the group's most respected and successful editors were sacked. In Lowe's case this was from the relatively well-per-forming Bristol *Evening Post*. A few weeks later it was the turn of his deputy, another respected journalist who had won awards for his community cam-paigns (see Aldridge 2003). 'Unceremoniously booted out . . . his picture disappeared from the paper between editions' as he had been 'told to clear his desk in 10 minutes after more than 20 years' graft for Northcliffe' (*Press Gazette* 12 August 2005).

At first there was speculation that a policy of sharing editors was about to be applied even to papers of the importance of the Plymouth-based *Western Morning News* but eventually new appointments were made. Simply saving money was, therefore, clearly not the sole motive for this particular manifestation of the brutal management style characteristic of newspapers (Aldridge 1998). Part of the reason was the elimination of resistance: the Bristol editor 'did not look favourably at merging parts of his editorial operation with that of the *Post*'s sister morning title, the *Western Daily Press*', while his colleague in Bath did not wish to turn the daily *Bath Chronicle* into a weekly or bi-weekly (Press Gazette 1 July 2005). Not surprisingly, 'The new *Bath Chronicle* editor [is] "open to change"' (*Press Gazette* 5 August 2005). Beyond the purely pragmatic needs of corporate management, however, is the symbolic significance of the editor in any newspaper. Changing the editor is an essential ritual when claiming to make a dramatic move forward, even where the true position is desperate. (For further discussion of this newspaper trope see Aldridge 1998.)

Reducing staff costs

Getting rid of 'awkward squad' editors enables, as the Bristol example makes clear, the imposition of another method of making newspapers pay: reducing staff costs. The most straightforward and unsubtle method is **low pay**, for which the regional press has become notorious, even within an industry where various forms of exploitative employment are traditional. According to the Campaign for Press and Broadcasting Freedom, some Newsquest journalists are 'paid so badly that they have to claim family tax credit', while at Guardian Media Group 'Fully qualified senior journalists on their weekly papers in Greater Manchester earn . . . £172 [per annum] more than a McDonald's trainee manager earns from day one' (Barter 2005).

Staff costs can also be 'contained' by **cutting the number of staff**. Unless the editorial content of the paper is slashed, there must be several further operational consequences. One is **intensified working practices**. Reporters undertaking the 'direct entry' of their text into the newspaper's data-handling system is now well established. In smaller papers they may also, as was noted above, take over some sub-editing functions, a process made easier by the fact that some papers now use templates for 'nearly all their pages' (Hastings 2004a). In other words, news must be slotted in around the space already committed to advertisements.

Economies in the collection and use of content

Fewer reporting staff inevitably determines the routines of news-gathering. Much more reliance will inevitably be placed on economies in the collection and use of content. For many entrants the attraction of journalism is that they may be able to carry out what McManus (1994) calls 'highly active discovery' – investigative journalism. While this remains the central value of occupational culture (Aldridge 1998), it has the fundamental disadvantage, in an environment where the biggest operators are driven by 'shareholder value', of being expensive and unpredictable. Staff senior enough to be working on their own initiative away from the office can be tied up for long periods, possibly with little or no publishable outcome. Whereas **being 'office-bound'** used to be regarded as the mark of the inept or burned-out, now a trainee on a London weekly writes: 'on-the-streets reporting was described to me early as "a luxury". The newspaper did not have enough journalists to allow staff to go daily to court, let alone out and about . . . across local newspapers, regurgitating press releases and sticking a couple of opposing quotes on the end has become the norm' ('Pecke' 2004: 30). (That the author needed to use a pseudonym needs no further discussion.)

Apart from using the cascade of PR from organizations of all kinds, from public institutions to large voluntary organizations to commercial firms, there are several other standard means of **passive news-gathering** – what McManus (1994) calls 'minimally active discovery'. These include making regular contact with reliable news sources, for instance, the emergency services; using material provided by news agencies, a source for over a century but now proliferating into specialist topics like weather forecasts and celebrity news; and – rapidly increasing – trawling the Internet. Even McManus's (1994) 'moderately active discovery', where a reporter takes the kernel of a story and develops it through gathering further background information and quotation from those involved, is now often done on the telephone rather than face to face.

The same salary/time/product calculation has **curtailed attendance at meetings** of local councils and other statutory bodies and **cut the numbers of specialist staff** such as education correspondents. Conversely, as we shall see when content strategies are reviewed in Chapter 3, many editors first (re)discovered **'community correspondents'** that is, volunteers working for nothing, and are now enthusiastically encouraging the public to supply content as **'citizen journalists'**.

A further economy of scope made possible by owning multiple titles is the **reuse of material**, however originated. Archant, a middle-range but expanding group, has set up a 'syndication system that aims to sell its own pictures and stories on to the nationals in competition with freelances and news agencies' (*Press Gazette* 25 November 2005). For the largest groups, worthwhile economies can be made internally. When Trinity (now part of Trinity Mirror) took over Thomson it inherited a 'central features service . . . serving all its titles' and quickly saw the possibilities for 'sharing generic content that does not have a local aspect such as food, personal finance and DIY' (Slattery 2002: 17). This, of course, is also advantageous – in both directions – where a group owns both national and local titles. From local to national secures a flow of useful one-paragraph news items or 'nibs'. These not only fill resource-hungry news pages but give them variety and help to fend off claims that newspapers are becoming little more than lifestyle magazines. Conversely, the national papers in a group provide stories that enable regional titles to exploit the all-important 'local angle', probably within a more positive interpretive frame as in '[fill in town/city] couple survive [fill in natural disaster]'. When the mass murderer Harold Shipman was first arrested, he was 'Nottingham-born' in the *Evening Post*, but not for long. In yet another version of this process, as we saw earlier in this chapter, the *Metro* franchise is based on the reuse of nationally gener-ated material packaged and distributed locally.

Multiplying and targeting products

Central to the *Metro* logic is that the core audience consists of sections of the population who tend not to buy newspapers. Their content is thus skewed towards younger people and women, part of a wider trend towards more active marketing, more targeting and more products. In traditional newspaper lore and rhetoric, the successful paper intuitively understood its readers, based on a brew of local involvement, letters to the editor and the daily contact involved both in the news-gathering process and, often, being a long-standing local resident. Successful editing was seen as having a strong element of non-rational intuition, very much like the inborn 'nose for news' (Aldridge 1998). In the new corporate world, much more use is being made of **market research**, particularly where a relaunch of presenta-tion and/or content is being contemplated. Trinity Mirror spent a sum so large that it would 'not disclose the cost' on discovering 'what key reader groups each newspapers should be targeting'. The groups identified included 'families with school-age children . . . sports fans, businesses – especially small and medium-sized enterprises, and baby-boomers' (*Press Gazette* 9 September 2003). Individual households are being canvassed in some areas, in the hope that they will agree to having the paper regularly delivered (Greenslade 2005a).

Titles are not only being sold more determinedly to readers. The Newspaper Society is pursuing advertisers and the advertising industry with its own market research on consumer behaviour, particularly in markets like recruitment where the online threat is greatest. (See www.newspaper-soc.org.uk for both current strategy and campaign materials.) The tension between financial imperatives and **editorial autonomy** is systemic in com-mercial media. That there are boundaries that should not be crossed is constitutive not only of journalism's professional ideology but, as previous discussion has illustrated, is implied in the definition of a 'newspaper' for legislative purposes. For some staff, at least, contemporary commercial pressures are attacking this boundary: 'Editorial staff at Trinity Mirror have written a protest letter to the company after 12 of its [paid-for] newspapers carried a wraparound advert which obscured front and back page news and sport' (*Press Gazette* 4 February 2005). The subtext is that this makes the paper look like part of the freesheet category, defined as lower status products precisely because they are well understood to be entirely advertising-driven.

The search for new streams of advertising revenue lies behind regional media's development of 'a broad **portfolio of media products** in order to reach a wider range of consumers' (Newspaper Society 2005c) including 'supplements, niche publications, lifestyle magazines and web sites, as well as branching into radio, TV and other communication methods'. 'In 1994 the Manchester Evening News group had a total of 23 paid-for, free weekly and evening titles. Now it has 48 products, including a TV channel – Channel M' (Tomlin 2004b). Ironically, part of the major disinvestment/ new investors churn in newspaper ownership in the 1990s was caused by the failure of cable television to yield the expected alternative platform for the larger regional newspapers. One venture was versions of L!ve TV in Birmingham and Liverpool which ultimately went down with the London-based parent station. (See, for example, *Press Gazette* 20 November 1995 and 22 November 1996.)

Newspapers' development of associated **web sites** was initially hesitant. Some of the most informative sites were not, as might have been predicted, operated by the big players. For example, the independently-owned weekly *Newark Advertiser* had a regularly updated news-led site in the late 1990s, and still does (www.newarkadvertiser.co.uk). By contrast, the big city evening papers opted for leisure and listings-led sites, with the largest companies operating group-wide brands. Sites linked to Northcliffe titles are badged 'this is', as in 'this is Nottingham in association with the Evening Post' (www.thisisnottingham.co.uk), while Trinity Mirror's newspapers use the 'ic' brand, as in 'icWales' for *The Western Mail* (www.icwales.icnetwork.co.uk). Since that initial phase, newspaper sites have moved towards putting news in the foreground, based presumably on a realization that this is their core business and 'unique selling proposition' in the face of, for example, cinemas operating their own online facilities and the rapid development of the specialized commercial sites referred to earlier in the chapter. Many of these sites are now multimedia, offering audio and video content as well. For example Northcliffe/DMGT has a contract with the Press Association for bulletins 'covering a national news agenda relevant to the regions' (*Press Gazette* 7 October 2005). A visit to the Nottingham *Evening*

Post in August 2006, however, found the service flagged as 'national news', which may well increase traffic on the site, but does not expand the local news content.

Regional newspaper publishers were slow to grasp the scale of this challenge to their core revenue. In 2000 the president of the Newspaper Society declared that 'publishers' worries about the internet threat are receding' (*Press Gazette* 21 July 2000). This was at just the wrong time, according to a financial analyst, commenting on Trinity Mirror's purchase of a property sales web site, their stake in a recruitment web site and interest in buying United Business Media's *Exchange and Mart* and *Auto Exchange* with their associated web sites: 'I'm a bit surprised that they did not focus on buying these type of assets four or five years ago' (*The Guardian* 29 July 2005). Tellingly, DMGT/Northcliffe and Johnston were also reported to be interested in the UBM sell-off, presumably bidding up the price. The likely cost of *Exchange and Mart* was quoted at £100 million, while later in 2005 Trinity Mirror cancelled a planned £250 million share buy-back in order to fund further online acquisitions in 2006 (*The Guardian* 3 March 2006). It is not just the demands for increased shareholder value that impels the gathering of regional newspapers into ever-larger groupings with their expected economies of scale and scope: this kind of defensive move is only open to the very biggest players in the industry. Hardly surprising, therefore, that from the perspective of those working for – or even running – their component firms, the dominant logic seems to be not making news but being a lean and efficient wholesaling operation, with the newspaper titles as the retail arm.

3 Imagining the community

Taking 'community' for granted

In 1947 the first Royal Commission on the Press issued a questionnaire to newspaper publishers and their representative organizations in which Question 2 was 'What is the proper function of a newspaper?'. Ninety-five responses were received, most of them from regional newspapers. Looking at them 60 years later, what is striking is not their high-flown generality – just as typical of mission statements now – but their confident tone. 'To provide the public with a full and accurate account of all public affairs and facilities for expressions of opinion from all quarters', according to the owners of the *Perthshire Constitutional and Journal* (Royal Commission on the Press 1947: 97), or, as the Aberystwyth-based *Cambrian News* put it: 'The function of a newspaper is to give the news of the day and under sane management to direct public opinion' (Royal Commission on the Press 1947: 62). Clearly the authors felt that they could claim an assured and active place in the social order. Elaborating the point, the owners of the daily and weekly papers based in Burton-on-Trent wrote that their 'main consideration' was providing 'a sound and clean news service . . . the promotion of a proper respect and reverence for our national traditions and ideals, the development of a national and local patriotism and spirit of public service and the fostering of true progress' (Royal Commission on the Press 1947: 58).

These invocations of stability are the more striking because 1947 was a time of great hardship and *in*stability. The material problems caused by the 1939–45 World War were intensifying with shortages of food, fuel, housing, clothes and consumer goods – an almost complete absence in the last case. Families disrupted by war service, bombing and evacuation were having to deal with demobilized men expecting to take back their traditional place in the home and in employment. Both the divorce rate and the birth rate reached unprecedented levels. The Labour government, elected in 1945, was radically reconstructing health care, social insurance, education, land ownership and the planning of the urban environment. At the heart of this process of transformation, however, was an essentially unchanged institutional order in which the hierarchies of authority at every scale from national to local remained the same, even if new and unexpected individuals filled the positions within them. Paternalism was the normal mode. In 1946, for example, a government committee recommended that a significant proportion of the population be rehoused in new towns – self-contained communities built on rural greenfield sites (New Towns Committee 1946). Nor did its members limit their vision to the built environment. There were specific recommendations aimed at promoting 'high culture' in just the way that the chair, John Reith, had taken for granted that he should when setting up and leading the BBC in the 1920s and 1930s. Like all those involved in the contemporary social reforms, the New Towns Committee worked within an assumptive frame of one nation; one system of legitimate values.

This was the context in which newspaper owners and editors could treat the meaning of 'community' as self-evident and an everyday actuality, whether referring to the nation or their own small town. Now there are no such certainties. While, as we saw in Chapter 1, locality is still very important for most people, the decision-making that shapes their employment opportunities, or the quality of public services, or the range of consumption leisure activities open to them has become socially and physically remote. At the same time the political rhetoric of consumer choice portrays authority as performative, not an automatic attribute of formal position. Even more importantly, 'culture' itself is contested, not simply at the level of whether Western classical music is 'better' than rock music, but in the profoundest sense of moral and spiritual values. How do regional newspapers address a multicultural audience? Does this moral and demographic diversity, coupled with the changes in consumer behaviour driven by industrial change, explain why city daily papers are struggling more than paid-for weekly papers? The rest of the chapter will review these changed social realities, the similarities and differences in how the daily and weekly sectors have responded to them and conclude with a discussion of the exceptional aspects of the London newspapers market, followed by a case study of Birmingham, a city where the complexities of the contemporary UK are vividly visible.

Disappearing democracy; disappearing news; disappearing staff

There have been few research studies that have focused entirely on regional newspapers. Of those that have, three appeared over a short period in the early to mid-1970s, based on data collected in the late 1960s to early 1970s. All were primarily concerned with the extent to which the local press was providing an adequate forum for political debate and acting as an active independent player in the local polity: Jackson's (1971) wide-ranging analysis of their organization, content and editorial attitudes; Cox and Morgan (1973) who studied the daily and weekly papers on Merseyside; and Murphy's (1976) participant observation in two weeklies. All found the local press wanting, but Murphy is particularly scathing: 'The much vaunted disinterested role in the functioning of democracy claimed by the journalist is a myth. Whatever his intention, the objective outcome of his activities is frequently propaganda for the status quo' (1976: 31). These authors could not, of course, have been aware that they were capturing the same world that had existed in 1947 but was about to disintegrate; a world in which Jackson (1971: 43–5) could deploy the concept of a class of 'community leaders' and 'leaders of thought' as an explanatory variable, and where Murphy could argue that one reason why newspapers avoided robust critique was that for those in family ownership the proprietor would be part of the local elite. (The disintegration was not instantaneous. Until 1994, when Northcliffe/DMGT controversially took it over, the Nottingham *Evening Post* was in just this situation. Colonel Tim Forman Hardy 'just loved owning a newspaper . . . There were no financial pressures' – Slattery 2005.) The editor, too, would probably be inhibited as well as advantaged by strong ties to the area, as Cox and Morgan also observe. Those that they interviewed were 'local men, locally educated and locally recruited, trained and promoted. If not actually from Merseyside, then they had followed almost their entire careers there' (Cox and Morgan 1973: 110). The individuals featuring in both studies were indeed nearly all men, another aspect of local media that was about to change – but not entirely. See Chapter 7.

The disappointment evident in all these studies sprang from the lack of coherence and depth in the coverage of local politics. Events and outcomes were reported, rather than inputs and the process of decision. Nevertheless, Cox and Morgan could assert that 'political news of some kind almost always appears somewhere on the front page of the average issue of the [Merseyside] weekly and, not infrequently, forms the lead story' (1973: 71). No longer: on 28 October 2005 the *Newark Advertiser*, a notably successful and still family-owned weekly, led with a local church hiring security guards because of attacks by young vandals, while the *Isle of Wight County Press* gave most prominence to a dispute between the teaching unions and head teachers on the island. The *County Press*, also a successful title with a 'household penetration' during the first half of 2006 of between 60 and 70 per cent across its circulation area (www.newspapersoc.org.uk > Newspaper Society > Newspaper Search) appears to be self-consciously traditional in its presentational style. Its titlepiece is in a Gothic font; and not only is it one of the very few regional papers not to have moved to tabloid format, but its pages are slightly *bigger* than broadsheet. On the date in question there were nine stories on the front page, none of them about local participatory democracy.

According to Cox and Morgan (1973: 122), even in the late 1960s journalists 'learn[ed] to act on two premises . . . The first of these is that local government is dull, and that reporting it is a matter of civic duty rather than natural inclination. Most of the editors appeared to lean towards this point of view'. Nevertheless they gathered and printed this material; now they do not. Occupational ideology situates individual editors as the mainspring of editorial policy, but explanations like that of the then editor-in-chief of the Newcastle *Evening Chronicle* – 'we're not interested in political hot air. We're interested in what affects people's lives' (Marks 1997a) – are insufficient. (The editor in question was later to lead the Trinity Mirror 'Biggest and Best' rationalization policy referred to in Chapter 2.) Reduced coverage of local politics, the courts and other specialized topics is driven by two linked structural processes forces: cost-cutting and centralization/globalization.

As Chapter 2 demonstrated, in a labour-intensive and highly competitive industry, staff costs are always under scrutiny. Simple descriptive reporting of local government ties up a lot of staff time attending meetings. Providing explanation or informed critique demands not only that time, but also a sophisticated level of knowledge and good contacts built up over years. Today even large and well-resourced newspapers have tended to move away from allowing staff to specialize, in the belief that generalists are more productive. As the editor of the *Liverpool Daily Post* put it, when defending the halving of its arts coverage and sacking of three columnists 'We're not cutting [it] – we just no longer want it ghettoised on a specific page each day. We want to see it forcing its way on to the news pages' (*Press Gazette* 14 October 2005). When local authorities were first given the power to shift important decisions into 'cabinets' and to hold their meetings in private, there was some organized opposition from regional newspaper lobby groups (see, for example, Francis 2001). Tellingly, this pressure for access to detailed political and technical debate has not been sustained. A visit to the Society of Editors' web site (www.societyofeditors.co.uk) in October 2005 showed only two news releases on the topic in 2005, and none in 2004. The Newspaper Society (www.newspapersoc.org.uk) displayed a similar lack of priority given to the issue.

By contrast regional newspapers both collectively and individually have very actively resisted attempts to prevent publication of the names of young people involved with the civil and criminal courts, whether as victim, witness or defendant. Challenges to orders made under Section 39 or (less often) Section 49 of the 1933 Children and Young Persons Act feature regularly in *Press Gazette*, often following the folkloric narrative of 'young trainee reporter defeats self-important members of the establishment, thus showing what a good job we do in our legal training and how independent the regional press still is'. This is even more marked in relation to Antisocial Behaviour Orders (ASBOs). Highly politicized and occupying confusing terrain between criminal and civil jurisdictions, there is fierce controversy as to whether publicity is intrinsic to their purpose or is an infraction of the rights of those subjected to them which will, worse, make it impossible to escape from the deviant identity they impose. (For a full explanation of the legal complexities see Welsh et al. 2005.) Unsurprisingly, the typical stance of newspapers, as reported in *Press Gazette*, is that identification is both efficacious and morally right, 'following in the tradition of the stocks and public execution', as Clother (2001: 172–4) dryly observed in relation to court reporting in general.

This rather disingenuous advocacy of 'naming and shaming' is overdetermined: it links three key aspects of contemporary regional newspaper practice. First is the vital importance of names and faces, about which more will be said later in the chapter, as it will about the second element: campaigning. Third, it goes some way to explaining a paradox in the coverage of court cases. One might expect that the coverage of this guaranteed, predictable and sometimes dramatic source of news would be increasing, particularly since it is an opportunity for trainees to practise their shorthand and consolidate their knowledge of the law, both of which are compulsory. Reported crime has not declined and courts have multiplied. Nor is there any sign that public fascination with crime and deviance is diminishing, whether in fictional and 'reality' genres, or real. Faced with this abundance, however, and with limited staff to deploy, routine coverage becomes impossible. Court reports have become skewed to the more eye-catching cases, many of them relating to sexual offences, very young offenders, multiple offences, and 'public order' issues likely to resonate with the generality of readers – hence the preoccupation with Section 39 and ASBOs.

An unwillingness to commit staff time is not, however, the only explanation for the reduced coverage of traditional news beats like the courts and local politics in regional newspapers. Less and less is governed locally, and the organization of that which is has become barely comprehensible even to the educated and engaged. Piecemeal reforms of local government superimposed on top of the (relatively) straightforward two-tier system introduced in 1974 have increased anomaly and mystification. Are the powers of metropolitan districts and unitary authorities the same? Why is the City of Nottingham unitary authority responsible for only part of the greater Nottingham area? (See Turner 2006 for a clear account.) The introduction of optional elected mayors seems only to have amplified the problem. (Here, see Temple's 2005 commentary on the Stoke-on-Trent *Sentinel*'s fruitless attempt to go against the trend and participate actively in the politics of a mayoral election.)

Beyond this, as Turner (2006) points out, local authorities' capacity for independent action is circumscribed in a range of ways. Many services formerly run directly, for example transport, refuse collection or even housing, have been contracted out to the private sector or very large not-for-profit operators. Neither category is answerable to the local population. Even where the service is a municipally owned enterprise run on business principles, limited company legal status inevitably adds another layer of insulation between it and the electorate.

Where local government services remain in the public sector they, too, are constrained by nationally imposed guidelines and performance standards on matters like the curriculum in schools or methods of practice in social services, to say nothing of the intricacies of the overall fiscal regime. Beyond local government, other public services delivered locally have either passed wholly into the private sector (like water and sewerage), or have such a staggeringly complex structure that their supposedly decentralized structure is impenetrable (like the trusts of the National Health Service), or have been made answerable to central government. The probation service, for example, used to be run by semi-autonomous local committees involving members of the judiciary, local (lay) magistrates and probation professionals. Even where they were not long-standing locals, such people were deeply embedded in local networks and involved in local events: a potentially newsworthy fraction of the elite 'leaders of thought' to which Jackson (1971) referred. First the probation service became subject to ever-stricter national practice guidelines, then probation officers became employees of central government, then national management took over and the probation service underwent merger with the Prison Service to form the National Offenders Management Scheme (NOMS) – and some of probation officers' work with offenders is to be tested in the marketplace, that is, privatized. Local probation boards still exist but they are answerable, as is the Chief Probation Officer for the area, to the National Probation Directorate, part of the Home Office.

Prisons have always been Crown Property and therefore not subject to the usual local authority planning controls. It was just this supra-central power that was used to set up a unit for post-sentence sex offenders within HM Prison Nottingham, thus avoiding public or local media protest until the situation was effectively irreversible. (For a full account of the local newspaper's handling of the furore, see Cross and Lockyer 2006.)

Key decision-making functions in the for-profit sector (including newspapers, as we saw in Chapter 2) have not merely been centralized but in many cases have become transnational, if not expatriated altogether. In late 2006 Corus, a British/Dutch group which owned the steel-making plants central to the economy of the Bridgend/Port Talbot area of south Wales, was taken over by Tata Steel of India. Birmingham's industrial economy was based around 'metal bashing', from jewellery to cars. Longbridge, the vast car manufacturing site which used to dominate the life of south Birmingham was finally sold to a Chinese company whose intentions were so opaque that, as we shall see in the case study at the end of this chapter, the evening daily *Birmingham Mail* ran a long campaign to try and get some explanation. In this operating environment the workforce and trade unions struggle to make any impact on company strategy, the local political system is simply bypassed, and the regional press often left with nothing but frustration and failure to report on. Even the vital news-generating tactic of campaigning becomes risky.

As with the centralization of public sector decision-making, globalization of capital has further dismantled the elites who used to provide a rich seam of news because, liked or loathed, they were celebrities at the local scale. Nottingham used to be known for machine-made lace and, later, the 'needle trades' more broadly, cigarette manufacture, Raleigh cycles, and pharmaceutical manufacture and retailing. The family names of Boden, Player and Boot are still visible around the city, historically in road names and, more recently, through higher education: for example, one of the Player's cigarette factory sites has become Player's Court student accommodation. Jesse Boot was a particularly active local benefactor: he gave what is now the University of Nottingham's main campus and the adjoining public park to the college and the city in the 1920s. The Boots Company maintained this tradition of civic-mindedness and benevolent paternalism well into the 1990s with major donations to both of Nottingham's universities and a welfare service for its pensioners, now discontinued. By the early 2000s, ferocious competition from the supermarkets had undermined both Boots' sense of purpose and its profits. A succession of senior executives was brought in, replacing people who were born and brought up in the region and had worked for the company all their life. Presumably their interest in the locality is minimal, as is the interest of local people in them. In 2005 Boots merged with Alliance Unichem, a similar company with European as well as UK interests. Surely the moving of management functions away from Nottingham will follow.

Where it used to manufacture bicycles, lace and garments, Nottingham is now producing knowledge. A notable lace factory building in the city centre Lace Market area is a part of a further education college; the old Raleigh bikes/Sturmey Archer gears site is now a branch campus. Both universities have energetically pursued the logic of the funding regime and greatly expanded student numbers. Some neighbourhoods are now almost completely colonized by student housing. This changed population pattern is unpopular with all sections of the community – including students – but higher education policy is as globally driven as the pharmaceutical industry. Both are beyond the reach of the city and its media.

Where there was conflict, consensus; where there might be sensationalism, restraint

Three strands run through adverse criticism of news media: that they thrive only on bad news; that they sensationalize; and that an appropriate scepticism has decayed into cynicism. None of these are true of the regional press. For national newspapers their readers are an abstract category, even when they are addressed as directly as 'you' and deliberately mobilized as a source of political pressure. As far as those readers are concerned, editors – even of a progressive newspaper like *The Guardian* – are equally anonymous and inaccessible. In striking contrast, in many regional titles, including big-city evenings like the Nottingham *Evening Post*, the name and telephone number/email address of the editor are printed: a tacit invitation to contact her or him. In regional press trade talk the recurrent theme is responsiveness and accountability to the readership.

As we shall see in Chapter 7, this direct contact with readers is a source of real pride and pleasure to journalists on regional newspapers, but the sense of responsibility to which they often refer has a sound commercial as well as a moral basis. Inaccuracy of any kind is immediately obvious and provokes an adverse response, whether it is carelessness with the spelling of names, factual errors in the account of a major event, or casual condemnation of people or behaviour. 'Our customers are living with the stories we report. And they see straight through it if we try to flam or bend the truth' according to the editor of the Halifax *Evening Courier* (*Press Gazette* 20 May 2005). 'Louts' may damage a statue, but only when they are a general category. Specific people are another matter. The Norwich morning *Eastern Daily Press* fought a complicated legal case, which went to the High Court, involving a young man who had been convicted of dangerous driving and who was subsequently granted legal aid to try to enforce the Section 49 order which would maintain his anonymity. (See the discussion above and *Press Gazette* 22 April and 4 November 2005.). He lost the case. On 27 October 2005 the front page of the *Eastern Daily Press* was graphically dramatic but linguistically and semiotically restrained: a four-deck headline 'We unmask the "lethal weapon driver"' alongside a large picture of the youth looking serious, followed by a detailed explanation of the initial case and the legal issues. On 28 October 2005 *The Sun* devoted most of an inside right-hand page to a picture of the youth looking defiant, with the 160-point headline 'SCUMBAG' and a short account superimposed on it. In its leader column it described him as an 'irresponsible moron'. This kind of discourse simply cannot be applied where the circulation area includes the young man's family, their friends, his friends – and even people who have never met him but may have heard a more complex and nuanced account of him and the events. The arrogance often displayed by national newspapers would destroy a regional paper's standing in the locality and lose readers. Losing readers drives down advertising revenue in two ways: first, those same readers do not place the all-important classified ads; second, falling sales will eventually affect the rates that can be charged for both those same classified ads and for the display ads elsewhere in the paper. (See Chapter 2 for more discussion of the logic of advertising finance.)

The same fear of alienating sections of the readership has driven regional newspapers towards the political neutrality which was already becoming the norm in the 1970s (Cox and Morgan 1973; Murphy 1976). Paradoxically this was the outcome of a round of closures in the 1960s (see Jackson 1971: ch. 2) which led to most paid-for regional papers' being 'solus', that is, having monopoly status in their circulation area. Achieving maximum market penetration henceforth required a consensual approach, rather than being controversial. Presumably a reputation for unrelenting political partisanship would also have raised questions over 'plurality' with the competition authorities when mergers were planned, as we saw in Chapter 2.

Other considerations also underlie this avoidance of conflict. Question 5 asked of publishers by the Royal Commission on the Press (1947: unnumbered preface) was: 'To what extent if at all do you consider that the accurate presentation of news or the adequate expression of opinion is distorted or restricted by . . . the interests of advertisers?' The replies are typified by denials of a vehemence and piety which suggest that a nerve had been touched. In contemporary regional newspapers cooperation between the editorial and the marketing function is more active, and to an extent more overt. It is hard to believe that this does not operate as a 'chilling' effect when deciding how to cover local business news, whether routinely or where wrongdoing is a possibility. As regional newspapers include ever more 'lifestyle' content, inextricably bound up with consumption in the home and in leisure activities, symbiosis with local advertisers can only increase. How likely is it, for instance, that local pubs and restaurants would want to pay a premium price to appear close to an advertising feature on eating out if the paper had been too enthusiastic in following up the shocking findings of local authority environmental health officers' visits to catering establishments in the city? Tunstall's (1971) classic study of the journalist–source relationship pivoted on the permanent tension between an ideology of editorial creative autonomy and the financial realities of advertising-driven media. Every aspect of the environment in which regional newspapers now operate has increased this tension, sometimes to breaking point, as the fate of some editors referred to in Chapter 2 demonstrates. Journalism is more 'market driven' (McManus 1994) than ever, and the echoing silence about the real influence of advertisers remains.

As well as being – like all commercial media – wary of the sensitivities of advertisers, regional newspapers have always been careful to maintain good relations with their regular news sources, most of whom are institutional contacts in the local authority, the police, the emergency services and the courts (Cox and Morgan 1973: ch. 7; Murphy 1976: ch. 1). Increased pressures on staffing mean that a reliable and plentiful flow of news from these is vital, the more so given that there is little time to cultivate informants by informal face-to-face contact. One of the few aspects of news-gathering where this still continues is sport, notably football (soccer). One might even argue that, within reason, this is a part of the paper where stimulating controversy can be a viable strategy. Another folk narrative that appears in *Press Gazette* is 'local paper's respected football correspondent banned from ground of struggling lower division club for pointing out what every knowledgeable fan grasps, but the local businessman chairman is too obtuse to understand'. Excoriating criticism in relation to other holders of important offices is much rarer. Where it occurs, the risk is usually offset by the target being under formal investigation as, for instance, occurred with senior political figures in Lincoln, where the editor of the *Lincolnshire Echo* said that a county council scandal was 'Mismanagement on such a scale that nobody disagreed with the stand we took. The council officers and the 17,000 people working for them were very supportive. I also got fantastic backing from my newspaper group' (*Press Gazette* 29 April 2005).

These distinctive characteristics of regional newspapers' mode of address and orientation to their audience, sources and advertisers are common to both weekly and evening daily papers, despite the differences in the resources at their disposal and the size of the territory which they must cover. Widely advocated devices to make their content more eye-catching and easier to follow include briefer items, fact files and digests of content (for example, the *Hull Daily Mail* – *Press Gazette* 25 February 2005), colour coding and increased print size (for example, the biggest-selling weekly, the *Kent Messenger* series – *Press Gazette* 6 May 2005). Nor is there any systematic difference in graphical style. Many have moved to tabloid size, which has the multiple advantages of being easier to handle; having more right-hand pages for which advertisers can be charged more; and being culturally linked with accessibility and liveliness. The semiotic borrowings from the national mass tabloids can also be seen in the use of devices like very large fonts, white-on-black (or on colour) headlines, and dramatic 'poster-style' front pages dominated by a single picture with little or no text. As with the *Eastern Daily Press* story referred to above, however, their typical linguistic structures and vocabulary are much more restrained than any national paper. They do not print four-letter words in full, as do *The Guardian* or the *Financial Times*, nor assassinate by adjective *Daily*

Mail-style. Compare 'POLICE: SEE THE FACTS BEHIND THE FIGURES' (front page of the *Lincolnshire Echo* 28 October 2005) with 'MY RAPE AGONY by B[ig]B[rother] Lesley' (front page of *The Sun* 28 October 2005). Yet in their contrasting ways they both hope to be attention-grabbing. As we saw in Chapter 2, regional newspapers are now very reliant on casual sales, as mass tabloid newspapers and consumer magazines always have been. For the same reason, and also because it appeals to advertisers, many regional papers are trying to move to colour printing to attract generations of readers for whom a black-and-white format is completely alien.

Summarizing the perspectives of Merseyside newspaper editors in the late 1960s, Cox and Morgan (1973: 122) report 'that they believe in something real called "the good of the town"'. Can this still be invoked as an operating principle? In the remainder of the chapter I will argue that for many weekly newspapers 'the town' is an emergent reality in which their role is essentially to let it talk to itself. For city daily papers, by contrast, the institutional structures and social networks which allowed this reification are now much less dense and more fragmented. For those papers, active editorial strategies of 'imagining' are required.

Weekly papers: allowing the town to talk to itself

Applying his humanities background, Jackson (1971) carried out a systematic analysis of the typical narratives in regional newspapers. His overall conclusion (Jackson 1971: ch. 6) was that the weeklies focused on individual and institutional order, while the dailies included more news of 'disorder'. Contemporary weekly newspaper texts and discussions within the trade press about the characteristics of successful newspapers show the continuing relevance of Jackson's neat summary.

The Nottinghamshire *Mansfield Chad* series was the second biggest-selling weekly at mid-2005. On 19 October 2005 'Your more local paper' was 160 pages long, including 62 of houses for sale and rent and a 16-page supplement, '50 plus', for 'the mature reader'. (Older people are an important segment of regional papers' markets.) Most of the first 33 pages, aside from display advertising, were taken up with news. Two of these were given over to one-paragraph items of 'community news' from villages in the town's rural hinterland, with a photograph and contact details of their community correspondent, all three of whom were women. The *Chad* series can rightly claim to be 'more local': there is an *Ashfield Chad* with an overlapping but distinctive set of items on the news pages and a different set of readers' letters. Sutton-in-Ashfield is 3 miles from Mansfield.

In an age of electronic media it is surprising that 'having your picture in the paper' still provokes excitement, but it undoubtedly does. Selling copies of their photographs is a significant activity for regional papers, even in a big city like Nottingham. When the sales desk of the *Evening Post* was asked why people still wanted them when they can so easily take their own, the reply was that the quality of professional photography is better, but this cannot be the whole explanation. Appearing in the paper yourself, or knowing someone who has, seems still to be a validation of self-identity as a member of the community, which axiomatically has a public as well as a private and domestic dimension. Whatever the underlying cause, including as many 'names and faces' as possible is a widely endorsed editorial tactic, particularly in weekly papers whose overarching strategy is usually to aim for the maximum possible volume of news items with local relevance. In the free-standing small towns where weeklies flourish, this is likely to gen-erate identification and interest on a purely probabilistic basis. The *Newark Advertiser* of 30 September 2005, for instance, had a page of 'names in the news', followed immediately by most of a page reporting a local agricultural show. Every prize-winner was listed, necessitating a font point size so small that it was a challenge to read it. Where the town is or, more often, was dominated by a small number of major employers – as agriculture and its associated industries like sugar beet processing are important to Newark – the social networks of family, residence, leisure and work are superimposed on each other. The likelihood that seemingly trivial descriptive items of good news will have personal significance therefore rapidly increases.

One of the most distinctive features of all regional papers is that they are the site of birth, marriage and death announcements (BMD) for ordi-nary people. To place such a notice is another way in which people affirm public selves, but would be pointless if there were no imputed audience to whom it would have meaning. 'In memoriam' small advertisements not only remind the audience that the subject was loved, respected and well embedded in the social fabric, but are a symbol of social continuity and sta-bility. Jackson (1971: 101–4) notes the prominence given to golden and diamond wedding anniversaries and to one-hundredth birthday celebra-tions, as in this sixtieth anniversary notice: 'Mrs S contributed to the war effort by working at a factory making bomb detonators but the majority of her working life was spent at Peek Frean's [biscuit factory]' (*Isle of Wight County Press* 28 October 2005). As he points out, these anniversaries not only allow for this kind of reminiscence about working conditions, war service, running a home and so on which will appeal particularly to older readers, but are also a coded reference to the moral virtues of hard work and steadfastness and to social progress.

The *Mansfield Chad* of 19 October 2005 contained five pages of obitu-aries ranging from 9 to 36 column centimetres. All included a picture of the deceased, brief biographical details and a list of mourners. This is more typical of French regional newspapers than those in the UK. What

Mansfield has in common with provincial France is that, until the virtual destruction of the deep coal-mining industry in the 1980s and early 1990s, the town was economically, and thus socially, unusually self-contained. In such a context, there is little need for a newspaper to do other than be an effective and responsive machine for news-gathering and dissemination. Being controversial in order to raise its public profile is not necessary. The *Isle of Wight County Press* of 28 October 2005 had no editorial column, but a full page of letters, many of them not only about local politics, but party politics – and some of them so trenchant that the paper must surely have checked them for possible libel.

Weekly newspapers from the Isle of Wight, Mansfield and Newark have been used as examples because they are successful (and the Isle of Wight is also the subject of a community study discussed in Chapter 1). In most respects these locales could not be more different, but they have two crucial characteristics in common which have provided the potential for the local newspaper to prosper simply by providing a rich description of local life. First, as we have seen, they are relatively self-contained, although the mix of causal socio-economic and topographic factors is different in each case. According to the January to June 2006 sales figures for weekly titles (*Press Gazette* 8 September 2006), six of the ten best-selling titles were based in this kind of bounded community. (Of the remaining four, two were series covering predominantly rural areas.) Second, they are monocultural. At the 2001 Census, the England and Wales average of people who self-identified as 'white' was 91.3 per cent and 'born in the UK' was 91.1 per cent. For the Isle of Wight the figures were 'white' 98.3 per cent, 'born in the UK' 96.0 per cent; in Mansfield 'white' 98.3 per cent, 'born in the UK' 97.3 per cent; in Newark and Sherwood: 'white' 98.5 per cent, 'born in the UK' 97 per cent. The figures for Nottingham City were 'white' 84.9 per cent, 'born in the UK' 90.1 per cent. In Nottingham 7.5 per cent of Census respondents specifically declared themselves as members of a religion other than Christianity, compared with 1.2 per cent in the Isle of Wight, 0.9 per cent in Mansfield and 0.8 per cent in Newark and Sherwood.

Most of Britain's big cities are, like Nottingham, now multi-ethnic and multicultural. Assumptions about common life histories or employment experiences or curiosity about, for example, what the town square looked like in the 1920s or even 1970s cannot be made – nor should be. This is the terrain on which most daily papers operate. How can they address a diverse potential readership?

Daily papers: imagining the community

Appealing to a population with divergent priorities and points of reference is actually not a new problem for daily newspapers. A large section of their potential consumers are commuters, people who work but do not live in the area. For this group, much of the news of social networks (for instance, the BMDs and the doings of voluntary organizations) and issues that relate specifically to being a resident (for instance, the level of council tax or a controversial new housing development or road scheme) will be irrelevant. As we saw in Chapter 2, tailoring content for specific demographic groups is a common device when trying to stem falling sales. Consistent with the Hargreaves and Thomas's (2002) research discussed in Chapter 1, people at the household and family formation stage of life are a prime target because they will be consuming more of the kinds of local goods and services advertised in regional papers and, at the same time, their attachment to the locality will be increasing, notably their interest in education and health services. These are another irrelevance for many commuters, who might, however, be very interested in news of business, employment-related issues and that vital source of revenue, the 'situations vacant' classified advertisement. But that only points to a further dilemma for regional newspapers. Older people are acknowledged to be an important section of the readership, yet they are least likely to be interested in employment issues or the job advertisements.

Regional daily titles must, therefore, operate in an environment where not only are declining sales the norm and commercial pressures savage, but the divergent interests of the audience can be hard to reconcile. Hardly surprising, then, that so much trade talk is about battle strategy and tactics. Nearly all of it relates to daily publications, reinforcing the point that weekly paid-for titles inhabit another universe with its own logic.

The Newspaper Society makes much of the fact that many of their readers do not take a national daily paper. Nevertheless, one of the longer-established conventional wisdoms among regional evening dailies is that competing with radio, television and the Internet is hopeless: there is no point in trying to cover national, let alone international, news unless there is a 'local angle'. Instead, regional papers should exploit their 'unique selling proposition': localness (Tunstall 1996). Accordingly, while in 2005 the Nottingham *Evening Post* typically published one page of 'World and National' news, the *Lincolnshire Echo*, winner of a trade award, printed none. Now rolling news services accessible all the time and everywhere – the 'ambient news' phenomenon discussed in the previous chapter – have led to many local daily papers questioning the value of 'breaking news'. In other words, to what extent should daily routines and staff resources be pivoted on printing today's news today? Even by the late 1990s the

Nottingham *Evening Post* sometimes consisted entirely of pages that had been completed the night before. At mid-2005 the paper produced three weekday editions, with the last arriving for distribution at 2.00 p.m., having been brought from the printing works at the *Derby Evening Telegraph*, fifteen miles away.

As we saw in Chapter 2, this typical economy of scale is becoming more commonplace, and with it a shrinking time/space window for today's news, particularly since the steep decline in home deliveries requires the hard copies to be in the shops when people are out and about returning from school, work and shopping trips. Some regional daily papers have acknowledged that they are, in reality, mid-morning to mid-afternoon papers by dropping 'evening' from their title, as has the *Swindon Advertiser* (*Press Gazette* 15 July 2005); others have reduced the number of editions produced. Rapidly extending access to the Internet has provided a solution to the dilemma of late-breaking news. Like a growing number of papers, the *Norwich Evening News* moved to placing it on their web site (*Press Gazette* 14 January 2005) as did the *Bolton* [Evening] *News*, one of the regional dailies which have gone one stage further by repositioning themselves as morning titles. From June 2006 it was 'printed overnight to reach the news-stands by 6.30 am' (*Press Gazette* 26 May 2006). A survey in *Press Gazette* (18 September 2006), ironically titled 'Hot off the press?' showed that few 'evening' papers now have more than two timed (as opposed to geographically distinct) editions and that nearly all have a 'print time' for the last edition before midday on the day of publication.

How will this strategy, which puts the paper in direct competition with the national daily press, play out? By mid-2006 there were only 19 long-standing regional morning papers in the UK. As we saw in Chapter 2, the most successful are those in regions with some combination of self-containment and strong self-identity, for example *The Northern Echo*. Contrary to the current regional paper nostrums about localism, according to the editor of this Darlington-based paper 'The aim is to show our readers that this is the only paper they need . . . Around 70 per cent of our readers only buy *The Northern Echo* and so our core philosophy is local, *regional, national*' (*Press Gazette* 13 January 2006; emphasis added). Papers like the *Bolton News* are essentially relying on their readers' seeking national and international news from radio and television, but according to one sceptical editor 'I suspect that some former evening titles will bitterly regret their move the first time there is a major [local] story in the later morning or afternoon' (*Press Gazette* 18 September 2006).

Logistics are not the only reason for these production practices, however. The editor of the Nottingham *Evening Post* has long argued (*Press Gazette* 22 March 1996 and personal communications) that the best use of journalists is to generate as many stories as possible that are exclusive to the paper. Only that way will it compete successfully with local radio, its main rival in that it combines real localism with immediacy. By their nature, these stories will not be unexpected and will probably not be highly time sensitive. The paper's lead on 3 November 2005 about the reorganization of local further education colleges provides a good example: 'EYESORE TO GO IN COLLEGE REVAMP' – lots of people directly or indirectly involved; lots more people interested in the cityscape; pictures and plans essential, which is not easy for local radio to cover, and the issue is too localized for the regional television news (see Chapters 4 and 5).

In the newspaper industry status hierarchy, any regional daily paper ranks above all paid-for weeklies. Nevertheless, in the prescriptions for success in *Press Gazette* the common – but never stated – linking theme is that daily papers seem to be trying to mimic weekly style, in the hope of capturing their greater reader loyalty and more resilient sales. Some papers have increased their visibility by re-establishing the city-centre presence lost when both editorial and production moved to a more modern site (see Chapter 2) or by reopening offices in outlying districts of their circulation area. The Ipswich morning *East Anglian Daily Times* has done this in several Suffolk market towns because 'The amount of community affection this provides cannot be quantified in terms of pounds and pence' (*Press Gazette* 18 June 2004).

Systematic attempts also are being made – or at least actively discussed – to counteract the effect of the takeover of journalism by graduates. Not only does this mean that recruits tend to be from a middle-class back-ground, but they are unlikely to have any previous local affiliations through which to pick up and interpret stories so that, in the view of a respected former editor, 'A lot of regional papers have lost touch with their readers' (Slattery 2005). This lack of fit between those gathering and pro-cessing news and the social composition of the potential readership arises in particularly sharp form in relation to ethnicity. All print media have been slow to pursue active diversity policies, but by 2005 the composition of the workforce had become enough of an issue for the Society of Editors (2005) to commission a report. (For further discussion of working in journalism see Chapter 7.)

Various ways to make news more micro-local are being pursued, for example more editions (like the *Birmingham Mail* example discussed later), although these have heavy logistical and financial implications, or by including 'neighbourhood news' often supplied by volunteer community correspondents. The Ipswich *Evening Star* launched a weekly pull-out sup-plement, while in the Nottingham *Evening Post* City edition, outer areas are clustered geographically and covered on a designated day each week. Items about forthcoming illustrated talks to the local history society certainly have that authentic local weekly feel!

Alongside this new enthusiasm for the micro-local is advocacy of more 'good news', not just 'fire brigade journalism' as the editor of the *Evening Star* put it. In Coventry, as in Ipswich, market research had reported readers saying they were depressed by a constant stream of bad news (*Press Gazette* 24 September 2004 and 16 September 2005). But what is the social scale at which good news is salient? Journalism folklore defines non-news as 'small earthquake in far-off country; no one hurt' but 'smallish hurricane in Birmingham in summer 2005; amazingly no one seriously hurt' was national news. This came not only from its geographic and cultural proximity (see Galtung and Ruge's 1962 classic analysis of newsworthiness) but its 'what-might-have-been' quality, which assists the all-important reader/viewer identification. It is also important to hold in mind that the over-representation of news of 'disorder' identified by Jackson (1971) is not simply the outcome of editorial decision interacting with the affective inclination of the readership towards drama. Heavy reliance on institutional sources like the courts, the police and the emergency services makes the supply of bad news reliable, plentiful and cheap.

We have already seen that weekly papers can be reactive and reflective, rather than high profile, and still be enough of a local presence to be successful. This is not an option for daily papers: they must keep promoting themselves not only to attract the attention of readers for whom, unlike many weekly papers, reading them is not a regular habit, but as an active and important player in local affairs (Aldridge 2003). How can this be achieved alongside the simultaneous imperatives of party political neutrality, lack of social divisiveness, not too much negativity, news coverage that can be planned in advance to make maximum use of limited staff, reader identification and – with luck – the direct audience involvement now common with electronic media? A single device seems to promise all this: campaigning, which has been taken up as the regional paper cure-all to the extent that a trade web site runs a list (see www.holdthefrontpage.co.uk).

Advice from successful campaigners warns that even this reliable generator of news needs to be undertaken with care. 'An initiative without proper planning and research won't even get out of the starting blocks' writes Maguire (2004) under the classic military-style headline 'How to fight a winning battle'. For the sake of the paper's reputation, obviously there must be a reasonably high probability of success, or at least a reflection of what the readership seems to be thinking. A major campaign by the Nottingham *Evening Post* to prevent the closure of Nottinghamshire elderly persons' residential homes was mounted only when it was obvious that this was a popular cause (Aldridge 2003). When the paper was still in family ownership and widely believed to be at heart a Conservative-leaning paper, it was nevertheless very vocal in opposing the Conservative government's policy of closing deep coal mines, given the industry's then domination of

Nottinghamshire life and politics. To do otherwise would have been commercial suicide (see *Press Gazette* 26 October 1992). Campaigns likely to end in heroic failure can only be taken on when the stakes are similarly high, as happened in Newport over the Llanwern steelworks. The editor of the *South Wales Argus* maintained that 'If people feel you were on their side and it was a cause worth fighting for then you haven't lost everything even when you've lost the campaign' (Boden 2003).

Topics to campaign on cannot be relied upon to offer themselves, as those above did. How, given the diversity of the readership – in age, life stage, gender, ethnicity and income, employment or non-employment, area of residence – can a consensual topic be found, let alone one that will attract positive approval? Unfortunately, as I have argued elsewhere (Aldridge 2003), the inexorable logic is that campaigns will tend to rest on either common-sense populism, or an appeal to supposedly universal human values at an affective and sentimental level, or are simply addressing people as consumers, rather than as citizens with rights and responsibilities in the public sphere. In Richardson's (2007: 116–27) analysis of a 12-month sample, health emerged as the most frequent focus of campaigns, usually linked with an appeal for cash donations. Tellingly, cancer charities were particularly prominent: not only is this a group of diseases where research is manifestly yielding results, but it is grimly inclusive, striking at all ages, classes and ethic groups. The second most frequent topic was crime.

Populist 'solutions' are particularly likely to be seized on in relation to deviance, because a more far-reaching deconstruction of cause is usually unsettling. Thus the Bristol 'Clubsafe' campaign (Aldridge 2003; Maguire 2004), while no doubt effective in many ways, rested on the assumption that violence against young women is a problem that they must solve themselves, by appropriate changes in their behaviour and demeanour. The possibility that violence is culturally inscribed in masculinity is too unwelcome to confront. As at 4 November 2005, the most recent addition to the Hold the Front Page list of campaigns was the success of a joint effort by the *Birmingham Mail*, the *Cambridge Evening News* and the Newcastle *Evening Chronicle* to increase the maximum penalty for causing death by dangerous driving. Clearly anything that reduces fatalities must be supported but, as with many other crime-related issues, a common-sense model of deterrence is being reinforced. Does *anyone* think that they are a bad driver, let alone calibrate their driving technique on the basis they will get away with a light sentence if they drive badly enough to kill someone? If the motive is not deterrence, then such campaigns could nourish another easy populist trope – the skewing of the criminal justice system towards retribution.

The topics of the next ten campaigns listed on www.holdthefrontpage.co.uk were animal cruelty (two), taking more 'pride' in the local area (two), saving a struggling football club, cancer prevention, 'reclaiming the neighbourhood' from yobs, and two which related to individuals in dramatic difficulties (being detained at Guantanamo Bay and being in debt to the Benefits Agency because of someone else's action), while the *Surrey Comet* had been 'taken aback' by the response to an appeal for victims of the earthquake in Kashmir. This last instance is the exception that tests the rule: a weekly paper taking up a non-parochial cause, the scale of which justifies its appeal to universal values. As far as the rest are concerned, the common element is their careful blandness.

Perhaps, however, this dull virtue should be applauded. If campaigns are intended to unite by artificially obscuring real social divisions, constructing 'the stranger' is very seductive. This, I and others have argued (Kitzinger 1999, Aldridge 2003, Cross and Lockyer 2006), has been a crucial impulse fuelling the never-ending moral panic about paedophiles in the community, rather than the empirically more likely paedophile in the family. Although famously taken up in the form of a national crusade by the national Sunday tabloid *News of the World*, the first such campaign was launched in 1996 by the *Bournemouth Echo*. Bournemouth is a large and long-established holiday resort with an unusually varied and fluid social composition. Then, as now, it was a very popular retirement destination, but is also the base for a growing number of financial institutions, producing a population split between the affluent and those in the kind of low-paid jobs associated with the service sector, particularly in hospitality and tourism. Alongside these permanent residents were the transient groups of holidaymakers and large numbers of students at the university and at the language schools typical of English south coast resorts. According to the 1991 Census, 15.64 per cent of the population was aged under 15 years, compared with an England and Wales average of 20.07 per cent. No one can dispute the importance of child protection, but in terms of direct relevance to the potential readership in 1996 – manifestly crucial to any newspaper campaign – paedophiles seem an improbable topic. It is this very indisputability that provides the key. Paedophiles occupy that relatively small social space of the universally condemned, the outermost ring of Hall et al.'s (1978) 'signification spiral'. They are the ultimate 'stranger' and thus can be made to do the sociological 'work' of uniting an otherwise socially fragmented locality.

London: locality, community and democracy uncoupled

Central London is experiencing a blizzard of newsprint. At late 2006 there were three weekday titles, two of them wholly free, and an auction was taking place for the rights to distribute two further titles. And, like the rest of the UK, every district of the capital has its own paid-for and free weekly newspapers. Does this mean that those who live in London are unusually well informed as citizens? Far from it: a strong argument can be made that the structure of the London newspaper market makes it a poor basis for debating issues relating to the immediate locality of residence.

London's established daily paper the *Evening Standard* is owned by Associated Newspapers Limited (ANL), a subsidiary of DMGT. Distributed throughout Greater London, until December 2004 the paper was only a paid-for, sold through newsagents and by street vendors who still shout their ware ('St*aaaa*ndud!'). Rather than London residents, the *Standard*'s primary 'address' is to London workers. In reality it has long been an afternoon paper: its last edition goes to press at 3.45 p.m. to accommodate the commuters who form a third of its readership (Greenslade 2004a). As Greenslade points out, the paper likes to measure its performance against the national, not the regional press, to the extent of aiming to 'set the agenda' for national media output later in the day. Both for reasons of business and of prestige, therefore, dramatically falling sales demanded a radical solution: the introduction in 2004 of a free *Lite* edition, distributed in the central area between 11.30 a.m. and 2.30 p.m.

This 'slimmed down, snappy read with more focus on celebrity, lifestyle, shopping and sport' (*The Guardian* 15 December 2004) was aimed directly at the same section of the population as the *Metro*, for which ANL holds the London franchise: young adults who would not otherwise buy a newspaper. In London the *Metro* is distributed during the morning rush hour via dump-bins placed at railway stations under a contract with Transport for London (TfL), Network Rail and some train operating companies. Following a complaint to the Office of Fair Trading (see OFT 2006), ANL gave up this monopoly agreement, opening up the possibility of *two* further afternoon free titles being launched: one at underground stations, the other at stations serving above-ground lines.

Even in this crowded 'market', News International (NI), owners of *The Sun*, *The Times*, *The Sunday Times* and the *News of the World*, saw a 'gap for a quality freesheet' (*Press Gazette* 4 August 2006). In September 2006 NI launched *thelondonpaper*, with an initial print run of 400,000 to be distributed by on-street agents around central London and Canary Wharf from 12.30 p.m. The challenge to the *Evening Standard* was obvious. Despite trade speculation that the latter would respond by becoming completely free, instead it announced that it would drop the *Standard Lite* in favour of a *London Lite*, also distributed in central London from midday onwards (*Press Gazette* 18 August 2006). At the same time the *Evening Standard* tried to reposition itself upmarket. Its price was raised to 50p and the claim 'London's Quality Newspaper' was incorporated into the masthead.

According to the section of its web site addressed to advertisers (www.esadvertising.co.uk/esta/brand/es), it has 'the ultimate cash-rich, time-poor audience', who earn '78 per cent more than the national average'. It also proclaims itself as 'the only newspaper dedicated to London', although if the edition of 13 October 2006 is typical, a smaller proportion of its mainstream news content is London-specific than that in *thelondonpaper* of the same day.

News International's economies of scale and scope are legendary, enabling it, for instance, to bear the vast losses inevitable in the early days of satellite television and thereby achieve total dominance of the platform in the UK. Not only can it use its existing news-gathering infrastructure to produce a new product at relatively low marginal cost, but it has the financial resources to carry it until it establishes itself – or not. If *thelondonpaper* succeeds, it could siphon off advertising not only from the *Standard* but from the London *Metro* too. This would be doubly bad news for ANL/DMGT. While *London Lite* can draw its content from the *Daily Mail* as well as from its paid-for sister paper, 'the *Evening Standard* does not make money' (*Press Gazette* 18 August 2006) – and the *Standard*'s sales in October 2006 were 19 per cent down on the same month in 2005 (*Press Gazette* 20 October 2006).

Alongside all this, *City A.M.*, a free financial weekday paper, was launched in 2005, again by hand and from dump-bins in the City of London, Canary Wharf and Mayfair (home of hedge funds). A year later its business model seemed to have paid off. It was claiming to be 'the most widely-read business newspaper in London' (*Press Gazette* 14 July 2006), closing rapidly on the venerable *Financial Times* and with a high proportion of the sought-after younger audience.

The common factor in these launches and would-be launches is that audiences are defined entirely in terms of age and imputed income. Titles based on this business model have no interest in the less affluent, whether working or not, nor in diversity in all its meanings because, as all these ventures demonstrate, what is being sold to advertisers are the more prosperous fractions of the population. Trainee distributors for *thelondonpaper* were instructed only to offer it to people who appeared to be in the ABC1 (that is, upper income) category. Even more than is typical of regional newspapers, therefore, readers are addressed as consumers first and citizens second, if at all. Hardly surprising, then, that one of the elements present in the *Evening Standard* but missing in both the rival frees is comment. Also missing from *London Lite*, to an even greater extent than in *thelondonpaper*, is political and business news – or much London-specific news at all. In these respects it is indeed 'the *Metro* in purple' (L. Thomas 2006), a series whose proud boast is that it does not have opinions – a sociological impossibility of course.

Where policy and politics are concerned, only transport and crime are guaranteed to 'speak' to all readers of London's daily regional papers. Topics particular to distinct areas or communities within London cannot be covered in depth, just as they cannot in regional television news (discussed in Chapter 5) How, then, can residents of London find out what is happening in their own locality, not just what is on at the multiplex cinema, but about housing, health, the environment, even local history? (Contrary to the discourse in medialand, many Londoners in all social groups have lived in the city for all or most of their lives.) For this they must rely on weekly papers, but even in this sector London is less well served than the rest of the UK.

In terms of a functioning local public sphere the terrain looks promising. London boroughs are unitary authorities, and thus semi-autonomous in terms of not only district council functions such as street lighting and cleaning, but education and social services – and are the same size as many provincial cities. The 2001 Census returns show, for example, the City of Nottingham as nearly 267,000 people and Wandsworth as over 260,000; Norwich as nearly 122,000 compared with Hammersmith and Fulham at over 165,000. Yet while Norwich and its hinterland sustain one of the few remaining regional daily morning papers (the *Eastern Daily Press*), no single weekly paper effectively covers the whole of Hammersmith and Fulham. According to the Newspaper Society database, the *Fulham Chronicle* reaches almost twice as many people in Fulham as in Hammersmith – but even then only about 4.5 per cent of households. This may be an extreme case – the borough is an artificial amalgam of historically separate communities and marked by extremes of wealth and poverty – but even the *Hackney Gazette*, in an ethnically diverse but less socially polarized area, achieves only 17 per cent penetration in its core area. Compare this with the *Newark Advertiser*'s near-49 per cent in the town itself and more than 10 per cent in several of the surrounding areas. Across London 'many paid-for newspapers have been struggling in terms of circulation' (*Press Gazette* 20 January 2006). Falling circulation, falling revenue, cuts in staffing and other resources, less salient and interesting content, further falls in circulation: a downward spiral is hard to avoid.

Outside London, as we have seen, daily evening titles are increasingly dealing with the 'today's news today' problem by putting breaking news on their web site. Many weekly publications apply a similar strategy to make their content more immediate and to intensify the imagined relationship between newspaper and community of readers. See for, example, the *Mansfield Chad*'s site (www.mansfieldtoday.co.uk). London titles are, however, notably absent from the list of newspaper web sites provided by the Newspaper Society (www.newspapersoc.org.uk). In part this is because many are under group management, and therefore linked to a group site, as is Trinity Mirror's South London Press (Tuesday) group: icsouthlondon. icnetwork.co.uk. But to what extent can the titles in such a cluster – or the site itself – act as a forum for the day-to-day concerns of residents? Visiting the site reveals links to Charlton Athletic *and* Crystal Palace *and* Millwall football clubs. It would be hard to imagine a more powerful indicator that these newspapers are not a distinctive presence in the communities they claim to serve nor have the capacity to be a recognized and effective player in local affairs.

Outside London there are few areas of the UK with a more diverse population than the West Midlands. Birmingham, which still supports a morning daily as well as evening daily and regional Sunday titles, provides a vivid case study of all the challenges – in both its literal and euphemistic usages – now facing the regional daily press.

Is anybody out there? Newspapers for a multicultural and globalized Birmingham

In England there are now very few regional morning papers. *The Birmingham Post* is one of them: upmarket, still broadsheet, but struggling with average daily sales of only 12,550 for the first half of 2006, compared with 17,858 for the *Liverpool Daily Post* or 68,504 for the Norwich-based *Eastern Daily Press*. The *Birmingham Post* is published by Trinity Mirror, which also owns the regional *Sunday Mercury* and the daily *Birmingham Mail*, which dropped 'Evening' from its title in 2005, a tactic that has been adopted by a number of regional evening papers, as we saw earlier in the chapter. The *Birmingham Mail* also faces seemingly intractable problems with declining circulation.

In terms of population, Birmingham is the second largest city in the UK. Yet, as Chinn and Dyson (2000) point out, lacking any distinctive geographic feature, or strategic importance or natural resources, it was an insignificant market town until the Industrial Revolution. Suddenly Birmingham became the 'city of a thousand trades', most of them in metal-bashing, from jewellery to motor vehicles. From the mid-nineteenth century until the 1970s the city and its West Midlands region dominated British manufacturing industry, the foundation of the national economy. One of the biggest employment sectors was volume car manufacture (that is, not specialist or luxury marques), for which Birmingham was famous.

Like other successful manufacturing centres, the city relied on migration to meet its need for labour. In the industrial expansion after the 1939–45 World War period many migrants came from south Asia and the Caribbean, attracted by the abundant opportunities for relatively well-paid work, particularly for men. By the 2001 Census, 30 per cent of Birmingham residents declared themselves to be of Pakistani, Indian or Black Caribbean origin.

Since the 1980s, manufacturing industry in the UK has collapsed. In Birmingham 40 per cent of jobs in the sector had gone by 2000, radically changing the city's economy, its social structure and the texture of every-day life. The history of Birmingham is the history of the UK, so the 'career' of two very well-known Birmingham workplaces has wider resonance, as do the problems of its newspapers as they try to identify, address and retain their readership.

Herbert Austin bought what is now the site of the Longbridge car plant, 7 miles out of Birmingham, in 1905. The attraction of the location was its potential for expansion and the unpolluted air needed for a good paint finish (Chinn and Dyson 2000: 6). 'The Austin' employed 400 people and produced 147 cars in 1907. After the disruption caused by the 1914–18 World War, the firm was in severe difficulties, averted only by the develop-ment of the Austin 7 in 1922. By 1934 90,000 cars per year were being pro-duced on a completely self-contained site, including a foundry. Longbridge did not simply assemble cars, it made them from scratch.

In 1961 the site covered 165 acres, produced 193 810 cars, and employed 21,000 people, of whom 'about 3250 employees had worked at the factory for between 25 and 50 years. For many of them, Longbridge was their life and that of their families' (Chinn and Dyson 2000: 17). By then part of a larger conglomerate group, the Longbridge works produced one of the UK's iconic cars – the Austin version of the Mini-Minor – and one of its most successful of the period, the Austin 1100. As Chinn and Dyson's history points out, however, engineering brilliance was not matched by robust financial planning: both were underpriced, an element in the under-investment now seen as causing the long decline of the indigenous British car industry. The history of Longbridge from the mid-1960s to the late 1990s is saga of 'rationalizations' and 'rescue plans' as depressing as it is complicated (Chinn and Dyson 2000: 18–29). In 1999 BMW, who had bought what had become known as Rover Group in 1994, threatened to close the entire site, risking the loss of the estimated 50,000 jobs which depended on Longbridge when direct employment, jobs in the myriad of suppliers, and services like local shops and supermarkets were taken into account. If some workers had 'Longbridge running through our family like words through a stick of rock', with several generations and branches of the family having worked there (Chinn and Dyson 2000: 17, 39), the plant had also become multi-ethnic, as can be seen from many of the illustrations in the Chinn and Dyson history, notably that of the protesting No. 3 Paint shop (2000: 118). In the event, BMW sold parts of the company to the Phoenix Consortium for £10, but the jubilation that this caused was tem-porary. After abortive talks with a Chinese car maker, in April 2005 the firm was put into receivership in such controversial circumstances that formal inquiries both by Department of Trade and Industry (DTI) inspectors and accountancy profession regulators were set up (*The Guardian* 1 June and 18 August 2005). Later in 2005 another Chinese company, Nanjing Automobile, acquired Longbridge, but for a long time remained silent about their intentions for the site, the plant itself or the 5000 remaining employees.

Halfords, the car and cycle accessory retailer, has a happier history but is equally representative of the UK's changing industrial structure and ecology. The firm was founded in 1892 as a hardware store in central Birmingham. Gradually the shops became specialists in cycle parts and then motor accessories. By 1929 there were 200 'depots' (branches) served by an imposing purpose-built combined headquarters and warehouse on Corporation Street, one of Birmingham's landmark main streets (Jones 1981: 40). Halfords remained a family-run firm even after its takeover by Burmah Oil in 1969. For a period in the mid-1970s the grandson of the founder was a senior executive. The 'family' theme was not confined to the board: ritual and long service were prominent in company life. In 1972 a member of the cashier's department retired after nearly 50 years' service and a manager with 47 years' service was promoted; in 1974 eight employees retired with between 44 and 49 years' service (Jones 1981: 201, 204, 246).

For Halfords, as in many other areas of UK economic life, the late 1970s were the end of tradition. Burmah Oil over-expanded and came close to collapse in 1975, only surviving through government and Bank of England support. Senior executive positions in Halfords were no longer customarily held by 'Halfordians'. In 1984 the company was sold to another retail chain who then sold to The Boots Company in 1989 which, facing its own difficulties with over-expansion, sold it to a venture capital group. As at early 2006 the company had 402 branches and around 9000 employees. The directors have, according to their biographies (www.halfordscompany.com), impressive business backgrounds, much of it with international companies, but none appear to have held senior positions in the motor or cycle industry, or have any visible West Midlands links.

A further aspect of Halfords' development also typifies UK industrial change. When its 1929 headquarters became too small, two further storeys were added to the building. In 1971 when this, too, became inadequate, both the offices and the warehouse were moved to a 12-acre greenfield site at Redditch, a new town 15 miles south of Birmingham. Distribution problems caused by traffic congestion and the need for a single-storey mechanized warehouse had become higher priorities than a visible presence in the city centre or easy access for the staff.

Saunders's (1980) study of the political and business elite in Croydon reveals an active network, busy cultivating their local contacts. Even by that time, however, most were not proprietors or autonomous chief executives, but senior managers working within company policies determined elsewhere. The trajectory of Halfords, from local firm to part of a series of large conglomerates, back to a public limited company (plc) with a single focus, might suggest its re-embedding into regional life. Neither the nature of its management, nor the global sourcing of its stock suggest, however, that this is likely. What has happened to Halfords is a direct commentary on what has happened to *The Birmingham Post* . Once the paper was a vital source of intelligence about local industrial and business life, and the local political dynamics and decisions upon which much company policy-making depended. Beyond that, it recorded the social events so important for the solidarity of traditional paternal firms, for making potential profitable contacts, for getting valuable inside information and for establishing one's position in the local hierarchy. Does the section of Birmingham society that used the paper in this way still exist? If so, does it need what the paper offers? According to the *Post*'s management the answer is 'yes', but on a smaller scale and in a range of formats. (*Note*: the following account is based on an interview with Mike Hughes, deputy to the Acting Editor, in December 2005 with a brief follow-up in August 2006.)

From the point of view of advertisers, readership is at least as important as sales. Much of the *Post*'s circulation consists of office copies each read by several people – as many as ten in some cases, the paper believes. As these are individuals with attractive amounts of disposable income, in terms of advertising revenue the paper is more viable than raw sales figures would suggest. Typically these 'aspiring decision-makers' are in their thirties, or even late twenties, and team leaders with at least some corporate expenditure under their control. Just as much as their older and more autonomous predecessors, they need to know what their rivals are doing and what is happening on the local political scene. One of the *Post*'s key editorial strategies is to support a team of very experienced specialist correspondents in key areas such as local government so that it can offer informed assessments of the likely impact of local as well as national policy decisions. Such writers get plenty of space and prominence, which encourages continuity and allows the paper to 'trade on its reputation for good journalism'. The same principle is applied to photographers: the new-style business elite are, apparently, just as interested in the regular social diary page and in seeing a highly professional photograph of themselves in the paper.

Ultimately, though, a newspaper pitched at the business community is competing with electronic sources of information even more than other sectors of the printed media are. One tactic used by the *Birmingham Post* is to push its printing deadline as late as possible, so as to maximize the chance of covering late-breaking local events. Here the relatively small print run consequent on its limited sales is a positive advantage. In mid-2006 the paper launched a subscription-based electronic version. Early indications were that the new venture fitted well with the inclination of its target audience to turn to the Internet: online readership rapidly reached 1 per cent of the total for the hard copy version. Further investment in this new platform, however, depends, like every other aspect of the paper, on corporate decisions by Trinity Mirror, who operate on the national scale in a global market. In that sense, those who produce *The Birmingham Post* daily are all too familiar with the terrain on which their potential readers operate.

Where the *Post* is for the would-be bosses, the *Birmingham Mail*, like all regional 'evening' dailies, tries to be for everyone. But who is 'everyone' in UK cities today? What kind of jobs do they do and who employs them? When a new editor was appointed in 2001, he was much more explicit than is customary in the industry: it needed to transform itself from 'a white man's paper' where 'female and ethnic minority readers were conspicuous by their absence' (*Press Gazette* 9 November 2001; Graham 2003). He was right. In the late 1990s I interviewed a number of journalists in the Post and Mail group. Some were very critical of the extent to which the papers were not just run for men but by men, and sometimes on the basis of outright sexual discrimination. 'The *Mail* is just very traditional . . . I think that if they can see a man who can do the job then they'd rather have him than a woman . . . I think they just feel more comfortable with keeping it all in the club, so to speak' (sub-editor/page planner: personal communication 4 August 1997).

Despite very extensive focus group-based research with readers and a major relaunch in 2003, sales continued to fall, although some of the decline was attributable to the correcting of the accounting irregularities of the late 1990s referred to in Chapter 2. The editor lost his job (*Press Gazette* 11 March 2005). (Even more than other industrial sectors, news media managements work on the sociologically naive principle that systemic problems will be overcome if the right leader can be found.) Steve Dyson, Birmingham born and bred, and a former deputy editor who had played a central role in the 1999 'battle for Longbridge' replaced him. In a further relaunch, much more emphasis was placed on locality-based news, with seven editions of the paper defined geographically by areas of the city and its hinterland (*The Guardian* 3 October 2005; *Press Gazette* 7 October 2005; Steve Dyson, personal communication 7 November 2005). This, Dyson believes, provides the kind of useful and recognizable information that people want: street-level news of anniversaries, planning applications and court proceedings. Asked whether this was the adoption of 'weekly paper news values' discussed earlier in this chapter, Dyson argued that it is more of a return to the buoyant days of the 1960s when the *Mail* had 13 geographical editions. Given the distribution of the population, the effect of this reorganization – although the editor sees it as a positive by-product of a deeper editorial principle about localism – is to sidestep the artificial selection of content based on particular sections of the population, for instance, women or readers of Asian origin. Covering festivals such as Eid ul Fitr is news; providing a 'fact box' about its significance is potentially alienating for some sections of the readership and patronizing for others: 'We would not do it for Easter.' The sustained effort put in by the previous editor to recruit journalists from the ethnic communities and to educate the staff about diversity has been continued; otherwise editorial policy is that news values dictate content. There is to be no mechanical formula for representativeness, based on 'face-counting'.

Like all regional dailies, the *Birmingham Mail* is a keen campaigner. Ironically for Dyson, one of the most high profile issues when he returned to the paper was Nanjing Automobile's refusal to say what they intended for Longbridge. The 'No more Chinese whispers' campaign consisted of printing the same 12 questions every day for 34 days, delivering them to the Chinese embassy and putting the slogan on the front page in Mandarin. Finally clarification was forthcoming, which Dyson sees as all that could be reasonably achieved as the 'rôle of the paper is to provide factual information' so that the former workforce and the wider community can move forward.

In July 2006 Nanjing Automobile finally announced that it planned to build 15,000 cars per year under the MG marque, employing at most a couple of hundred people. They will be assembling kits of components made in China using equipment shipped there from Longbridge (*The Guardian* 18 July 2006). Meanwhile sales of the *Mail* were continuing to fall but Steve Dyson 'remained bullish' although conceded that 'it will probably get worse before it gets better' (*Press Gazette* 10 March 2006). And it did: sales in the first half of 2006 were 18 per cent down on the same period in 2005 (*Press Gazette* 8 September 2006).

Like its sister paper *The Birmingham Post*, the *Mail* reflexively experiences the world it reports. Its readers are employed by companies which, if not global in scale, lack local loyalties. And it, too, is facing staff cuts in the face of the search for 'shareholder value' when an editorial strategy of providing fine-textured local news in a big city context entails more investment in news-gathering. Family ownership, mused Dyson, like that of the rival *Express and Star* based in Wolverhampton, usually means poorer salaries and limited career prospects, but also a longer-term view. How will Trinity Mirror define success and how long will they wait for it?

4 Local broadcasting: what price public service?

Regulating broadcasting: from Reith to Ofcom and back?

Contemporary debate on public service broadcasting (PSB) tends to deploy the discourse of 'market failure', with its implication that PSB is an unfortunate default from the normal and desirable state of things. This would appear to be the assumption behind the often quoted passage from the Peacock committee (Cmnd 9824 1986: para. 580), set up when the Conservative government headed by Margaret Thatcher was at its most confident and radically pro-market. They wrote: 'The best operational definition of public service is simply any major modification of purely commercial provision resulting from public policy.' In paragraph 581 they define the broadcasting market as 'highly imperfect'; 'In particular it provides an inadequate supply of medium appeal and "minority programmes", which most people want to see or hear some of the time . . . the public service institutions have been necessary to provide the listener with what he or she wants as a consumer'.

In fact the UK had a purely commercial broadcasting market only for a very short period before the BBC was established in 1926. Under John Reith, its founding Director General, the BBC was set up as a royal chartered public corporation. That its work should be framed as a public service logically followed: it was not simply an expression of high cultural paternalism or an assumption that there was a mandarin class bound to rule. Franklin (2001: 19) draws on Reith's memoirs to summarize the principles which he believed should determine the provision of public service broadcasting: it should be protected from commercial pressures; it should provide services to the whole community, that is, its reach should be universal; it should be unified, and not subject to regional or sectional interest; and it should be closely regulated to ensure high standards.

Eighty years later the institutional form of PSB has been modified, but Reith's tenets are still visible in the regulation of UK broadcasting. This is not, however, only a matter of high principle – although there are undoubtedly very important issues of 'public goods' and the relationship between communications media and the public sphere at stake. As we saw in Chapter 2 in relation to media ownership rules, even the most competition-friendly governments regard the media industries as exceptional, precisely because of their importance as a forum for enabling (or containing) public debate.

From its inception broadcasting has everywhere been subjected to heavy regulation, not only because of its 'reach' but because of its perceived impact on attitudes and behaviour. Commercial broadcasting in the UK is regulated by Ofcom. Set up by the Office of Communications Act 2002, the new body was explicitly intended to move towards 'light touch' regulation. As one of its 'regulatory principles' puts it: 'Ofcom will operate with a bias against intervention' (www.ofcom.org.uk > About Ofcom, accessed 26 July 2006). It was only relatively late in the legislative process that the public were recast as 'citizen consumers' rather than simply 'consumers'. In other words, Ofcom's domain assumption is the economic rational actor. Nevertheless, the first paragraph of its 'new definition of PSB' for television reads: 'Given the power of television and its ability to reach and influence large numbers of people, public intervention to secure such [valued] content remains justified' (Ofcom 2005a: 7).

In the UK PSB may still be with us, but it is always under challenge precisely because it involves market intervention or, to put it another way, has the potential for raising costs or cutting profits. Heated debate and high stakes are not conducive to careful analysis: it is important to distinguish public service broadcasting as a *form of output* with aims that are not determined solely in commercial terms, from *public ownership*, *public funding* or the *regulation* of broadcasting. As later sections of the chapter will indicate, most of the wrangling over PSB is about cash – the implications in terms of extra costs or lost revenue; and the impact on the marketplace of the BBC as a largely publicly funded organization – and the more so, the more successful it is. Beyond this skirmishing, however, are elements of PSB-inspired regulation that are rarely or never questioned. The most important is the concept of 'due impartiality', which governs *all* news broadcasts based in the UK. Put on a statutory basis by the Broadcasting Act 1990, it was then incorporated in the BBC's 1996 Charter and Licence Agreement and re-established in the Communications Act 2003. Essentially, it prevents broadcasters from taking an editorial position on 'matters of political or industrial controversy; and matters relating to current public policy' (Communications Act 2003: s. 320) either by direct expression of opinion or by the way that news and current affairs programmes are constructed. Arguably this legislation is the key distinguishing feature between broadcasting and the press in the UK. On the one hand, it underpins the public's high regard for broadcast news and, on the other, it provides 'operating space' for national newspapers to make political partisanship and outrageous opinionizing part of their selling proposition.

Less consensual, but also widely approved, is the concept of the 'listed event', a category of sporting events considered so important as part of our shared cultural experience that the exclusive rights to broadcast them cannot be sold to channels that are not free-to-air. The dramatic England/Australia Ashes series of 2005, shown on Channel 4, caused renewed interest in the game. Cricket test matches had, however, been 'delisted' and the rights bought by satellite channel Sky, so subsequent series would only be available 'live' to their subscribers. When this became known, the general public reaction was of puzzlement and anger, demonstrating the extent to which many elements of market intervention in UK broadcasting are entirely taken for granted. (The current 'list' can be found in DCMS 2005a.)

One of Ofcom's wide-ranging statutory duties is to carry out a five-yearly review of public service broadcasting, the first two of which were published in 2005 for both television (Ofcom 2005a) and radio (Ofcom 2005d). In the event, both reluctantly confirm that the broadcasting market is imperfect. 'Our starting point is the promotion of more choice and competition . . . There are, however, some aspects of television which even a better functioning market would not provide, or would under-provide, which society as a whole values enormously, and which should be available to all' (Ofcom 2005a: 7). In relation to radio – although the analysis is just as appropriate to television content – they write:

> our hypothesis was that radio is sufficiently important in people's lives to warrant intervention to address any market failures . . . resulting from the advertising model which meant that broadcasters are likely to cluster round the most lucrative demographic group for advertisers and to reach the maximum geographic audience, so depriving some listeners of the types of service they want – in particular local programming and a wide range of genres, such as specialist music and speech.
>
> (Ofcom 2005d: 18).

Even more significantly, they continue: 'For citizens, we argued that even if the radio market is working effectively for consumers, it may not provide things that are good for society. For example, listening to news on the radio . . . helps to make listeners better informed and therefore better able to participate in a democratic society, *to the benefit of everyone*' (Ofcom 2005d: 18, para 4.10; emphasis added). Much of Ofcom's reasoning is based on the extensive social research which, consistent with its consumerist assumptions, was commissioned as part of these reviews. (These explorations of audience attitudes will be discussed in more detail in Chapter 5.) By a nice irony it seems that the popular voice has endorsed public service broadcasting, even if indirectly in the sense of expressing a high level of approval of the content produced under the current heavy regulatory regime inspired by John Reith.

When the Peacock Committee specified what the market might not provide adequately, it listed particular types of broadcast content (Cmnd 9824 1986: para. 563): informational genres like news, documentary and educational programmes; high-quality arts performance and criticism; and 'critical and controversial programmes covering everything from the appraisal of commercial products to politics, ideology, philosophy and religion'. In most respects this style of regulation, by prescribed types and hours of content, has been rejected – but with one very telling exception. As we shall see, the Communications Act 2003 imposes detailed requirements on public service broadcasters in relation to the amount and scheduling of local and regional news. Apart from being a powerful symbol, three practical effects of the statute demonstrate the centrality of news media to the contemporary public sphere. First, this is one of the very few respects in which the BBC must answer to Ofcom. Second, regional news has emerged as the 'floor' of PSB output required from Channel 3 television. Third, in respect of the 'localness' of commercial radio news production, Ofcom has been compelled to develop just the kind of detailed regulatory guidelines that it had previously rejected as typical of yesterday's 'legacy regulators' (see Ofcom 2005d).

News obligations apart, Ofcom's reworking of PSB is framed according to a set of 'public purposes' for television clearly directed at the consolidation of national culture and social structure through programme content intended to:

- inform ourselves and others and to increase our understanding of the world through news, information and analysis of current events and ideas;
- stimulate our interest in and knowledge of arts, science, history and other topics through content that is accessible and can encourage informal learning;
- reflect and strengthen our cultural identity through original programming at UK, national and regional level, on occasion bringing audiences together for shared experiences; and
- make us aware of different cultures and alternative viewpoints, through programmes that reflect the lives of other people and other communities, both within the UK and elsewhere.

In addition, public service broadcasting should be characterized by programmes that are:

- high quality – well-funded and well-produced;
- original – new content, rather than repeats or acquisitions;
- innovative – breaking new ideas or reinventing exciting approaches, rather than copying old ones;
- challenging – making viewers think;
- engaging – remaining accessible and enjoyed by viewers; and
- widely available – if content is publicly funded, a large majority of citizens need to be given the chance to watch it (Ofcom 2005a: 7–8).

Ofcom uses its testing of public attitudes to legitimate these criteria, but there is no escaping that social and cultural judgements have been made and inscribed in them – as they must be if public service broadcasting is to be maintained. John Reith might wonder why the PSB 'purposes' are so preoccupied with 'different cultures' and 'other communities', but would presumably happily endorse the importance attached to informing and educating the public and celebrating nationhood.

The BBC: national symbol *versus* local demand

The BBC was established as a royal chartered corporation on 1 January 1927 to provide radio services, in which it had a UK broadcasting (although not reception) monopoly until 1972. In 1936 it launched one of the first television services in the world, in which it had a national monopoly until 1955 (Crisell 1997; Curran and Seaton 2003; DCMS 2005: 107–11). From the first, however, its mission as an embodiment of national sentiment and cultural identity was in tension with the breadth of 'address' – including in geographic terms – that justified this claim. Despite its origin as a consortium of commercial firms, the BBC quickly acquired the classic profile of a public bureaucracy: rigidly hierarchical with centralized decision-making. Naturally its main base was in the administrative capital of the UK: London. As Harvey and Robins (1994) point out, as early as the 1930s this was being questioned, for example by Robson (1935: 475), who proposed that there should be semi-autonomous 'miniature BBC[s]' which would be allocated a proportion of the licence fee and make their own programmes 'for regional purposes'. Given that autocracy was the natural inclination of the corporation's founding Director General this was never a likely move – and it became even less so under the command economy established to fight the 1939–45 World War and deal with the severe social problems that succeeded it.

This tension has not been resolved. By the time of the negotiations over the Ninth Charter – expected to run from January 2007 for ten years – the contradictions had become even more marked. The BBC is one of the biggest players in the global television market (in wildlife programming, for example, it is the world leader), yet the reasonable expectation exists that, as a publicly funded institution not unlike the National Health Service, it should have a visible, accessible, physical presence throughout the UK.

BBC television in the regions

The BBC's duty to provide regular bulletins of regional news at specified times was formalized by a 2003 amendment to the 1996 Charter and Licence Agreement. Regional programming must be 'of regional interest', 'of high quality' and, in the case of news, in or near peak viewing times (Cm 6075 2003: S5G.1). At the time that the amendment was drafted, these arrangements were the responsibility of the BBC itself, through its self-regulation by the Governors. Henceforth, however, any proposals for changes to them were subject to agreement by Ofcom (Cm 6075 2003: S5G.3), one of the first formal breaches of the BBC's corporate autonomy.

At late 2006 the weekday cycle on BBC1 consisted of a half-hour early evening bulletin with shorter versions early in the day, at lunchtime, mid-afternoon and after the late evening news – a very similar pattern to that on Channel 3. According to the corporation's statement that preceded the Green (government consultative) Paper on the BBC (DCMS 2005b), 'BBC One's 6.30pm [weekday] news programme for the Nations and regions of the UK are the most watched news programmes in the country – over six million viewers tune in every day' (BBC 2004c: 66). Eighteen different programmes are provided: England is divided into 12 regions with 'sub-opts' from Oxford, Cambridge and the Channel Islands, and there are services for Wales, Scotland and Northern Ireland, with further versions on BBC2 and (at the time the document was compiled) two digital services (BBC 2004b: 31–2).

Neither Briggs's (1995) magisterial history of the BBC nor the key statement on the BBC's 'role in representing the nations and regions' (BBC 2004b) in the summary history of the corporation provided in an Appendix to the Charter Green Paper (DCMS 2005b) provide a clear account of when and why the corporation started providing regional news and other programming on television. Briggs provides a detailed history of the protracted internal debate about the potential value of local radio, but his section on 'the regional and the local' in England (1995: 623–69) moves seamlessly into a discussion of television without, tellingly, a separate sub-heading. One powerful reason for resisting regional television was its cost; any programmes made in the regions should be suitable for the whole national network. Accordingly, for instance, the BBC in Bristol came to specialize, as it still does, in wildlife and nature programmes.

But there may also be a more powerful underlying reason for this opacity: the BBC's own long-standing ambivalence about its relationship to the English regions (see, for example, Lewis and Booth 1989: 95–7). Reading the 'nations and regions' document (BBC 2004b) one gets a sense of confusion and anxiety that what was once marginal and secondary is suddenly central, not only because the regional news service is already so popular, but because of growing pressure on the corporation to sustain and strengthen it. The BBC's standing as a news provider at every level from worldwide to local is crucial to defending its continued existence as a pub- licly *funded* public service broadcaster. At the same time this concentration of responsibility has allowed Channel 3, particularly ITV plc, operating space radically to reduce the priority it gives to regional news.

The semi-autonomy of the BBC, based in its governance under royal charter, became one of the central controversies in the process for renew- ing the charter for the ten years from January 2007. It was particularly ironic, therefore, that in its eagerness to strengthen its regional presence, the BBC yet again attracted criticism for seeming arrogance in taking major policy decisions without external consultation. The BBC's vision for the next charter period (2004c: 66) simply announced: 'We intend to launch a new highly local television news service for . . . 50–60 areas across the UK with up to 10 minutes an hour of genuinely relevant local news and infor- mation . . . We will explore the relative costs and feasibility of launching this service on digital television, including Freeview, and on broadband'; this '"ultra-local" news service will harness the growing power of video journalism'. A month later a pilot scheme for five areas of the West Midlands was announced, running from late 2005 until mid-2006, with separate services for Shropshire; Hereford and Worcester; Stoke-on-Trent and Staffordshire; Coventry and Warwickshire; and Birmingham and the Black Country (that is, around Dudley and Wolverhampton). 'We are talking about "local TV" in the same sense as our 40 local radio services across England' wrote Griffee (2005), the controller of the BBC's English regions. His article in *Press Gazette* was part of the BBC's attempt deal with angry reaction from the regional newspaper industry, including a '63-page submission to the Government' by The Newspaper Society (*Press Gazette* 22 July 2005). As had already happened with local Internet sites, 'Our staff are paying through their licence fees for the BBC to compete with them' as the editor of the *Hull Daily Mail* saw it, although other editors of major regional dailies were more sanguine. 'We feed off each other anyway. TV feeds off newspapers, newspapers feed off TV . . . and if we have to sharpen up, so be it' was the response of the editor of the *Manchester Evening News* (Lagan 2005a). A month later the BBC Director of Nations and Regions was offering another 'olive branch' with assurances that the new services would come to agreements with regional papers for the use of their content and staff for this 'new content on existing platforms' (*Press Gazette* 21 October 2005), a reassurance repeated to the Society of Editors in the period when the pilot services were being evaluated (*The Guardian* 7 November 2006).

BBC local radio

Why was the regional press so exercised by the BBC's proposal for more fine-grained local television service? According to the editor of the *Tamworth Herald* 'there seems to be an inexhaustible public demand for local news in whatever media it's delivered' (Powell 2005) and both BBC and commercial local radio had operated on their territory for over 30 years. Presumably it was the possible cumulative impact. As we shall see, commercial local radio has not competed with newspapers for the advertising of local products and services as much as might have been expected, and its provision of local news has become vestigial – where it exists at all. Not only would the proposed local television news be free, possibly on multiple platforms and moving towards ambient, on-demand provision (see Chapter 2), but it might attract the young adult audience. The only direct challenger as a news provider, BBC local radio, much as it is valued by the audience (see more detailed discussion in Chapter 5), historically has 'tend[ed] to have a higher proportion of ABC1 and older listeners than commercial services' (Ofcom 2005d: para. 3.21) while 'Commercial radio continues to dominate listening among the . . . markets most often targeted by advertisers – notably, 15 to 24 year-old listening' (Carter 2003: 46). In 2004 the mean age of the audience for all local radio was 39 years, but for the BBC it was 55 years – a figure which the corporation seemed happy to embrace as an indicator of its distinctive public service contribution (BBC 2004b: 25, fig. 3.6)! Moreover the BBC takes a much smaller share of the local radio audience. While the validity of television and radio audience figures is hotly contested because of the intractable and long-running methodological issues surrounding their measurement (see Tacchi 2001), in terms of 'share' these problems are less significant. As at late 2005, figures from Radio Joint Audiences Research Limited (RAJAR) gave local commercial radio 76 per cent of the audience (*Press Gazette* 4 November 2005).

Initially there was 'no real demand for local radio', write Lewis and Booth (1989: 94) citing the Pilkington Committee (Cmnd 1753 1962), one of the landmark government reports on broadcasting. Nevertheless the idea was established on the political agenda in part, according to Crisell (1997: 143), because the highly publicized 'pirate' broadcasters of the mid-1960s operated at a relatively local scale and included some coverage of local events. (The 'pirate' tag was apt because the best-known stations sidestepped the BBC monopoly by broadcasting from ships moored just outside territorial waters on the east and south coasts of England.) Radio Leicester became the first BBC local station in 1967 (Crisell 1997: 143; DCMS 2005b: 108).

By late 2005 there were 40 such stations. These are mapped in the BBC's 'nations and regions' document (BBC 2004b: 32) although, with unintentional symbolism, the map is difficult to decipher. The passage that follows the map is an annotated example of a typical daily cycle of radio and television output from six of the regions: WM (West Midlands), Cumbria, Jersey, Scotland, Wales and Northern Ireland – illustrating their range, variety and inclusiveness. 'Local phone-ins, public debate, faith, sport and community action remain at the heart of the schedules' of these 'distinctive speech based local stations'. For instance: ' 12.00–2.00pm News and topical debate on both Radio Wales and Radio Cymru' (BBC 2004b: 33–5). It could be argued, however, that the six areas chosen are hardly typical: three are 'nations', which operate on a rather different plane from local radio in the English regions, as we shall see in Chapter 6. Two (Cumbria and Jersey) are geographically isolated and self-contained, which provides a more assured demand from the audience. Only WM has to compete for an audience in a diverse English region whose boundaries may not be those perceived by the audience in their daily lives, an issue to which we shall return in the discussion of content in the next chapter.

BBC Internet-based local news

Alongside the deliberately traditional – even cosy and parochial – style of its regional radio and television output, the BBC has quietly become a driving force in Internet-based news. Interestingly, the first column of the table of output referred to above contains the same text in every cell: '58 *Where I Live* sites updated every 2 mins'. Initiated in 2000, these include a wealth of news, weather, webcam images of traffic troublespots, and listings of community and leisure events organized, in England, on a county-by-county basis. In fact the 'news' is little more than a bulletin board, resembling a 'news in brief' newspaper section of one-paragraph spot news items more than the conventional BBC radio or television bulletins. On the other hand it is an easily accessed, trustworthy, rolling news service heavily used by the all-important younger segments of the audience: 46 per cent were in the 15 to 34 age group according to 2003 figures (BBC 2004b: 20).

To an even greater extent than the 'ultra-local' television proposals described above, the BBC's move into Internet news produced vehement protest from the regional press, including a campaign by the Newspaper Society. 'Now we are faced with a largely unregulated non-commercial competitor threatening to stamp on the seedlings shooting up in the local online space' wrote a senior manager of one of the medium-sized newspaper groups (Davies 2004). News was not the problem: it was that the BBC's local pages included listings of commercial leisure events, a key selling point for regional newspapers. Partly in response to this lobbying, the DCMS commissioned an independent review (DCMS 2004), which concluded 'What's On listings sites do not seem . . . to be sufficiently distinctive from commercial alternatives or adequately associated with public service purposes' (DCMS 2004: 10). The BBC's reaction was, in part, injured innocence, arguing that these listings promoted 'activities which bring people together for collective, community experiences' (BBC 2004b: 26). As at early December 2005, this included a '360 degree virtual tour' of a Nottingham microbrewery. The news pages of local sites now have links to other media sources so that users can 'check out a different perspective on the same story with a longer-term view of improving media literacy', according to the BBC's rather disingenuous response (*Press Gazette* 15 October 2004).

Unity in diversity? The BBC's contradictory mission

Writing of the perpetual struggle against the BBC's centripetal tendencies, Harvey and Robins (1994: 43) suggest that 'the regionalist argument was primarily about a more representative balance of programmes reflecting the cultural diversity of Britain'. It still is, but 'diversity' is no longer a code for metropolitan versus provincial, or even dominant bourgeois values versus the more 'authentic' cultural practices of ordinary people. Today 'diversity' is a multi-layered concept that must be operationalized and addressed by all public sector agencies, despite its being simultaneously fugitive and freighted with sensitivities.

In *The BBC's Role in Representing the Nations and Regions* (BBC 2004b), much is made of the geographical dimension of diversity: 'Lives are lived locally' it declares, clearly referring to the commissioned research on daily life discussed in Chapter 1 above; 'The area where people live, the realities of the community and society immediately around them gives them stability and roots in their lives' (BBC 2004b: 3). This 'opening vision' goes on to mention the local web sites and the contentious proposals for local television explained earlier. The following chapter begins 'Local radio is the foundation of the BBC' (BBC 2004b: 5) but then rather spoils the effect by, in the second paragraph, continuing 'Within ten months of going on air, the BBC took a giant leap forward with the first ever UK-wide simultaneous broadcast out of London, on 19 August 1923'.

Ambiguities like this infuse the whole document. For example, 'new ways to connect with communities' are listed as BBC Open Centres,

Community Buses and local partnerships delivering education and training in media literacy (BBC 2004a: 14, BBC 2004b: 3). Manifestly these are extremely worthwhile and appropriate for a publicly funded institution of the scale and scope of the BBC, but surely what is being addressed is not 'community' but inequality of wealth and skills. This becomes much more explicit in the final statement of purposes submitted to charter review, in which they are described as 'focusing on cities and regions where audience need is highest' (BBC 2004c: 14). Vital non-geographical dimensions of community are also prominent in *The BBC's Audiences*: 'Some programmes are designed for communities of interest . . . Others portray members of different communities reflecting the wide diversity of the country' (BBC 2004a: 12). Here diversity of ethnic origin is being signalled, as well of 'interest' in, say, gardening. Pursuing the same theme, the 'nations and regions' document talks about the corporation's support for 'faith communities' but again demonstrates that perhaps the implications of diversity have not been rigorously interrogated by declaring 'All of the BBC's 46 radio stations provide religious output on a Sunday' (BBC 2004b: 8).

Both documents catalogue an impressive array of valuable and valued activity. Both make large claims about the BBC's role in sustaining democracy and active citizenship, confirmed in *Building Public Value* (BBC 2004c). One of the BBC's 'five main ways' of creating 'public value' is 'Social and community value: by enabling the UK's many communities to see what they hold in common and how they differ, the BBC seeks to build social cohesion and tolerance through greater understanding' (BBC 2004c: 8). But both documents are also confused, repetitive and sometimes contradictory, conveying the strong impression that 'nations and regions', however conceived, have not been at the forefront of corporation policy. Rather, the sense is of a slightly desperate round-up of anything that might be relevant, compiled under pressure. Key organizing concepts and distinctions are not thought through, for example that already discussed: between 'community' as locality, of whatever degree of self-containment, and as non-place communities of affiliation or shared activity or disadvantage. Why does the latter appear in a document about 'nations and regions' at all?

Another slippage is between BBC output addressed *to* a nation or region and its activities *in* that region. Apart from the educational projects already mentioned, a table of the BBC's activities around the UK lists, under the English regions, 'production for BBC television and radio networks' (BBC 2004b: 30). In other words, the BBC as a source of investment and employment, a theme which emerges much more strongly in *Building Public Value* (BBC 2004c) and the Charter Green Paper, where the licence fee is described as 'venture capital for creativity' (DCMS 2005b: 27). Again, who would want to argue against this potential for contributing to economic regeneration, but the categories need clearer demarcation. Logically the BBC could decentralize all its production while producing nothing reflecting life in a particular geographic region.

One of the more coherent and confident of the strands in the documents is that relating to news. Of seven aims relating to the support of 'civic life and national debate' (BBC 2004b: 6), five are directly connected with gathering and broadcasting news, although even here there are contradictions between its purposes of unifying and of serving diverse needs. The '3000 journalists stationed across the UK outside London' are positioned as being part of a 'regional news-gathering service' 'feeding into the overall BBC news machine'! Similarly, *Building Public Value* asserts 'The BBC . . . will continue to invest strongly in news-gathering at local, national and international levels', but then continues 'It will commit to keeping a broad range of *specialist* correspondents and *foreign* bureaux, prioritizing expert first-hand reporting, careful verification and a comprehensive *international* agenda of foreign reports and analysis' (2004c: 65; emphasis added).

Quite so, but again the national and international is privileged without any qualifying comment.

Perhaps the inexorable logic of the BBC today is that it must, in the last analysis, give priority to 'uniting the country' (BBC 2004a: 12) via the 'high holy days of television' (Dayan and Katz 1992) ranging from the Olympics to royal funerals to instant but thorough coverage of national and international disasters. These must have precedence over the competing demands of diversity of any kind, including regionality, not least because it is widely believed that the BBC's status as a unifying force in national culture and anchor of national identity protected it from outright privatization under the Conservative governments of the 1980s and early 1990s. Take this immutable order of priorities. Then add in increasing costs. The White Paper on charter renewal (Cm 6763 2006) confirmed the corporation's traditional function as a leader in advancing broadcast technology: it is now expected to carry much of the responsibility for, and financial cost of moving ahead with digitalization. At the same time – yet again – its public funding and central place in a leading industrial sector have driven renewed demands that it decentralize its operations, which itself will generate large capital costs. Finally, factor in major expenditure cuts, which in a labour-intensive industry are bound to fall heavily on staffing. These are the outcome in part of real budgetary pressures but are also a strategic response to the renewed political struggle over the level of the licence fee. In this environment, additional funding for the BBC's regional newsrooms is not the likely outcome, let alone enough to generate extra content for the new 'ultra-local service' at a level which would allow self-originated stories or a 'highly active discovery' (McManus 1994) style of news-gathering.

Regulating commercial broadcasting

Ventures into print media no longer need a licence, but in the UK every person who wishes to broadcast still does, even though digitalization has removed the historic justification of 'spectrum scarcity'. As we have seen in the earlier discussion of 'public service broadcasting', the underlying rationale is the assumption that broadcast media are potentially more powerful in their impact on the audience than print. With the exception of Internet-based services, the structure and content of all non-BBC broadcasting in the UK is regulated by Ofcom, who determine what licences will be available, at what price, who holds licences and the terms on which they do so. Overall content standards are set down through the *Ofcom Broadcasting Code* (www.ofcom.org.uk/tv/ifi/bcode) but some licences come with specific content conditions (for example, the public service broadcasting-related duties discussed above and below) or that bids should be for a specific format (for example, in the case of radio, be speech rather than music based). Beyond that, the developing practice is that bidders should set out their own 'format' proposals (Ofcom 2005d: s. 7). Ofcom then monitors licensees' performance on the basis of these, backed by a range of sanctions including fines and, ultimately, withdrawal of licence. (For a full account of Ofcom's powers, activities and adjudications for both television and radio, see www.ofcom.org.uk.)

The declared aim of the Communications Act 2003 was to 'deregulate where possible in order to promote competition and attract new investment, ideas and skills' (www.culture.gov.uk/broadcasting/media_owner-ship, accessed 27 September 2005) but, as we have already seen in relation to newspapers, exceptional statutory limits are placed on the operation of the market where news media are concerned. Thus the very next paragraph of the DCMS explanatory notes quoted above goes on: 'The aim is to retain a balance of different media viewpoints (a "plurality" of debating voices) in society, and specific limits on the ownership of media assets (over and above competition law thresholds) are the best way to achieve this'.

For print media, 'plurality' issues are dealt with by media-specific aspects of general competition legislation (see Chapter 2) unless cross-media mergers involving broadcasting are involved, in which case Ofcom has a role in advising the Secretary of State. The ownership rules that it operates cover both who can hold a licence and the overall distribution of licence-holding thought necessary to sustain 'plurality'. Restrictions cover categories of 'persons' (in the legal sense, that is, they may be organizations). For example, since the Communications Act, companies based outside the European Economic Area can now bid for licences. Judgements are also made about the attributes of particular bidders: 'whether persons controlling or carrying out media enterprises post-merger are likely to comply with the spirit as well as the letter of the broadcasting standards set down in the Communications Act 2003' (Department of Trade and Industry 2004: 35).

In relation to radio, the 'plurality' goal is that 'in any local area there should be at least two commercial radio operators plus a BBC local radio service' (Carter 2003: 17). Domination of the commercial media output in any particular area by one company or group of companies is now limited by a 'points' system set out in The Media Ownership (Local Radio and Appointed News provider) Order 2003. (This can be found, together with a supporting explanatory note at www.opsi.gov.uk/si/si2003/20033299.) In general terms, points are allocated to types of licences according to the proportion of the audience in the area that they are expected to attract. 'Persons' who hold only radio licences are allowed to hold a '"cluster" of licences' which overlap with each other in an area up to 55 per cent of the total points available. The greater significance attributed to cross-media ownership is signalled by 'the dominant local newspaper provider' or the regional Channel 3 licence-holder being limited to one licence and 45 per cent of the points. Moreover 'No person may hold a local radio licence *and* the local Channel 3 television licence *and* be the dominant local newspaper provider in the same area' (Ofcom 2004b; emphasis added).

Commercial television in the regions: public service *versus* profits

Commercially funded television (henceforth Channel 3) started broadcasting in the UK in 1955. Although national in coverage, it was specifically intended by the Conservative government of the time not only to challenge the BBC's monopoly, but its monolithic organization and patrician, metropolitan style. Licences to broadcast were issued on the basis of geographic regions whose boundaries still stand, even though they were drawn up 'in economic rather than cultural terms' (Curran and Seaton 2003: 182). Because the new system was funded entirely by what are now known as 'spot ads', a region could only be financially viable 'if the joint purchasing power of the audience was sufficient to make up a marketing unit' (Curran and Seaton 2003: 182). Even so, in the early days some of the licences attracted little interest, or changed hands relatively cheaply because of their poor financial performance.

Not only the structure but the management style of the new channel contrasted with that of the BBC. The key players tended to come from a business rather than a public administration orientation. One of the most successful and visible was Lew Grade, a theatrical agent and impresario and, by a nice historical turn, uncle of Michael Grade, Chairman of the BBC

Board of Governors during the highly contested reviews of the BBC Charter and of the meaning of public service broadcasting, discussed earlier in this chapter. When Michael Grade took the combined role of the chief executive and chair of the board of what was by then ITV plc in November 2006, the sentimental connection was, Grade said, one of the reasons for his sudden and unexpected move.

In one crucial respect, however, Channel 3 remained within the traditional framework of British broadcasting: it was subject to close regulation both of structure and content. Not only were there restrictions on cross-ownership between newspapers and television licences, which remain in modified form, there were also limits on the number of regional licences that one operator could hold. Persuaded by the companies' arguments about the needs for economies of scale if UK companies were to compete in the global marketplace in television content, successive governments gradually permitted a greater degree of conglomeration through merger. The last restrictions on the holding of multiple Channel 3 licences were removed by the Communications Act 2003. Consequently, by early 2004 12 of the 15 licences – including all those for England and Wales – were held by one company.

ITV plc, the new monolith formed when permission was given for the merger of Carlton and Granada, immediately made a number of moves the business logic of which was compelling in a highly competitive environment, but which further undermined the reality of its supposed regional architecture. Just as we saw with regional newspapers, economies of scale are pursued not only because of the potential savings in fixed costs but for the opportunity – even if it is a one-off – to realize assets. Soon after the Carlton–Granada merger, ITV plc closed its studios in Southampton, at New Hythe in Kent and in Nottingham. Two hundred jobs were lost at the Nottingham site, at which major networked programmes had been made, as well as its being the base for *Central News East*. Opposition to the closure came not only from the workforce but from local residents and local politicians worried about ITV plc's commitment to active news-gathering in the East Midlands region. Despite assertions that these rationalizations would not affect news-gathering capability – and indeed would underwrite a major modernization of equipment (Azeez 2004) – scepticism remained. At the time of the Nottingham studio closure no premises for the promised regionally-based news hub had been identified, and the transmission of the bulletins themselves was moved permanently to Birmingham, 50 miles away in the *Central News West* region. Eventually a news-gathering operation was established on an industrial estate 5 miles east of Nottingham and the former Central television studios were sold to the University of Nottingham as a branch campus. A couple of years later further adjustments to ITV's regional news operation were announced. From the management perspective these would ensure that realigned boundaries would 'ensure that ITV broadcasts to identifiable regions'. Employee reaction was predictably different: 'You cannot expect to cut 40 to 50 jobs out of the service and expect it to be as good' *(Press Gazette* 9 June 2006). Concerns that the search for savings could undermine the effectiveness of the regional news operation received tangential support when ITV plc was fined by Ofcom for broadcasting an East Midlands late evening regional bulletin pre-recorded because of staff shortages (*The Guardian* 5 April 2005). Broadcasting news bulletins live is a condition of licence.

Shortly after the merger an 'editor of the ITV regions' was appointed, based in London. Then a more standardized ITV1 'brand' was imposed with a newly designed opening sequence for both national and regional news bulletins and other on-screen markers like station 'idents'. At the time of this centralization the new editor defended the strategy on the basis that it would be a way of sharing best practice rather than a reduction in regional editorial autonomy: 'I'm not going to be telling the heads of news what they ought to be leading on' because ITV newsrooms 'historically have been better connected to the communities they serve than the opposition' (Tomlin 2004a).

The doubts raised about ITV plc's long-term commitment to regionality fed by these organizational changes were further reinforced when the company began to lobby Ofcom for a reduction in its public service broadcasting-related content responsibilities, deploying all the familiar themes about international competitiveness. Apart from providing good quality regional news at agreed times, long-standing regulatory requirements had placed three further duties on Channel 3 licence-holders: to produce a prescribed weekly amount of non-news programming of specific interest to their region (quite separate from producing material for the network with a distinctive regional flavour, classically *Coronation Street* by Granada); to broadcast religious programmes; and to show programmes for children. None of these non-news programme categories are particularly expensive to produce, but they cost more than buying ready-made content and are unattractive to advertisers. Thus they are a net cost to the broadcaster (Ofcom 2004a: paras 3.22. and 3.26) – even more so if they have to be broadcast in 'peak hours'. ITV plc claimed that in 2004 this amounted to £250 million per year (*The Guardian* 30 June 2004). In 2005 Ofcom announced, in effect, the phased ending of all non-news PSB demands on Channel 3 in England. Part of the justification was overt: research for the review of public services broadcasting had shown the non-news regional output to be little valued by audiences. Accordingly, the hours per week in the English regions were to be reduced from three to 1.5 hours a week in the English regions, reducing to 0.5 hours per week after digital switchover (Ofcom 2005a: ch. 3). (In Scotland, Wales and Northern Ireland different considerations and rules apply: see Chapter 6.)

Evidently the decision on religious and children's programming was seen as potentially more embarrassing: it was not so much announced as buried in the small print. The relevant news release (Ofcom 2005b) is soporifically headed 'Ofcom accepts commercial public service broadcasters' proposals on Tier 3 obligations'. After consultation, Ofcom had allowed ITV plc to reduce children's programming from 11.5 to eight hours per week, and religious programming from two to one hour per week, applying for the first time the criterion that this type of output from all 'public service channels' should be 'taken together'.

These concessions demonstrate that the news/citizenship nexus is the most entrenched element of the bundle of ideas that make up public service broadcasting. The specific inclusion of 'a suitable range of programmes (including regional News programmes) which are of particular interest to persons living in the area for which the service is provided' is one of the rare acknowledgements that an effective public sphere must operate locally as well as nationally. While Ofcom has since dispensed with some of this 'range of programmes', the commitment to news remained unchanged, including that 'some Regional News must appear in peak-time', thus establishing the baseline PSB responsibilities for holders of Channel 3 licences.

As the chapters on regional newspapers have shown, even when passive and office-bound, gathering and producing news is labour-intensive and thus expensive. Ofcom's review of public service broadcasting revealed that the costs are so great that even its popularity with regional television audiences is not enough to make it profitable in terms of the sale of advertising. Accordingly, ITV plc began to argue that Channel 3 licensees should receive a subsidy to offset their remaining PSB responsibilities, in addition to the cost reductions outlined above. As an industry commentator lamented 'Regional news and regional current affairs – once the USP of ITV – are apparently now regarded as nothing but an expensive burden . . . the trouble with putting a financial cost-benefit analysis on a public service tradition such as local news provision is that it ignores the brand loyalty value of that provision' (Shaw 2005).

At the time, this tactic of staged withdrawal from the expensive commitment of providing good quality regional news was interpreted as part of a larger strategy: making ITV plc into an attractive takeover target. Ironically, it was rapidly overtaken by other changes in the media landscape. Advertising revenues were falling, in part because of accelerating competition from online, but also because of a declining share of the audience caused by the twin pressures of multiplying channels/platforms and seemingly less successful programme output. 'The numbers just don't add up' according to a newspaper report on takeover speculation (*The Guardian* 29 August 2005), presumably because advertising space on its main channel, ITV1, still accounted for 70 per cent of the company's revenue

(*The Guardian* 9 December 2005). The downward spiral continued into 2006, with the share price tumbling and the departure of the chief executive. A large deficit in the company's pension fund further exacerbated the company's problems, but the fundamental reason for investor scepticism was that holding a Channel 3 analogue licence was seen as a less and less profitable proposition. As the Chair of the Ofcom Board put it in the 2006 Ofcom Lecture 'after digital switchover . . . [broadcast] licences will no longer be scarce' (www.ofcom.org.uk/media/speeches/2006/11/annual_lecture). There seems, therefore, almost no prospect that ITV plc, or any successor, will invest substantially in regional news output, a form of content that is by definition incapable of being sold on to other UK commercial broadcasters, let alone in the international marketplace.

Local commercial radio: the 'light touch' gets heavier

All histories of commercial radio in the UK (for example, Lewis and Booth 1989; Carter 2003; Curran and Seaton 2003; Ofcom 2005d; Crisell and Starkey 2006) comment on its haphazard development. When the first licences were issued under the 1972 Broadcasting Act, it was on the basis of locality, not because there was an established audience demand or robust commercial model, but because it was thought that 'localism' rhetoric would win over a sceptical government. But, as Lewis and Booth (1989: 99) astringently point out, 'commercial broadcasting is in the business of selling audiences to advertisers' and for most purposes what interests advertisers is age as a proxy for life stage, activities and spending patterns. Moreover, in the 1970s those advertisers who wished to appeal to a geographically defined audience had well-established relationships with regional newspapers, as they still do. At its inception, then, local radio had to look for advertisers of national products, for whom they faced competition from national newspapers, specialist printed media and commercial television. Worse, 'except in densely populated urban areas, local stations could not deliver a large enough chunk of the audience to interest advertisers of products for the mass market' (Lewis and Booth 1989: 100).

Given this very fragile financial basis, it is unsurprising that holders of local analogue licences made the books balance by reducing the cost of their content coupled with minimal compliance with their regulatory obligations. Most offered predominantly national rather than local news, bought from Independent Radio News, based in London. By the late 1990s some had even been allowed by the then regulator, the Radio Authority, to drop news bulletins altogether (*Press Gazette* 8 May 1998). The rest tended to offer only 'capsule' news generating local content from passive sources: 'on diary' events; news beats like the police and the courts and, of course, press releases. The outcome, Crisell observes (1998: 30) was typically 'derivative and lacking in distinctiveness' with less depth than that provided by the local newspaper.

Gradually station formats converged, so that by Ofcom's review of radio regulation the 272 local licensees 'mainly focused on mainstream music output' (Ofcom 2005d: 9). Or, to put it another way, '80 per cent of the population have no commercial local news and speech service' (Brown 2005). As with television there was also a consolidation of ownership as restrictions on the ownership of multiple licences were progressively removed, particularly by the Communications Act 1990 and the Broadcasting Act 1996. Even as sympathetic a commentator as Carter (2003: 39), writing an official obituary for the Radio Authority before its merger into Ofcom, summarizes the process as a 'shift from an industry run by a network of local fiefdoms through the emergence of regional groupings in the late Eighties to a Nineties industry dominated by half a dozen or so major ownership groupings'. By 2005 two companies (Emap and GCap) owned '60 per cent of all commercial radio listening' but the really significant development according to Robinson (2005) was that Ofcom had, for the first time, granted a licence to a non European Economic Area (EEA) company. CanWest, a Canadian-based company transnational media group with very extensive media holdings in anglophone Canada and Australia, acquired the Solent FM licence.

Radio's great advantage is that it is flexible and cheap to produce. Until the arrival of 'citizen journalism' via email, texting and cameraphone, the first accounts of unexpected breaking news were usually provided by radio. It is particularly piquant, therefore, that what should have been a classic local news event exposed the inadequacy of many commercial stations' news-gathering infrastructure. When the M11 was brought to a standstill by a blizzard in January 2003 it emerged that almost none of the contiguous local commercial stations had a journalist on duty. The direct result was the incorporation into the Communications Act 2003, despite the inevitable lobbying from the industry (Brown 2005), of a duty on Ofcom to provide a test of 'localness'. With evident reluctance, given its 'premise that . . . where possible the regulator should avoid determining how the programming is made' (Ofcom 2005d: 57) Ofcom has underwritten the 'input regulations' set out by its predecessor, the Radio Authority. Both the guidelines and the preceding discussion (Ofcom 2005d: 63–7; 70–2) make interesting reading because of the insight they provide into how, left to themselves, commercial radio stations might deal with the expense of originating genuinely local news. Studios must 'be in the area to which they broadcast' (Ofcom 2005d: para. 7.35). Station formats must 'ensure that an appropriate proportion of programming is made locally' (Ofcom 2005d: para. 7.41). 'Specific limits on automation [may] be reintroduced if we found that stations were not generally reacting to local and national events in the interests of their listeners' (Ofcom 2005d: para. 7.49). (In relation to this, para. 7.50 reveals that commercial radio stations can be 'unmanned at certain times'.) News-hubs – 'whereby the news for a number of local stations in different areas is presented from a single location' (Ofcom 2005d: para. 7.54) – are permitted, but each station must 'provide direct and accountable editorial responsibility . . . equivalent at least to full time professional journalist cover for all of the hours . . . that it will provide local news programmes (Ofcom 2005d: para. 7.56).

These requirements come at a price. 'The balancing act of delivering a profitable, commercially-focused business while providing a locally based radio station with strong ties to the locality has always been tricky'. So much so that in late 2006 the owners of Star 107.9 handed their licence back to Ofcom, blaming '"heavy-handed" regulation' (Ackerman 2006).

Commercial radio of course faces exactly the same market pressures and risks of a downward financial spiral as does commercial television – and in an environment where technical change is an even more immediate challenge. The iPod provides people with 'a virtual radio station in their pocket' (Gibson and Day 2006), while provision via the Internet allows both real-time and 'on demand' listening to stations worldwide. The Internet is also taking advertisement revenues, with commercial radio revenues falling by 5 per cent in 2005 (Gibson and Day 2006). As with television, investment in expanded regional news output seems unlikely. There are, of course, always exceptions that test the rule: the news-driven Real Radio Network has succeeded to the extent that it can claim the longer 'listening hours' (that is, for how long members of the audience typically tune in) that lever up sales of advertising airtime. 'News defines local radio for a community' according to the group programme director (Pike 2006). Can the Real Radio formula be repeated elsewhere, or is it contingent on it having tapped into audiences with a particularly well-defined sense of identity already: Yorkshire, Wales and Scotland?

5 Must broadcast regional news be anodyne?

Audiences: what they say

Ofcom is consumer oriented and committed to evidence-based policy-making; the BBC, as a predominantly publicly funded public service broadcaster, ultimately depends upon public support. Unsurprisingly, therefore, the simultaneous government review of the BBC's Charter (for the period from January 2007) and Ofcom's first five-yearly analysis of public service broadcasting both drew heavily on specially commissioned audience research, using a range of social survey methods (Hargreaves and Thomas 2002; BBC 2004a; Ofcom 2004a; 2005c).

In Ofcom's review of the public purposes of **television**, all types of news emerged as the public's most highly valued programme genre, both in terms of 'personal importance' and 'societal importance'. Regional news was ranked fifth: the BBC's half-hour early evening regional news bulletin is the 'most watched news programme in the UK' (Ofcom 2004a: 34–5). Across the English regions the highest rankings on both dimensions tended to be in more self-contained Channel 3 regions like West Country and Tyne Tees, while the lowest personal importance ranking was in London, where respondents rated the societal importance of regional news higher. Whether this was because of the capital's perceived importance or because they saw regional news as having some potential integrative function is interesting to speculate upon. Earlier research for the BBC had placed regional news as the second most important responsibility for a specifically public service broadcaster (BBC 2004a: 16). In most regions respondents named television as their main source of information on their local area. This aligns with Hargreaves and Thomas's (2002: 64) findings that, overall, 45 per cent of their interviewees named television as their main source of local news. In regions with region-wide newspapers, like (East) Anglia and West Country, however, the statistical gap between television and the press was smaller

Ofcom's review of **radio** deployed both focus group and large scale survey methods to construct a definition of the medium's 'six key "purposes and characteristics"' (Ofcom 2005c: 11). Again local news emerged as important: interviewees in a questionnaire administered to a national sample ranked it as the fourth most important attribute (Ofcom 2005c: 15) from a list of ten, just behind national news.

Despite – or perhaps because of – the high level of interest expressed in regional news, levels of satisfaction were lower. Ofcom's research on television audiences shows a consistent pattern of satisfaction rated at half the level of 'importance' (Ofcom 2004a: 32). (It should be noted, however, that this does not separate out news from 'programmes that reflect the needs of different regional communities'.) This replicates Hargreaves and Thomas's observation (2002: 63) that although a large number of their respondents regarded themselves as 'well served' in terms of news of their locality (from all sources) only '27 per cent declared themselves "very well served"' – half the levels of satisfaction for national and international news. Hargreaves and Thomas draw particular attention to the higher levels of dissatisfaction among black and Asian respondents for whom 'television is also more likely to be the preferred source . . . This is a worrying picture in that most television news does not even attempt to focus at the truly local scale: the geographical areas served are, for the most part, much too large' (Hargreaves and Thomas 2002: 64). Quite so: Meridian, for example, stretches from Weymouth to Essex and covers a population twice that of the whole of Denmark' (Ofcom 2004a: 50). It is also striking that the Channel 3 Central (England) region is one of the few in which newspapers were rated above television as a regional news source (Ofcom 2004a: 36). At the time not only did it stretch from the Welsh borders in the west to Cambridgeshire in the east and Oxford in the south, but the region is well served by both daily and weekly newspapers. As we shall see later in the chapter, this geographical incoherence is reflected in the content and presentational style of the Channel 3 regional news bulletins.

Radio is 'unique in many respects, most notably in being the most *accessible* medium' (Ofcom 2005c: 4; original emphasis). Stations are multiplying and listening is rising (Carter 2003: 46). Yet even here there was mild dissatisfaction. Local news emerged as below par when its rating of 'importance' was mapped on to 'quality of current provision' (Ofcom 2004a: 36). Unfortunately this finding is very difficult to deconstruct because the research seems to have covered both national and local output *and* both BBC and commercial stations. Local news is provided only by local stations. Commercial broadcasting dominates in terms of audience share but most stations provide a minimal local news service, as we saw in Chapter 4. Which section of which audience is dissatisfied?

In all these analyses it is important to keep in view the link – or lack of it – between expressed attitudes and actual behaviour. All these audience studies are, quite reasonably, based entirely on self-report, although the

Ofcom-commissioned research on radio refined this by setting up focus groups according to patterns of consumption of the medium. (See the discussion of methods in Ofcom 2005c: 5–8.) Just as subjects of social surveys always underestimate their consumption of alcohol, there must surely be an inclination towards the 'good citizen' stance of being interested in news in general and local news in particular.

Audiences: what they do

Despite the public's declarations of support when responding to surveys, the general UK-wide trend in actually watching regional news on **television** is downwards, particularly in 'multi-channel' homes. Over the period between 1994 and 2003 Channel 3 lost audience share at a faster rate than the BBC, although ITV claimed that its 2004 figures showed an improvement (Hargreaves and Thomas 2002: 33–5; Ofcom 2004a: 34).

Trade talk attributes much of Channel 3's falling behind to what became known as the 'News at When?' saga. Feature films are a very popular (and relatively cheap) form of television content. To open up the possibility of showing films for an adult audience uninterrupted, that is, to start after the 9.00 p.m. 'watershed', the Channel 3 licensees moved the main news bulletin from 10.00 p.m. to 10.30 p.m., only to be instructed by the then regulator to move it back again. Several regulatory and political turns later it settled at 10.30 p.m. on week nights. The late evening short regional bulletin is now just before 11.00 p.m., but for a while it was very unpredictable: 'Suddenly you were losing viewers who were not necessarily the teatime audience but they knew you existed' according to the then news controller of one of the Channel 3 licensees (Azeez 2003). Arguably 11.00 p.m. is still too late for many in the Channel 3 audience, of whom 60 per cent are in social classes C2, D and E (Hargreaves and Thomas 2002: 32) and thus more likely to be employed at workplaces that start early in the morning. Even at the time of Hargreaves and Thomas's research, the audience share for the Channel 3 late evening news was lower in multichannel homes (2002: 35). Presumably the rapid spread of Freeview, providing access to 24-hour news channels, has accelerated this.

Despite remote control, the proliferation of channels, on-screen programme guides which invite 'channel surfing', and increasingly sophisticated technologies to consume broadcast output according to a personally constructed pattern, television schedulers still have faith in 'inheritance'. This is a supposed boost in the audience driven by a propensity not to change channels through inertia. Accordingly, the competition for viewers in the early evening is intense. Channel 3 has moved its early evening national news bulletin several times in recent years: from 5.40 p.m. to

6.30 p.m., briefly to 7.00 p.m. and then back to 6.30 p.m. In all of the latter configurations it was *preceded* by the day's main regional news bulletin. This pattern enabled the national news to be followed immediately by episodes of Channel 3's most popular soaps, but 'Most people are used to – and it naturally seems right – watching the national news and then see the impact of some of those stories on your region' (Azeez 2003). Unpredictably and 'unnaturally' positioned, and pitted against the BBC's early evening national news and very popular programmes on the other terrestrial channels: taking all these together, it is hard not to conclude that Channel 3 was tacitly ceasing to fight for an audience for its regional news service, despite the confirmation that this PSB obligation will continue. (See the discussion of public service broadcasting obligations in Chapter 4.)

Auditing the television audience is undertaken principally by Broadcasters' Audience Research Board Limited (BARB). Monthly viewing figures and trend data are freely available (at www.barb.co.uk), but breakdowns by specific programme and by audience share are only available to subscribers.

Radio audiences are measured by RAJAR, whose web site makes more extensive information available without charge. For the quarter ending in September 2006, BBC local/regional radio had a 9.8 per cent share of the total audience, while local commercial radio accounted for 32.6 per cent. No information is routinely available on the consumption of local news because, as we shall see, bulletins are characteristically short, frequent and mix national and local items. (For information and an account of RAJAR's methods – which have been the subject of controversy in the industry – see www.rajar.co.uk and Tacchi 2001.)

If the regional news on **television** is so popular with audiences, and so potentially important as part of the local public sphere, as Chapter 1 argued, why are the bulletins so unsatisfactory? In the following sections I will argue that the combined effect of the arbitrary regional boundaries, production imperatives, limited resources, and the nature of the imputed audience work against their being effective in terms of the public's understanding of events and issues in their locality. This emphasis on the informational purpose of news should not be seen as academic advocacy of worthy dullness: the quality and popularity of wildlife and nature programmes vividly demonstrates that television can entertain and inform at the same time (Aldridge and Dingwall 2003).

Examples will be drawn from the early evening bulletins in the South West (ITV *Westcountry Live*; BBC *Spotlight*); the East Midlands (ITV *Central News East*; BBC *East Midlands Today*) and London (ITV *London Tonight*; BBC *London*). All were recorded on 3 November 2005. The complex issues of regional media in the UK's nations of Scotland, Wales and Northern Ireland will be discussed in Chapter 6.

News on regional television: relevance *versus* complexity

One of the few television studies to include regional news is Harrison's account of the BBC and Channel 3 operations based in Leeds. Her analysis of one week's output in 1993 (Harrison 2000: 178) found no coverage of most aspects of politics, economics and finance, science, religion and, oddly, education, either in relation to central government or schools. Health issues did not figure in the BBC's bulletins, while the environment and conservation were absent from ITV. Even more strikingly, local government received no coverage on ITV's regional programme and accounted for only 1.6 per cent of the BBC's coverage.

This pattern was still evident in the 2005 bulletins. Among the four bulletins outside London only four items (of 48) could be said to contain material that viewers might draw on in the future as citizens and electors: an account of the social impact of the ban on hunting with dogs (BBC *East Midlands Today*); a dairy farmer's lone protest about the effect of agriculture policies on farm incomes (BBC *Spotlight* and ITV *Westcountry Live*); and an interview with the recently elected mayor of Torbay (BBC *Spotlight*), including an explanation of how this new post fits into the structure and budgeting of local government.

In the ITV bulletin in particular, rather than being about politics, the farmer's story was placed within a personalized interpretive frame of individual struggle as he telegenically poured perfectly wholesome milk down the drain. How the farmer's problems connected with industry-wide problems, UK agricultural policy and the European Union (EU) did not become clear. As Cottle put it in his landmark study of regional news (1993: 80, 79) the premium on 'empathetic understanding' transforms what could or should be interpreted as 'public issues of social structure' into 'personal troubles of milieu'.

Clearly contextualized or not, however, the farmer and his milk manifestly had very widespread relevance in a largely rural region, even for those viewers with no direct connection to agriculture. More important still, for Devon and Cornwall, is the coast, source of both distinctive identity and livelihood. Both bulletins for the region had extensive coverage of storms the previous night and the consequent flooding, complete with boilerplate (but nevertheless riveting) visuals of wave-lashed promenades and so on. The BBC bulletin even reinforced the inclusiveness of the events with an aerial tour of the region.

By contrast, the East Midlands is probably the limiting case of an incoherent television region, lacking any common topographical features, industrial history, dominant industry or administrative infrastructure. What has Matlock (the former spa and now county town of Derbyshire) got

in common with the fen country around Spalding? It is also demographi-
cally diverse: Leicester has become a centre of south Asian culture, while the
sparsely populated agribusiness countryside and former mining towns of
north Nottinghamshire have, as we saw in Chapter 3, an almost exclusively
white population. How does one address such an audience? ITV's strategy
seems to be to include as many items as possible – 15 on the sampled
day, compared with the BBC's nine – with a notably wide geographical
spread, from Mansfield in Nottinghamshire in the north to Corby,
Northamptonshire, in the south, and Derby in the west to Louth in
Lincolnshire in the east. Multiculture was briefly acknowledged with greet-
ings to the audience for Eid ul-Fitr, the celebration of the end of Ramadan.

An obvious solution to the relevance dilemma would seem to be more
coverage of universal concerns, for instance health and education, frequently cited as of particular salience for the 'family audience', as viewers
of the early evening news are characterized. Indeed, these topics get
markedly more coverage in the *national* early evening bulletins. For
example, the BBC1 6.00 p.m. bulletin on 13 December 2005 included a
'special report' on malnutrition among elderly people, but there was no
mention of this at 10.00 p.m.

The central dilemma for regional news is that the specificity needed to
explain, as opposed to simply describe events, is in permanent tension with
their relevance for the entire audience. Being an historical legacy of the
location of analogue transmitters, the English television regions are too
large to mean anything to the audience for whom, as we saw in Chapter 1,
most of the activities of routine daily life take place within 20 miles of
home. Nor do they map on to any aspect of the structure of government.
The East Midlands, for instance, covers several counties and a number of
cities responsible for education services. Health care under the National
Health Service (NHS) is organized through a complex reticulation of trusts,
covering primary care, hospitals and other provision like mental health and
emergency ambulance services. As in the case of education, within any television region there will probably be more than one trust for any given
aspect of health care.

Or take the privately owned water and sewerage services, increasingly
controversial as charges increase and questions are raised about the ade-
quacy of future supply. (Some of the driest regions like East Anglia are those
where the population is increasing fastest.) Issues do not come more
'domestic' than water metering and hosepipe bans, but a visit to the industry regulator's web site (www.ofwat.gov.uk; search for 'boundaries') soon
establishes that there are very few regions in which a controversy about a
particular water company's policy would be relevant to the whole audience.

Hospital ward closures, a perennial topic of regional news, provide an
illustration of the presentational problem. A properly detailed explanation

of the proximate cause instantly reduces the relevance of the event for everyone in the audience except those who might need to use the hospital in question. Moving the explanation 'up' to the workings of NHS budgets, and then 'across and down' to how it could affect hospitals everywhere is a possibility, but requires a complex and resource-consuming 'package' of the kind more often seen in national news. For local bulletins geographic inclusivity and varied texture are higher priorities. It is, therefore, almost inevitable that the hypothetical ward closure will be covered in a way that, as is often observed of all news media, concentrates on events and outcomes: video footage of the public protests; *vox pops* (street interviews with members of the public) with those affected; and such a brief interview with an authority figure that explanation of the background is impossible. Relevance is thus achieved by placing the issue within a soft focus 'it could be you' interpretative frame in which the universalizing human interest dimension is in the foreground. Paradoxically, this probably explains the stand-out explicitly political item about the mayor of Torbay: the abstract issues were quite legitimately personified. Having an elected mayor is still exceptional, but the possibility that it could be proposed for their own area makes it relevant to viewers elsewhere. Moreover, as the item explained, 40 per cent of his budget is for education. Even the potentially inhibiting statutory requirements of election law and on impartiality were sidestepped because the election was over.

While the selection of news items and styles of textualization reflect the imputed audience, they are also constrained by the linked factors of resources and working practices. It cannot be said often enough that front-line news-gathering is (or should be) very labour intensive. Exclusive stories achieved through investigative reporting – what McManus (1994) calls 'highly active [news] discovery'; the kind of complex 'package' that provides a clear explanatory frame into which are fitted both expert exposition and the real experiences that make the abstract accessible; or even taking a story that originated elsewhere and developing it ('moderately active discovery') – all require hours of work. (Exclusivity through sensational 'buy-ups', whether downmarket kiss-and-tell or upmarket 'Behind the scenes at Downing Street' is not a tactic directly available to broadcasters.) The more complex the topic, the more specialized knowledge is needed to render it straightforward and comprehensible, as national news coverage of economics or the European Union amply demonstrates. Specialist correspondents are expensive because of their seniority and relative inflexibility, so media organization managements are very parsimonious in their deployment. Harrison (2000: 104–5) writes of the Leeds-based *Look North* in the mid-1990s that it adhered to the BBC policy of having specialist correspondents which, by implication, suggests that Channel 3's *Calendar News* did not, or not to the same extent. The areas covered 'reflect[ed] the different types of news covered by a regional organisation . . . education, transport, community affairs (mainly ethnic), health, business and industry, and environment'. She goes on, however, to observe that although their role was to 'seek out and generate stories and provide in-depth analysis . . . in practice the correspondents generate few such stories' but instead were allocated to follow up known news events in much the same way as general reporters.

Nevertheless, BBC's national news-gathering infrastructure continues to put the corporation at an advantage, as Harris (2003: 91) found when interviewing journalists about their response to 'food scare' stories. Her BBC regional television respondents were 'bi-media correspondents, who produced news reports for regional television, local radio and national BBC news as well as making the occasional documentary'. How this works on a daily basis is illustrated by an item broadcast on BBC Radio Nottingham (16 December 2005). Changes in the contractual basis of NHS dental services were concisely set out, followed by the results of a telephone survey of local dentists for their reaction. The explanation was provided by the specialist health correspondent, based on an item he had developed for BBC1 *East Midlands Today*, while the telephone survey enabled it to be grounded in greater Nottingham, which is only a small part of the East Midlands television region. By contrast, Harris's respondents in Channel 3 news were all general reporters and emphasized the flexibility of their working: 'There are four or five different shifts that I do, they alternate quite a lot . . . cutting pictures and writing up stories for each bulletin and that's what I did most of the day yesterday' (Harris 2003: 114).

Beyond the problems of relevance generated by large, baggy television regions, the statutory duty of impartiality on broadcasters also creates difficulties when dealing with contentious issues. Even assuming that the conventional for/against binary structure can be imposed on the topic, achieving 'balance' consumes scarce resources. Competing voices must be found to speak for and against, and the outcome then edited, all in order to produce an item that risks being judged both too long and too boring for bulletins that aim for wide appeal. An inclination towards anodyne or at least apparently consensual topics is therefore, I would argue, systemic for this as well as for the audience-related reasons discussed in more detail below. Thus recurrent themes include law and order (usually within an unchallenged inferential framework provided by the criminal justice system), sport, 'nature' and 'heritage'. In the last case the passage of time has helpfully erased the social conflicts of the era in which the practice or artefact originated. This process was vivid in the unexpectedly successful BBC2 series *Restoration*, in which advocates for a wide range of crumbling buildings competed on a regional basis for substantial grant support. The first series was won by the magnificent Victoria Baths in Manchester (www.victoriabaths.org.uk). Was there such widespread acclaim in 1906 when ratepayers were asked to pay for a 'no expense spared' municipal facility for ordinary working people?

Addressing the family audience: reassurance and narrative closure

Simon Cottle's 1993 study of *Central News West* (the Channel 3 regional news programme for the West Midlands, based in Birmingham) combined a content analysis of bulletins broadcast between 1982 and 1988 with an ethnographic study of the production process, carried out in the late 1980s. While most other television genres are much changed, his observations about regional news remain startlingly fresh.

In terms of audience 'address', Cottle's regional journalists modelled their output on a respectable mid-market newspaper (1993: 54): 'deliberately seeking to engage viewers through affective, as much as informative, involvement; purposively fashioning stories in such a way as to heighten their human interest appeal; and consciously seeking to incorporate the views and experiences, hopes and fears, of ordinary people' (1993: 64–5). This is not a reflection of some sudden 'softening' of the news agenda during the 1980s. In his fieldwork Cottle observed (1993: 63ff) a tension between the more 'hard-news' oriented journalists on the programme who saw themselves primarily as providers of information and those staff who had worked on predecessor regional 'magazine' programmes, and were happy to see themselves as delivering entertainment.

Magazine programmes were the quintessential 'family viewing', chosen for this reason as the basis of Brunsdon and Morley's (1978) classic audience study. One of the texts they used was the BBC's *Nationwide* of 19 May 1976, which included an interview with a man released that day from prison, having served seven years of a life sentence. This was a well-known and controversial case with heavy political overtones but 'From the beginning the emphasis is on the dramatic, emotional aspects of the situation and the focus is on [his] subjective feelings and responses to his experiences in prison . . . [He] tries to talk about the political background to the case but . . . each time the interviewer brings him back to whether he feels bitter about the experience' (Morley 1992: 102).

In the final analysis, no commercial or royal chartered news organization can have an interest in disrupting social stability, but Cottle argues that regional television news *actively* aims to reassure (1993: 65), through presentational style, choice of items, focus on the individual and subjective and, I will further argue, the narrative structure of the items. It goes without saying that in an increasing competitive broadcasting environment, news programmes must also be entertaining, in the loose sense of viewers gaining some sense of enjoyment as well as knowledge.

Family audience, 'family'-style **presentation**: with the interesting exception of BBC *London*, all the early evening regional bulletins are presented by a woman/man pair. As was noted in Chapter 4, when ITV's regional news service was brought under unified management, one of the stated aims was to impose a clear visual 'brand'. In late 2005, this consisted of a standard studio set, very bright with a lot of white, pale grey and chrome, consisting of an arc of couches and a low table, behind which the presenters sit, with slightly self-conscious informality, the man on the left of screen, the woman on the right. Other participants, such as the weather forecaster or interviewees (although this kind of 'talking head' format is rare compared with national bulletins) sit further round the arc, very much as one would to chat in a stylish sitting room. A backdrop indicates the region. *Westcountry Live* confidently put up a picture of the Tamar Bridge (not only a striking landmark, but the Devon/Cornwall boundary); *London Tonight* featured St Paul's Cathedral; while *Central News East* was suitably equivocal: an image of Nottingham, but so indistinct as not to over-privilege the city within the region.

Demographic precision was also embodied in the presenters: mainly thirty- to forty-something, now the typical family-formation life stage. On the sampled day, however, *Westcountry Live* featured an older male presenter who, together with the signed summary at the end of the bulletin, reflected a region with a large retired population. The female presenters for both notably multicultural regions, *Central News East* and *London Tonight*, were of south Asian origin; one of the reporters for *Central News East* was African Caribbean. By contrast all the presenters and reporters in *Westcountry Live* were white, as they were in the BBC bulletin. Such care with representativeness was somewhat let down, however, by the Birmingham accent of the male *Central News East* presenter. As protesters feared when the Nottingham studio was closed (see Chapter 4), despite the script, he was not speaking of 'his' region.

Nationally and globally the BBC is very aware indeed of the value of its brand, as *Building Public Value* (BBC 2004c) makes clear. This did not (as at late 2005) extend to imposing a standard format on regional news studios, the semiotics of which nicely signified their region. *London*'s set was gleaming silver; the lone and informally dressed presenter moving restlessly from standing to sitting to perching. On *East Midlands Today* the 'smart casual' presenters sat very close to each other at what looked incongruously like a breakfast bar (since replaced by a curved sofa). In the Westcountry, *Spotlight*'s format was strikingly similar to that of the late evening national bulletin: formally dressed presenters sat behind a round desk for much of the time, and made slightly didactic use of graphics. Where *Central News*

East's weather forecast was delivered in T-shirt and jeans, *Spotlight*'s weather presenter wore collar, tie and smart blazer – connoting the maritime traditions of the region perhaps?

Egalitarian coupledom was further emphasized by carefully tasteful banter between the presenters and by sharing the task of presentation, even to the extent of speaking alternate sentences, while the other member of the pair looked on with an expression of involved but restrained amusement, concern, sadness – whatever the news item called for.

When Harrison sampled the news bulletins in the Leeds-based newsrooms (2000: 178) she found that 34 per cent of the BBC items and 27 per cent of the Channel 3 items came into the violence/control of violence/court proceedings category. In the 2005 sample this theme is far less prominent, suggesting that reassurance is even more of a priority in the **choice of news items**. The overarching theme was home and family – although this was not nearly as much to the fore in London. BBC's *East Midlands Today* included a visit to a family in Leicester who explained how they were celebrating Eid ul-Fitr; *Spotlight* included a regular 'consumer report', on this occasion about a rogue roof conversion company. Pet and 'wild' animals were also prominent, the subject of two of the nine items on BBC *East Midlands Today* and two on *Central News East*. Although this was a smaller proportion (in a total of 15), one of them related the safe recovery of a 4-year-old's pony, including then/now film and an interview with the girl. The cynical viewer might suspect an element of professional self-parody. Both the Westcountry bulletins included animals/livelihood stories as well as the farm protest described above. Even ITV's *London Tonight* indulged itself in an animal story, but with a very London inflection: swans disrupting road and rail transport by mistaking the sparkle of wet roads and railway tracks for open water.

Since Harrison's mid-1990s work, leisure appears to have gained more coverage, not only through the long-standing focus on professional sport in the regions, but participation sports and other leisure activities. BBC *East Midlands Today* interviewed two fans queuing overnight for tickets for their hero's concert, and both London bulletins featured the opening of the film *Good Night and Good Luck* directed by 'gorgeous' George Clooney. This, too, suggested an element of knowing reflexiveness. The subject of the film – which was highlighted, not simply alluded to – is Edward J. Murrow, the American broadcast journalist who vocally opposed the anti-Communist witch-hunts in the USA of the early 1950s.

Cottle's observations about the 'people-led' (1993: 60) style of regional television news were amply borne out. Nearly all the items in all the non-London bulletins were refracted through the **individual and subjective** – what did it mean for them/me? – as in the example of the Westcountry farmer, above. Where the news was not about the impact of events on the lives of named and pictured individuals (or the otherness of animals and nature) the appellation was often consumerist: rogue builders, travel and transport, flooding bringing insurance problems. Both the bulletins for London were, however, fascinatingly different in their presentational style. Personalization as an explanatory device hardly appeared. In part this must be because of the nature of London as capital of the UK: 'local' events are hard to distinguish from national events. The lead story on ITV's *London Tonight* concerned the terrorist attack on 7 July 2005, as no doubt it would have in the BBC bulletin, had they not had an 'exclusive' about alleged electoral fraud. Another BBC *London* story related to Ofcom raids on 60 pirate radio stations, revealing the regulator in a less 'light touch' mode!

So diverse is contemporary London that it must also be practically difficult to personalize. Who now is the equivalent of the 'man on the Clapham omnibus'? Interestingly, ITV's *London Tonight* included not one, but two devices to 'imagine community'. As in *Westcountry Live*, the programme featured community projects competing for £50 000 from the Lottery Fund, under the banner of 'The People's Millions'. Email responses to a story about a controversial police 'clampdown' were also called for, with a selection read out towards the end of the programme.

What, though, about the **narrative structure of the stories** themselves? In his book *Tabloid Television* (1998), Langer sets out to examine the 'other news', based on data collected in Australia, whose relatively small population and federal system of government means that much of the news is effectively regional news. Langer's focus is the kind of story that is simultaneously condemned and unexamined by those engaged in the transnational lament over tabloidization: so-called 'human interest' material, with its enduring popular appeal. This is not, he points out, easily dismissed as 'soft news' – a category the boundaries of which are anyway more ideological than clearly operationalized (Aldridge 2001a). Many of the events reported, for example major traffic accidents or natural disasters, are 'hard news' in the sense that the wider public and the polity are also implicated, not just the private lives of those caught up in them. The crucial characteristic of this 'other news' is that while in detail it is constructed to conform to the conventional 'objectivity' discourse of events and facts, it clearly demonstrates the other discourse of journalism: the drive to tell a satisfying story (Darnton 1975; Gripsrud 1992). Not, of course, that this is a particular deformation of local media or mass tabloid newspapers. Despite at the time occupying one of the most unequivocal of 'hard news' posts – BBC Political Editor – Marr writes (2004: 289) that the job of the programme editor is 'to create an engaging narrative which will persuade viewers to settle down for up to half an hour to watch, and listen'.

So stylized is the category of 'other news' that Langer suggests (1998: 35) four basic 'story types': the 'especially remarkable'; 'victims';

'community at risk'; and 'ritual, tradition and the past'. All the categories are immediately recognizable within UK regional television news, but in terms of its potential as an arena for public debate, the latter two have particular force. In complementary ways these narratives emphasize continuity and stability. The 'community at risk' story – classically fire and flood, in which the normally contained force of nature is released – customarily include the theme of 'restoration'. Even if the damage cannot instantly be undone, reassurance is provided through the effectiveness of the emergency services, the help offered by complete strangers and so on. 'There is an ordering process at work: the move from balance to imbalance and back again . . . to re-establish the balance of the social organism' (Langer 1998: 124). Imagining the community in these terms may not be intended to have any particular significance, but the symbolic power of organic analogies is clear, implying as it does that fundamental conflict is either unthinkable or, if thinkable, unbearably destructive.

Both the East Midlands bulletins sampled led with the continuing story of the death by stabbing of a school student in Lincolnshire. The initial event received heavy news coverage not only as a human tragedy, but as a dramatic disruption of life in an area which, while no rural idyll, is not known for that kind of violence. His parents had initiated a campaign against the carrying of knives by school students: this attempt at 'community repair' was the basis of the follow-up story.

Conforming even more to Langer's typology was the news, on both Westcountry regional bulletins, of the storms off Devon and Cornwall, during which a ship had lost power and was at risk of running on to the rocks. Dramatic pictures showed the heroism of the coastguard, the more reassuring and inspiring for being represented by them as entirely routine. Even a story about the postponement of an auction of caged birds on BBC *East Midlands Today* conveyed a message about ordinary people putting the community before personal advantage or preoccupations because of the possible risk of avian flu.

While this category of story inscribes 'us' in the community here and now (Langer 1998: 112), the category of 'ritual, tradition and the past' anchors us in history while also implying future continuity. Typical raw material includes regular events, commemorations, re-enactments and the use of historical discoveries which emphasize the timelessness of human experience and consolidate a sense of connectness to the past and each other. Langer draws on Hobsbawm (1983) on the 'invention of tradition', while Anderson ([1983] 1991) and Dayan and Katz (1992) have established the long-standing significance of news media in reifying an 'imagined community', but at the national level. At the regional level, I suggest, there is an even more powerful impetus to do this. First, there is the 'mission to reassure' alluded to above. Second are the purely practical considerations of news-making. These recurrent and planned occasions are the 'diary events' increasingly relied upon by all news organizations: a need very well understood by both professional and amateur players in contemporary promotional culture. The mother who is dissatisfied with the police investigation of her son's death in a street incident knows that being filmed visiting his grave on his birthday or the anniversary of his death will be more newsworthy than simply being interviewed, as did the Devon farmer shown actually dumping his milk. If Cottle's respondents struggled to generate sufficient material to fill their bulletins because of limitations on time and money, a very much more competitive production environment must put an even higher premium on reliable, predictable sources of news.

In the bulletins sampled, religious ritual featured in references to Eid ul-Fitr (BBC *East Midlands Today* in detail – see above; *Central News East* and BBC *London* briefly). More secular traditions covered included items on the Bridgwater Carnival (ITV *Westcountry Live*); and a wry reference to the 'dreaded' Christmas pop song (BBC *East Midlands Today*). Both London bulletins listed firework displays for Bonfire Night and, as the BBC version pointed out, the winter festivals of several non-Christian religions. These quintessentially 'family and community' events were not mentioned by the non-metropolitan regional bulletins, yet another indication that the regions concerned are on a scale larger than that of the everyday activities of their residents. How much resource would it take to discover and list every East Midlands town and village celebration in three complete counties and part of two others? (In 2006, however, viewers were directed to a list of such events on the BBC web site.)

Audience participation via email, votes on worthy community projects and so on, is presumably primarily intended as a means of constructing community, but an item on BBC *Spotlight* in the Westcountry also provided an example of 'invented tradition'. Its competition for the South West Sporting Heroes Award was not about Olympic medallists, but rather the extraordinary ordinary. On the day sampled, the nominees were an elderly couple who had for many years been teaching older, often very nervous, people to swim. Nor did they intend to retire, thus satisfactorily tying continuity, altruism and optimism together.

The BBC's 'ultra-local' television experiment

If financial imperatives have led ITV plc to equivocate about its regional television news service in the English regions (see Chapter 4), the same concern about core funding impelled the BBC to pursue a diametrically opposed strategy. Its final pitch (BBC 2004c) to government in relation to the 2007 Charter Review – upon which not only the level of the licence fee

but its whole financial regime depends – put its ability to serve 'the community' in the foreground. In doing this, the BBC was also looking over its
metaphorical shoulder at Ofcom's review of television and radio's 'public
purposes' (Ofcom 2005a; 2005d) which, as we saw earlier in the chapter,
revealed that the public puts a high value on local news. Meeting this
demand provides a powerful justification for the large expenditure on the
corporation's news infrastructure, particularly the Internet-based services
which have caused such nervousness in the regional press.

Pursuing this strategy, under the heading of 'supporting active and
informed citizenship', the BBC announced an 'ultra-local news service' for
'50–60 areas across the UK with up to 10 minutes an hour of genuinely relevant local news and information' (BBC 2004c: 65–6) available via the
Internet and Freeview. A pilot scheme covering five areas in the West
Midlands was launched in late 2005 under the banner 'TV just got more
local' (www.bbc.co.uk/localtv/). A sample viewing of the Stoke and
Staffordshire bulletin in early 2006, however, showed the breaking news
content to be rather less than that on the equivalent 'Where I Live' BBC
Internet news site, where items appear as paragraphs of print accompanied
by still photographs. Only a very small proportion of the ten minutes consisted of recently updated news; the rest was accounted for by five people-
centred features lasting around two minutes. All the topics could be
mapped on to the Langer (1998) typology discussed above, notably the
theme of community suffering and repair. And all could have been prepared well in advance, in most cases in response to commercial or voluntary association attempts at self-promotion. Nor was this simply a reflection
of the particular locality: at the same time the breaking news section of the
Birmingham local television bulletin contained only four items, three
sourced from the emergency services (two fires and a suspicious death) and
one probably from the public (a woman fined for stopping on a motorway
hard shoulder to ask the police for directions and who had then told all her
friends about it).

For all its vast scale and global reach, in many areas the BBC faces contradictory demands which stretch its resources very thin. The tone of
Building Public Value (BBC 2004c) was confident and expansive, and the
government's response (DCMS 2005b) encouraged this mood. Since then,
however, the corporation has faced both financial difficulty and renewed
political and media industry criticism of its ambitions. What prospects can
there be for the additional resources needed if news at the 'ultra-local' level
is to include any 'highly active discovery' (McManus 1994), or even the
kind of exposition required to meet the BBC's claims about 'active and
informed citizenship'? Without them, it would seem that those regional
newspaper editors who scoffed at the idea that the new service television
would undermine them were correct (Lagan 2005b).

Local commercial radio: not in the news business

Ofcom's blunt statement about what 'localness' in radio is and is not (Ofcom 2005c: s. 7; and see Chapter 4) indicates that, in most cases, local commercial radio's provision of regional news is vestigial, only forming a small part of an overall news service itself geared to the minimum required to meet regulatory demands. These are stations which certainly address their listeners as local residents, but as consumers rather than as citizens:

> news agendas have moved towards being dominated by entertainment and sports news . . . [at] the 2001 election when IRN, the ITN subsidiary which provides, in effect, a free news service to commercial radio, offered all 250 stations the opportunity to join a live phone-in to party leaders, including the Prime Minister. Only 12 stations were willing to take part.
>
> (Hargreaves and Thomas 2002: 62)

Their primary aim is to provide company and relaxation to an audience of young and early mid-life adults (Harris 2003: 94; and see Chapter 4) through their output of carefully calibrated music. Listeners are not expected to be listening closely, but to have the station on as background to other activities, as the volume at which the stations broadcast indicates. Continuous half-listening of this kind, an important consideration for advertisers, is encouraged by devices like (Nottingham) 96 Trent FM's 'task-force' that visits local workplaces and offers rewards to those with it turned on (www.trentfm.musicradio.com).

A sense of community is certainly an important element of local commercial radio's typical informal, lively, slightly frantic style of address, which is mirrored in their web sites. Like their on-air output, these 'imagine' a community based on consumption and the private sphere. In the case of 96 Trent FM, for example, the site features competitions, and links to online ticket buying, journey planning, job seeking and dating, all of them nationally run rather than local sites. Brief profiles of the regular presenters provide a sense of personal contact and the basis of a generic schedule of programmes, which does not vary on a daily basis. Despite the six-strong 'news team' shown, 'Your News' on 3 January 2006 consisted of five national news items and three items of sports news, none of which had a Nottingham angle. Only the 'traffic and travel' section had local relevance – and that consisted of an out-of-date list of problem locations.

To reiterate, news is not core business for commercial radio. As Harris (2003: 94) writes, bulletins which are 'often only three minutes long, covering approximately ten items within that time' cannot aim for depth and detail. Nor is a broad sweep of topics an objective: even more than other media, commercial radio's news agenda is driven by the imputed audience, rather than some abstract concept of informing citizens. One of Harris's journalist respondents described her audience as being 18- to 35-year-old women who, according to the station's own research, 'were interested primarily in stories about health and the environment' (Harris 2003: 121). If we take 96 Trent FM as reasonably representative, however, such stories were more likely to be national, rather than local.

News for the older citizen: BBC local radio

We have already seen that the BBC's share of the local radio audience is much smaller than that of local commercial radio and that its listeners tend to be older. 'Dave and Sue', who are in their mid-50s, are the 'prescriptive fictitious pair' constructed by the BBC's Project Bullseye to enable their typically young and highly qualified journalists to understand whom they are addressing (Debbie Wilson, personal communication). For rather different reasons, Dave and Sue are also thought to have a particular interest in health-related news. 'Our lead tomorrow is going to be the . . . conference on gerontology, basically ageing , my listeners are going to be interested in that. I did a story this morning about knee replacements', a BBC local radio reporter told Harris (2003: 122).

In all other respects, however, BBC local radio is utterly different from commercial stations. This is radio intended to be listened to closely: much of the output is speech, with a heavy emphasis on participation. Here, arguably more than in any other aspect of its general output, the BBC is unashamed about the 'inform' and 'educate' aspects of its three-part mission. (The third is to entertain – see www.bbc.co.uk/info/purposes/.) Campaigns, community action, news of not-for-profit events organized by local voluntary societies and outright exhortations to, for example, 'Get Active' (with links to a complete section of the BBC Radio Nottingham web site featuring possibilities from samba to sudoku) are all prominent, alongside the usual weather, traffic and transport information.

Constructing the community is, inevitably, a prominent theme in BBC local radio, driven by the BBC's cultural standing and public funding, coupled with the nature of the audience. As we saw in Chapter 1, not only do older people tend to be more attached to the locality, they are assumed particularly to value the companionable presence of familiar voices on the radio. Biographies of the regular presenters feature on all BBC local radio web sites; all emphasize their local roots. Of the ten presenters listed on Radio Nottingham's site, eight are either locally born or declare their attachment to the area: 'After 13 years with the radio station Karl regards himself as a true Nottinghamian' and goes on to explain 'what he loves about Robin Hood County' (www.bbc.co.uk/nottingham/local_radio/ presenters/index.shtml, accessed 4 January 2006). The same motif emerges in relation to areas much less notable for the stability of their population, for example Radio Kent (a rapidly changing county where many people commute long distances) and Radio Northamptonshire (another commuter area in which Northampton was designated as a new town in the 1960s and Corby in the 1950s).

In line with the BBC's cultural position, the community represented is also inclusive: Radio Nottingham's schedules include specialized music programmes for listeners of African Caribbean, Irish and Asian origin. Diversity is also systematically pursued on the BBC's very extensive 'Where I Live' web sites, of which the local radio pages are a sub-set with extensive cross-links. For example, in January 2006 the Northamptonshire pages (www.bbc.co.uk/northamptonshire/about_northants) included a black history project and two features about being gay in Northampton, while the Kent site incorporated a complete section devoted to 'Romany roots' (www.bbc.co.uk/kent/romany_roots/index.shtml).

First heard in the UK on Radio Nottingham in 1968, one of the earliest forms of interactive media was the radio phone-in: 'a genuinely new broadcasting development in the sense that it enabled the ordinary listener to become a broadcaster, not because she was a guest of the radio station or an expert or an interviewee, but simply because she chose to initiate the broadcast' (Crisell 1997: 143). These still feature prominently in BBC local radio schedules, steering a middle course between the kind of public controversy that raises regulatory problems over impartiality and the sensationally personal ('I discovered that I'd married my long-lost brother') typical of television audience-participation shows. Now digital technology has multiplied the linkages in the network of the imaginary community. Listeners are encouraged to email presenters, to participate in online debates, to become 'community correspondents', and to contribute their video and still photographs to online archives. 'Snowy Nottinghamshire' in December 2005 showed 86 photos submitted by members of the audience, compared with 59 in Kent, where the snow had been considerably more dramatic. A potentially fruitful sociological index of local attachment perhaps?

All these elements of BBC local radio indicate that its address to listeners is as active citizens; consumer issues feature even less than on regional television. This orientation is reflected in the news content. Aside from the extensive coverage of local news in the breakfast-time programmes, even the short hourly bulletins are several orders of magnitude 'denser textured' than those on local commercial radio. Moreover, unlike their equivalent on local commercial radio, local news predominates for two reasons. First, at least some content will be generated by the BBC's total news-gathering operation, from its local Internet sites and regional television setup, to its permanent international correspondents. Second, relating back to the BBC's mission, its local radio stations constantly complain about their low priority in spending terms, but are incomparably better funded than commercial stations. This level of resource is reflected in a typical bulletin from Radio Nottingham, both in the range of items and their presentation. Two were international news, one was national political news and the remaining four (including the first and last) were local news. Three items included other 'voices' than the news reader: an interviewee and two journalists, one of whom was reporting for the BBC from the USA.

Despite the constraints of relatively limited resources and the delicate path of impartiality that has to be trodden, BBC radio appears to be the medium that most closely approximates to a local public sphere. Its potential is, however, limited by two factors. First, there is the small size and demographic profile of the audience. It is young adults, not the over-55s, who are most disengaged from civic life and the political process. Second, the nature of the audience, with their imputed desire for virtual companionship, and the BBC's own claims about its 'public purpose' of encouraging social cohesion, seem to incline local radio news towards the same universalizing human interest interpretive frame as is typical of regional television. In the news bulletin described above, both international items were of human tragedy, the national item was about health policy and three of the four local items could be construed as 'soft news'. Only one – on the flooding problems of the Trent Valley – related to matters of collective provision about which they might be required to form and express a view as citizens.

6 A delicate balance: media in the nations of the UK

Politics makes news; making news is politics

In Anderson's ([1983] 1991) now-classic phrase, nations are 'imagined communities' of shared social practices. Communications media have been pivotal in creating this sense of common experience. Early newspapers were important contributors to the standardization of language driven, Anderson argues, by commercial opportunities created by the spread of literacy. Conversely, assertions about the growing irrelevance of the nation state often refer to the impact of electronic media. On the one hand is their capacity to extol the virtues of a market-driven economy to a world-wide audience. On the other is the potential of digitally enabled 'narrowcasting' to address the interests of small and specialized audiences, for instance speakers of minority languages.

As Billig (1995) emphasizes, nationalism does not only consist in its 'hot' form of active conflict, whether making new claims or desperately propping up past certainties. Many of the ways in which a sense of nationhood is inscribed and reinforced in the lives of individual citizens are, in his newly classic concept, 'banal nationalism'. Billig defines these as the 'ideological habits which enable the established nations of the West to be reproduced . . . Daily the nation is indicated, or "flagged", in the lives of its citizenry. Nationalism, far from being an intermittent mood in established nations, is the endemic condition' (Billig 1995: 6).

Thus, even in conditions of relative peace and stability, the rhetoric of nationhood is in constant use by core social institutions. Naturally, news media are prominent among them, as Billig demonstrates in his much quoted survey of a day's output of the British national press (1995: 109–22). Sports news is particularly rich in unsubtle constructions of 'we', the audience and consequently an implied 'they', the rest. Media are so deeply implicated in the sport/nationalism nexus as to be almost constitutive of it. 'Interview with our new rugby captain' formed part of a 'teaser' above the main headline on the Cardiff morning daily *The Western Mail* of 11 May 2006. As Billig points out, these linguistic devices are often so taken for granted as not to register: for instance, usages like 'the Prime Minister' with no qualifying name or country.

Billig himself acknowledges that 'the British press is not national in the sense that the same editions cover the whole of the United Kingdom ... [By] concentrating on the English editions, some of the conventional hegemonic semantics of "British" nationalism have already been adopted' (1995: 111). Daily reality is, however, even more complex than this. As we shall see, Scotland and Northern Ireland have morning daily newspapers that position themselves in relation to those nations in just the same way as, for example, the English edition of *The Sun* does in privileging news of England (Rosie et al. 2004: 448). Meanwhile in Wales the absence of a daily newspaper adequately reporting and reaching the whole of the country is a running political sore. Whichever flag they are waving, however, all the current titles in Wales and Scotland are owned by corporations based outside the nations concerned – and, in one case, outside the UK.

Nationalism can only be banal, Billig argues, once nations are securely established. At that point 'the poets are typically replaced by prosaic politicians and the epic ballads by government reports' (1995: 77), an observation which neatly explains Wales's seemingly-permanent liminal status: it has all these. But can institutional structures such as the regulation of broadcasting be a *cause* as well as an outcome of nation-building? Where the mechanics of full statehood are missing, culture may provide a stronger platform than politics for nationalist sentiment and action.

As what is sometimes described as a 'stateless nation' (Law 2001: 315, quoting McCrone 1999) this is precisely the position in Wales, where broadcasting has been so significant that it has even been argued that modern Wales is the direct product (Hannan 1999, quoting Davies 1994). First, it reaches the whole country which, for topographical reasons, print media never have. (Cardiff to Bangor is 16 miles further than Cardiff to London, takes more than twice as long by direct train – of which there are few – and realistically about twice as long by car, as there is no direct fast route.) Second, the public funding of the BBC, the creation of S4C (Channel 4 in Wales) and, to a much smaller and diminishing extent, the public service broadcasting duties placed on Channel 3 television, have bypassed the problem of an audience which, because it is small and widely dispersed, is not commercially attractive for broadcasting in English, let alone in Welsh. Inevitably the structure and regulation of broadcasting have become a site of struggle in Wales, to the threatened death in one case, as we will see later in the chapter.

In relation to the politics of broadcasting, the stakes may be highest in Wales, but the symbolic messages incorporated by institutional arrange-

ments are equally important in Northern Ireland and Scotland. For the purposes of a smooth transition to the new regulatory arrangements set out in
the Communications Act 2003, Ofcom was established by the Office of
Communications Act 2002. In both Houses of Parliament members of all
parties argued that the nations of the UK should have nominated representatives on the Ofcom main board. The government's view, however, was
that the new regulator should be 'small and lean', modelled on business
practice, rather than the governance style of not-for-profit organizations
(Andrews 2005: 38, 41). Board members should not, therefore, represent a
single interest – except, critics might say, that of the beneficiaries of a
market-led economy. As eventually set up, Ofcom has offices in the nations
(and English regions), the directors of which sit on the Senior Management
Group rather than the main Board. The second-tier Content Board includes
representatives of the nations, but these members are appointed as individuals rather than being nominees of, for instance, the Scottish Parliament.
Members of the third-tier Advisory Committees for the Nations are
'appointed through an open public process'. In other words Ofcom's lay
members have no formal line of accountability to the publics whose interests they are supposed to represent. These committees 'offer advice' to and
'work with' the Ofcom Executive, while the Ofcom main board meetings
make what sounds rather like an annual Royal Progress around the nations
and regions. It is hard to disagree with Plaid Cymru's description of the new
regulatory arrangements as 'centralist' (Andrews 2005: 43). Clearly Ofcom
is not ashamed to be centralized: one of the purposes of the Advisory
Committees for the Nations is to respond to 'specific consultation requests
. . . on matters where a non-metropolitan perspective will be valuable',
from which one may infer that most of the time it is considered to be
unnecessary. To put it in Billig's terms, both Ofcom's structure and official
discourse 'flag' the unquestionable primacy of the UK over its constituent
nations. (See www.ofcom.org.uk/ about/scg for full details of Ofcom structure and protocols.)

Since its foundation the BBC, too, has been accused of
'Londoncentrism'. Being explicitly 'British' and a broadcaster funded by the
public of the whole UK, the corporation consequently expends consider-
able effort trying to demonstrate that this centralization is only sustained
to the extent that it must be an integrated organization and must be based
in the capital of the UK. Accordingly, the BBC Trust (which succeeded the
Board of Governors under the new Charter running from January 2007) has
a specific member for each nation (see www.bbc.co.uk > About > How the
BBC is Run) – although they, too, are there as individuals, appointed by the
Queen in Council on the advice of ministers.

So not only are news media in and for the nations of the UK more
caught up in the political process that is typical of the UK-wide 'national'

press and broadcast media, but their regulation, ownership, content, language and style of address are *politicized*. Everything from masthead to sports coverage is laden with symbolism.

Scottish and 'Scottishized': newspapers for Scotland

According to a survey in 2003, 65 per cent of residents of Scotland 'declare[d] themselves Scottish only or more Scottish than British' (Bryant 2006: 62). Apart from the self-containment encouraged by geography, Bryant argues that this strong national self-identity is linked to the nation's having the institutional basis for its own distinctive civil society. The 1707 Treaty of Union with England left Scotland with its church and systems of law, education and local government unaltered (Bryant 2006: 35). Despite the union's being primarily a matter of economic advantage, even Scottish banks retained an element of autonomy: they still issue their own paper currency.

Politics and every aspect of the judicial system are constitutive of the 'hard news' on which newspapers' self-definition – even if not the actual composition of their editions – depends. For regional and local papers, with their address to a family audience, education news is also a staple topic. Against this background it is easy to understand why 'virtually all those daily morning papers bought in Scotland have, to a greater or lesser degree, Scottish content aimed at Scottish readers' (J. Thomas 2006b). These newspapers fall into five categories. Three are directly comparable to the English press discussed in earlier chapters: local weeklies, city daily evening papers and regional morning papers. In the last case, however, the distribution of Scotland's population makes them relatively higher profile than their English counterparts. For instance, *The Press and Journal* of Aberdeen 'covers an area twice the size of Wales with a third of its population' (Marks 1997b) and claims to reach 'over 1 in 2 adults in the North of Scotland every week', 57 per cent of whom are in social classes ABC1, and 38 per cent in the 35–54 age group (that is, more likely to be economically active) according to the paper's media pack (http://mediapack.thisisnorth-scotland.co.uk/). Celebrating the paper's two hundred and fiftieth anniversary, the editor said that the paper 'has never aspired to be a national' (Marks 1997b). Ten years later little appears to have changed: a visit to the paper's web site indicates that regional news predominates. Perhaps its assured position as a regional landmark – referred to familiarly as the *P&J* – rests in part on an ability to balance tradition and modernity. The paper remains in broadsheet format, with a Gothic masthead. Visit the web site, however, and it is possible to listen to a podcast of the weekly column in Doric, the regional dialect.

Two other categories of newspaper circulate in Scotland. One is the set of three that define themselves as Scottish-based national papers for Scotland. *The Scotsman*, based in Edinburgh, brands itself as 'Scotland's national newspaper' and adopts an upmarket compact format similar to *The Times* of London. Based in Glasgow, *The Herald* makes a semiotic counter-claim to authority through broadsheet format and two references to its 1783 foundation in its masthead. Neither paper, however, is locally-owned. Newsquest, whose parent company is US-based, owns *The Herald*. In 2006 *The Scotsman* (together with its Sunday and evening sister papers) was acquired by the rapidly expanding English-based company Johnston Press. Nor is the third and biggest-selling, the 'red-top' *Daily Record*. Owned by Trinity Mirror and long unchallenged in this sector of the market, it is now being successfully attacked, particularly in the east of Scotland, by *The Scottish Sun*, using News International's familiar price-cutting tactics (*Press Gazette* 18 August 2006).

The Scottish Sun belongs to the last, and unique, category of Scottish newspaper: rebranded editions of London-based papers which 'account for approximately half of morning papers that circulate in Scotland (J. Thomas 2006b). As well as *The Sun*, the *Daily Express* and *Daily Mail* all have versions with 'Scottish' in the title, alongside the *Daily Star of Scotland*. The re-versioning consists both of substituted and modified content. The principal areas of substitution are the main news stories, sport and entertainment, as James Thomas's (2006b) 'day survey' shows and my own observation in April 2006 confirmed. Sometimes, however, the changes are more subtle. Rosie et al. (2004: 451–2) make a telling detailed comparison of the English and Scottish *Daily Mail*'s versions of a parliamentary sketchwriter's account of the election of a Scot as Speaker of the House of Commons. After relatively minor deletions and insertions, in 'the version sold in England the point of the story was to deride the speaker's accent, in the version sold in Scotland, the point of the story could be read as a derisory comment on English prejudice'.

Where these re-versioned papers have had a veneer of Scottishness laid on them, the *Daily Record*, *The Scotsman*, and *The Herald* have been Scottish throughout: recognizably 'national' papers in nearly every respect, constructed from a distinctively Scottish perspective. The editor of *The Scotsman* 'used to be one of the pillars of Edinburgh society' (MacWhirter 2006). The appointment in 2006 of the former editor of *The News*, Portsmouth, to the post was therefore interpreted locally as an alarming signal that, for Johnston Press, the primary consideration was commercial success, rather than the role of newspapers in national civil society (MacWhirter 2006; *Press Gazette* 8 September 2006).

In the two more upmarket papers, the pages headed 'news' consist mostly of Scottish domestic news and are followed by international news pages. Scotland also dominates the news content of the 'red top' *Daily Record* which, like its London-based equivalents, does not have extensive international news on separate pages. In the *Daily Record* all the signifiers of the popular paper genre are consistently Scottish, from stories of family tragedy to the (fully clothed) students modelling for charity, pictured on page three and the 'Stunning Scots swimmer' featured in a fashion spread (all examples from the *Daily Record* 20 April 2006). In all three papers the feature, comment, business and, of course, sports pages follow the same home-grown pattern. In one telling respect, however, these 'national' papers signal that their relationship with their audience may be closer, and more analogous to that of the English regional morning papers – or those in Europe and North America – than the aloof style of the London-based national dailies. In both *The Herald* and *The Scotsman* many of the birth, marriage and death announcements appear to come from, and be directed to, members of the local community. By contrast, those in *The Daily Telegraph* or *The Guardian*, for example, are intended to reach nationwide social networks, often military in the former case and academic in the latter.

In terms of a functioning public sphere, this relative intimacy of address has two contrasting outcomes. Higgins (2006) used content analysis to compare the coverage of the 1999 elections to the newly devolved Scottish parliament in *The Herald*, *The Scotsman* and *The Press and Journal*, with that in *The Guardian*, *The Independent* and *The Times*. He concludes that the Scottish papers provided more, and more prominent, coverage and more background. Hardly surprising but, importantly, he suggests that they provided this information and advice at a stage in the campaigning when readers would be considering how to vote. The London-based papers, by contrast, focused, too late, on the 'dramatic climax of the process' (Higgins 2006: 30).

A lack of in-depth coverage by the non-Scottish press is ironic, because most UK-wide news organizations responded to devolution by increasing the resources devoted to Scottish politics: 'Papers with one correspondent suddenly needed two or three', but 'Once the parliament met, old hands from Westminster encouraged a pack mentality' (Nicoll 2005). Given that the parliament has limited powers, and is serving a population of only five million, there is restricted meat for the pack to chew on. According to Nicoll, the London-based Sunday *Observer*'s Scottish columnist, 'starved of policy to dissect, the media [has] concentrated on the process', resulting in the relentless pursuit of political gossip and personal peccadilloes, an outcome also highlighted by McNair (2006: 40–1) and MacWhirter (2006). Nicoll shares the view of other Scotland-based correspondents that, as a result, Members of the Scottish Parliament (MSPs) have become defensive and reluctant to take risks, thus further undermining the effectiveness of the new parliament. Nor is the quality of debate helped by there being, according to the editor of *The Herald*, 'still papers in Scotland that believe that devolution should not have happened' (Nicoll 2005). This sense of insecurity and susceptibility to pressure is confirmed by Birks (2006), who reports that the editor of the Glasgow *Evening Times* believes that a well-timed and sharp leader comment can produce a political response.

All roads and profits lead to London: newspapers in Wales

Even if the Scottish polity suffers from overexposure as multiple titles and Scotland correspondents of UK-wide media vie for content, at least the Scottish public is well provided with both countrywide and regional printed news on a daily basis. Neither is the case in Wales. As with Scotland, today's controversies over communication are rooted in history and topography. Before 1536–42, when Henry VIII annexed the lands now recognized as Wales, there had been many powerful leaders, including royal princes, but it had never constituted a single state with unified institutions (Bryant 2006: 119–20). After annexation, Wales became subject to whatever legal and administrative framework was operating in England. Not until the mid-twentieth century did autonomy and something approaching statehood develop, and even then it was incrementally and adventitiously with, for example, the designation of Wales as a National Health Service region in 1948 and the setting up of the Welsh Office in 1964 (Bryant 2006: 122).

In Wales, terrain explains a great deal. Much of the centre and north of the country is beautiful but barren upland and mountain country that only supports a small and scattered population. The main areas of settlement are around the coast, along the English border and to the south and west. East–west travel has always been easier than north–south, a situation that has remained unchanged with the development of roads and railways. Nevertheless, terrain in the sense that the French talk of *terroir*, is very powerful. *Hiraeth*, inadequately translated as a 'longing', affects anglophone and even part-Welsh members of the Welsh diaspora. Its very existence as a discrete concept signals that 'Wales' has existed primarily in its culture and only secondarily and recently as institutions. One might, therefore, expect that the Welsh language would have been the basis for cultural continuity and solidarity. Certainly historians have asserted that the translation of the Bible into Welsh in 1588 was crucial in establishing the written language (Bryant 2006: 128, quoting Williams 1991) alongside the much older oral traditions in poetry and music.

At the beginning of the nineteenth century four-fifths of the population were Welsh speakers; by the 2001 Census the figure was nearer one-fifth – although this was 2 per cent higher than that reported in 1991

(Bryant 2006: 128; Thomas and Lewis 2006: 18). Behind this transformation was the explosive expansion of the coal, iron and steel industries in South Wales during the nineteenth and the first half of the twentieth centuries. Large numbers of non-Welsh-speakers were drawn into an area in which Welsh-speaking was anyway less universal than in rural mid- and north Wales. Members of this new industrial, working class, predominantly English-speaking 'Labour Wales', as Bryant terms it, were and are just as fiercely Welsh as those in *Y Fro Gymraeg* – rural Welsh-speaking Wales. Rivalry over which way of being Welsh is more authentic and who is better guarding the flame of Welsh culture is a recurring feature of Welsh life. (For fuller background, see Hannan 1999; Bryant 2006; Thomas and Lewis 2006.)

When these complexities of identity and social structure are laid over very difficult topography it is easy to understand why Wales has never had a single daily national newspaper, despite the masthead claim, in both English and Welsh, of the Cardiff-based *Western Mail* to be the 'national newspaper of Wales'. Starting afresh it might be possible, with electronic composition and remote printing, to produce a paper that gathered news from across the nation and was then distributed countrywide, but the territory is already occupied or, as critics say, carved up. Whatever its claims, *The Western Mail* has always been identified with industrial southern Wales (see, for example, Williams's 1995 analysis). Residents of north Wales relied on weekly papers for local news in English. Among the resort towns of the north Wales coast and towards the English border of north-east Wales, sales of the morning regional daily *Liverpool Daily Post* gradually increased to the extent that in 2003 a separate paper, the *Daily Post – Wales* was spun off. With the Welsh red dragon at the centre of its masthead, the paper describes itself as 'North Wales' best-selling newspaper' and now operates out of a base at Llandudno Junction. Its format is the lively, tabloid but very 'respectable' style characteristic of the regional dailies described in previous chapters. The news pages are headed 'Wales' – although actually focused on north Wales – followed by very limited coverage of UK and international news.

Like *The Western Mail* and its evening and Sunday sister papers, the *Daily Post – Wales* is owned by Trinity Mirror, which also owns a large number of local weeklies throughout Wales. While the two papers do not pursue a common editorial line, they have established 'separate and non-competing markets' (J. Thomas 2006a: 7) and have no daily competitors. This, critics point out, means that there is no alternative countrywide editorial 'voice' and vehicle through which to debate specifically Welsh issues on a national basis in the way that there is in Scotland, Ireland and England. Following the establishment of the National Assembly for Wales (NAfW) in 1999, dissatisfaction increased markedly. At first this was centred on what was seen to be a lack of adequate detail and analytic depth in political coverage (Barlow et al. 2005: 61; J. Thomas 2006a: 13). Concern was sufficient for the Culture, Welsh Language and Sport Committee of the Assembly to hold hearings on issues relating to the policies of the English-owned press in Wales. At these, representatives of the newspapers argued that Assembly business was adequately covered by their use of Press Association (that is, news agency) routine reports and sending reporters only for 'items of special interest to their papers', because their readers are 'most interested in how Assembly business affects their readers directly for example schools, health the economy etc.' (National Assembly for Wales 2006) – in other words as consumers, rather than as citizens.

'Wales is basically a tabloid-reading nation', writes Williams (2003: 33). From a commercial point of view, therefore, it is not surprising that many interpreted *The Western Mail*'s 2005 'radical new editorial line', aimed at arresting falling sales, as a (further) move downmarket (*Press Gazette* 24 June 2005). A 'week survey' between 8 and 13 May 2006 certainly seems to vindicate this view. On five of the six days, pages two and three, customarily regarded as important news pages, were taken up with 'soft news' of leisure and entertainment. Political issues were covered at length with a two-page spread on four of the six days. Two of these concerned Welsh politics, the other two national politics, but in all four cases the interpretive frame was interpersonal rivalries over, for example, candidacy in a NAfW by-election.

In response to this shift, a consortium of business people was reported to be trying to launch a rival broadsheet-style paper, based on the calculation that it would attract more ABC1 readers and thus revenue from job advertisements in the expanding public services. Trinity Mirror was sufficiently concerned to warn staff at *The Western Mail* that 'if they ever worked on the rival title they [would] be banned from working for the Cardiff-based group again' (*Press Gazette* 21 October 2005). As of late 2006 there is no sign of the rival title launch, presumably discouraged by a combination of the rapidly growing uncertainty about the future of classified advertising in print media, and the success of *The Western Mail*'s relaunch in narrowly financial terms. Sales figures for 2006 (*Press Gazette* 10 March 2006, 8 September 2006) showed only modest declines – a relatively good performance in relation to other regional morning dailies.

While the lack of a genuinely nationwide *daily* title remains a sensitive political issue, in fact Wales does have a national newspaper. *Y Cymro* (The Welshman) is a very long-established weekly paper, owned since 2004 by Tindle Newspapers, an English company which has concentrated on similarly traditional titles, including several in Wales, for instance the *Brecon and Radnor Express*. *Y Cymro* may well have national reach (no breakdown of sales is provided on the Newspaper Society's web site) but inevitably its audience is predominantly in *Y Fro Gymraeg*, rural north Wales, as indicated by its having offices in Porthmadog and Aberystwyth. The extent of Welsh-speaking in north Wales is further demonstrated by *Yr Herald Cymraeg* (The Welsh Herald), founded in 1855, but now a weekly supplement circulated with the *Daily Post –Wales*.

In the 1970s campaigns to sustain the language, combined with an unusually high level of interest in news of the immediate locality (Ofcom 2004a: 43), produced a distinctively Welsh media form: the *papurau bro*, monthly community newspapers produced by volunteers. James Thomas (2006c: 54) quotes an estimate of their combined circulation in the mid-1990s as 280,000. As of June 2006 the BBC Cymru web site provided links to the content of 58 *papurau bro* from all over Wales – and one in Liverpool – although the heaviest concentration is in the north west.

Paradoxically, the Internet has also provided a platform for a campaign to found a Welsh-language national daily paper, *Y Byd* (The World), explicitly intended to act as a Welsh public sphere, both politically and culturally. According to its web site, which is also available in English, French, Italian, German and Castillian Spanish, 'Speakers of Welsh are dispersed throughout Wales and beyond . . . with lifestyles and patterns of work becoming increasingly diverse, a daily Welsh language newspaper will help bring the Welsh-speaking community together and allow it to express its plural identity' (www.ybyd.co.uk). With a planned launch in spring 2007 the venture is to be funded through sales of shares to 'supporters', casual sales and 'further capital from the commercial and corporate sectors'.

'A strong tradition of news awareness': Northern Ireland's flourishing press

'People here are news junkies, they feed off news as a topic of conversation . . . whether it is the farmer down the road done for drink driving, or the politicians spouting their party line, or the paramilitaries', according to the editor of the *Sunday World* (Crummy 2006). With a population of 1.5 million, of whom 800,000 live in the Belfast area, Northern Ireland currently has two morning dailies, one very influential daily evening (the *Belfast Telegraph*) which now also produces a morning edition, a regional Sunday (*Sunday Life*, sister paper of the *Belfast Telegraph*) and 50 paid-for weekly titles. Many titles produced in the Republic of Ireland are also on sale, notably the red-top *Sunday World*. Unusually in the UK regional Sunday newspaper market, sales of the *Sunday World*'s Northern Ireland edition have been rising despite – or because of – their exposés of paramilitary criminal activity and the threats to staff, distributors and newsagents that followed (G. McLaughlin 2006 67–8; *Press Gazette* 8 September 2006).

The enduring religio-political divide in Northern Ireland ensures that there are not only two parallel social universes to be reported, but two alternative interpretations of the news. As a consequence Newry, for example, with a population of 48,000, has two weekly titles. On the mainland, finding 'the local angle' is a standard editorial tactic for regional daily and weekly newspapers. In Northern Ireland, according to an academic observer, the obverse is true: an apparently local issue, like a school closure, will be used to take a position on a matter of national politics (John Brewer, personal communication). As well as multiplying potential content, social cleavages also generate funding. Many of the weekly titles do not issue audited sales figures (Crummy 2006). Nevertheless they, like the major daily titles, for a long time benefited from employment advertisements by government and other public sector bodies, which are duplicated in order to demonstrate that both communities are being addressed equally. In mid-2005, however, the government announced a review of this spending. But it is not only conflict that has fed the newspaper reading habit in Northern Ireland. Just as in Wales, many people live in small rural communities and have an appetite for very local news. In his review of the market, Crummy points out that the Belfast *News Letter*'s sales are 45 per cent higher on Saturdays because its *Farming Week* supplement is a 'crucial buy for the farming community'.

The *News Letter* has appeared continuously under that title since 1737 and claims to be the world's oldest surviving daily newspaper (see www.newspapersoc.org.uk > Facts and figures > History). Staunchly Unionist, the *News Letter*'s 'About Us' web page describes itself as 'useful, entertaining and on guard'. Whatever the fears for the future encoded in that phrase, the paper has been stable commercially, although sales figures for the first half of 2006 showed a decline (*Press Gazette* 8 September 2006).

Until early 2005 the only morning daily title which provided a political alternative to the *News Letter* was the family-owned *Irish News*. The paper takes a 'constitutionalist nationalist' position: it supports the Social Democratic and Labour Party (SDLP) which advocates advancing the interests of the Catholic population through the use of existing legal and institutional structures.

In competition with both of these is the evening daily *Belfast Telegraph*, owned by Dublin-based Independent News and Media. In an environment where all newspapers can reasonably claim to speak for a real, rather than an imagined, community and therefore expect to be heard, the *Belfast Telegraph* enjoys a particularly influential position. Although 'implicitly republican' it is widely read by both communities 'and knows it' (John Brewer – personal communication). The paper's stature is signalled semiotically by still retaining its broadsheet format, but it does not rely only on being magisterial: in 2005 its editor attributed its success to the popular appeal of a tabloid morning edition, the serialization of a local boxer's auto-biography and the death of footballer George Best, a major news event for Northern Ireland (Crummy 2006).

In Ireland demographic issues have particular salience. Changes in the population ecology of the Belfast area were a major factor in the launch, in February 2005, of a third morning title, the *Daily Ireland* which took a 'republican nationalist' stance in that it supported a united Ireland. According to its mediapack (www.irelandclick.com/media, accessed 5 May 2006) the paper 'targeted young nationalist readers', particularly in the northern and western parts of Belfast. The paper was a new venture by the Andersonstown News Group, which runs a very widely read and influential set of weekly and bi-weekly titles covering sectors of Belfast. References to the employment opportunities created by the group's expansion and bursaries for young people entering further and higher education further signalled its post-peace process aim of appealing to a younger, more outward-looking audience. In September 2006, however, the paper closed, blaming the withholding of both government business start-up finance and the public sector advertising which it had 'expected to receive on the same basis as other local dailies' (*Press Gazette* 15 September 2006).

Another indication of social change in Ireland is the group's ownership of *Lá Nua* (New Day), known until January 2007 as *Lá* (Day). Formerly a weekly paper and acquired by Andersonstown News Group in 1999, it is now 'the only daily newspaper in the Celtic language', with a web site (www.nuacht.com) and 'busy offices in Belfast and the Donegal Gaeltacht' – that part of the west of Ireland where the language has remained in daily use. Significantly, the Group's mediapack, addressed to potential advertisers, refers to the paper's 'well-educated and largely affluent readership'.

Where once using the Irish language was a badge of highly committed political nationalism, it is now attracting middle-class Catholic learners and government funding for its teaching in schools. Relative peace has opened up 'space' for a cultural nationalism reminiscent of that in Wales – and with some interesting parallels in ambiguous mechanics of statehood.

Bearing the cost of plurality: public service broadcasting in the UK nations

Nowhere is the tension between the commercial funding of broadcasting and the interests of minority audiences more evident than in the nations of the UK. In terms of financial logic, the nations simply consist of audiences which can or cannot be addressed profitably. Where radio is concerned, the complexities of linguistic and cultural pluralism are effectively side stepped by the dominance of music-based formats. In Wales, for instance, Barlow et al. (2005: 108) report 'a growth in group ownership . . . The idea that Welsh radio should be locally owned and strongly related to the local community' has ceased to be a 'main regulatory goal'.

In television, as in radio, the same pattern of corporate consolidation applies. The Channel 3 licences for Wales and for the Scotland/England (and Isle of Man) Borders region are held by ITV plc; the two for the rest of Scotland by Scottish Media Group (SMG) under the common brand of STV; and for Northern Ireland by Ulster TV plc. For commercial television companies, the nations are only exceptional in the sense that they are the subject of heavier public service broadcasting requirements than those which apply to the English regions. The difference is, however, marginal: a matter of symbolism and political nuance. In mid-2005 Ofcom announced that dedicated output for the nations should be 5.5 hours per week for news and 4.0 hours per week for non-news programming, although the latter will reduce to 3.0 hours per week 'when the first UK region achieves [digital] switchover' (Ofcom 2005f: paras 1.4 and 1.7). (The comparable figure for English regions will be 0.5 hours per week.)

As we saw in Chapter 4, for commercial broadcasters this activity is an unwelcome loss-maker. Regional programming is relatively expensive because news has virtually no shelf-life and very little of the rest can be sold on. Meanwhile, multiplying digital television channels are eroding the Channel 3 licensees' audience share and thus their advertising revenue, with consequences that the 'Tartan 10.30' saga illustrates very nicely. This separate Scottish edition of the main Channel 3 evening news bulletin was proposed by SMG in their evidence to Ofcom's review of programming for the UK nations (Ofcom 2005f: para. 3.3). Faced with a positive response, however, SMG claimed that 'The programme is not viable in commercial terms' and that Ofcom had 'failed to find an appropriate funding mechanism' (*Press Gazette* 17 June 2005). To this Ofcom responded tartly 'it is not in Ofcom's power to award direct public funding for such a service . . . it is for SMG to decide whether this new service could be commercially viable on its own terms and decide whether or not to proceed with it' (Ofcom 2005f: para. 3.6). The prospects were not promising. In the latter part of 2006 SMG's corporate trajectory mirrored that of ITV plc: deteriorating advertising revenues; the removal of its chief executive; and a falling share price, culminating with a 'severe profits warning' (*The Guardian* 30 October 2006).

The last sentence of the same Ofcom paragraph (2005f: para. 3.6) reads 'Many respondents to the consultation felt that such a service was an important and valuable proposal', a telling insight into the conflicting forces affecting Ofcom too. We have already seen that, consonant with its mission, many of Ofcom's proposals on the 'public purposes' of broadcasting and their practical enactment have been legitimated by substantial social research, for example *Views in the Nations* (Ofcom 2005g). In broadcasting terms, the public appears to have expensive tastes. News of their nation, preferably from more than one provider, is 'overwhelmingly' the top priority (Ofcom 2005g: 7), while other dedicated programming should be of high quality, stimulating, not preoccupied with the main centres of population (that is, Belfast, industrial south Wales, and Scotland's Glasgow/Edinburgh 'central belt') and shown at peak times. More extravagantly still, broadcasting in the indigenous languages of the nations received consistent support, particularly for Welsh, but also for programmes in (Scots) Gaelic and Irish. In the last case the younger people surveyed were more positive than older people, suggesting that demand may rise, rather than fall away (Ofcom 2005g:10).

Ofcom's proposed solution to this public response is that 'dedicated digital services are the most effective way of meeting the needs of Welsh, Gaelic and Irish language speakers' (Ofcom 2005f: para. 1.8 and S.4). In Wales the vehicle for this already exists as S4C (*Sianel Pedwar Cymru*/Channel 4 in Wales). For Ireland, Ofcom suggests that the BBC in Northern Ireland and the Republic's Irish language channel TG4 should explore a relationship (Ofcom 2005f: paras 1.13, 1.14 and 4.51–4.63). Gaelic language analogue programming has been provided both by the BBC and SMG in Scotland. In Ofcom's view the BBC should take on the responsibility of the digital channel, partly supported by a 'cash-and-kind contribution' from SMG in return for 'reductions to its broadcast commitments' to Gaelic output, ultimately to zero (Ofcom 2005f: paras 1.11, 1.12 and 4.29–4.50).

The common theme is clear: that the BBC must take responsibility for these loss-making but popular and politically sensitive cultural activities. (See Ofcom 2005f: S.4 Fig. 1 for a summary.) Here, however, one meaning of 'plurality' bumps up against another: Ofcom is formally dedicated to the encouragement of competition, which makes placing the BBC in the position of monopoly provider undesirable in principle. Accordingly the *Statement on Programming for the Nations and Regions* (Ofcom 2005f) is larded with references to 'contestability' being achieved through alternative sources of funding, although from where and over what timescale remains opaque in all instances but one. The most specific proposal is that the BBC should transfer some of the 'licence fee revenues spent by the BBC on Welsh broadcasting', to provide partial support to a 'Welsh Public Service Publisher' (Ofcom 2005f: para. 1.10), as well as ceding more control to S4C (Ofcom 2005f: para. 1.9). 'Contestability' in this context means transferring money between not-for-profit organizations in order to lash together the rhetoric of the market and the 'complex and changing requirements of a devolved society with diverse cultural identities', as Ofcom itself puts it (2005f: Box 3.1, para. 5). Meeting those requirements is intractably unprofitable and yet politically unavoidable, as the history of S4C illustrates perfectly.

S4C: 'the most heavily subsidized broadcaster in the world'?

Sinanel Pedwar Cymru – S4C – was the outcome of a determined campaign by elite cultural nationalists: a very Welsh tale in its specificities, but with clear resonances if cultural nationalism were to become more high profile in the other devolved nations of the UK.

During the 1960s and 1970s Welsh national identity became a 'hot' political issue (Billig 1995). An important stimulus was the spread of television ownership among ordinary people from the late 1950s on. What would be the effect of consuming yet more popular culture be on the everyday use of Welsh, particularly among young people? This is, of course, an oversimplified model of the media–audience relationship, as Barlow et al. point out (2005: 149), but it has always had a tenacious grip on the public imagination, demonstrated by the constant iteration of moral panics about the supposed impact of media messages. The institutions of broadcasting were, therefore, a prime target for the civil disobedience staged by the Welsh Language Society, which had been formed in 1962. In the early 1970s, for instance, several impeccably respectable citizens were taken to court for not paying their radio/television licence fee. By the mid-1970s the Labour government of the day had accepted the need for a Welsh-language service, even if it required public subsidy, only to suspend the project when the economic situation deteriorated. In 1979 the newly elected Conservative administration reneged on a pre-election commitment to the new service. Language activists responded with tactics that proved politically irresistible. Later that year a television transmitter was switched off. Then, in the spring of 1980, Gwynfor Evans, president of Plaid Cymru, the Welsh nationalist political party, announced that from October he would fast to the death. He was believed: 'Fear of widespread political unrest in Wales and pressure from prominent figures in the Welsh political establishment . . . resulted in the government's reversing its decision' (Barlow et al. 2005: 138). (For a full account of these events see Barlow et al. 2005: ch. 6, particularly pp 134–8; and Hannan 1999: ch. 7.)

S4C first broadcast in November 1982. It was established as, and continues to be, a non-profit 'publisher/broadcaster', meaning that it does not make its own programmes. According to its web site (www.src.co.uk/abouts4c/corporate, accessed 19 June 2006) S4C broadcasts an 'average of 32 hours per week', of which ten are provided from the licence fee by the BBC and the rest commissioned from independent producers, including

ITV plc which holds the Channel 3 licence for Wales. During peak hours the 'majority must be in Welsh'. A parallel digital service was established in 1998; this now broadcasts 80 hours per week, with 'a substantial proportion in Welsh', including that being broadcast on the analogue channel. Before 1998 S4C output had displaced part of Channel 4's programming in Wales (and still does in analogue-only homes), causing some resentment among English-speakers. S4C was not only a response to Welsh language activists but also to English-speakers who wanted Welsh output shifted off mainstream television channels (Hannan 1999: 141; Thomas and Lewis 2006: 7). A further digital channel, S4C2, was established in 1999 to provide live coverage of the National Assembly for Wales.

In UK television ecology, the structure of S4C is a unique hybrid. Since 1993 it has sold its own advertising but, being not-for-profit, 'ploughs the net revenue back into the service' (www.s4c.co.uk/abouts4c/corporate). Much the greater part of its income, however, is a government grant-in-aid administered by DCMS: £88,690 million for the financial year to December 2005. The Secretary of State for Culture, Media and Sport also appoints the Chair and Board of the Welsh Fourth Channel Authority, which not only governs the channel, but also acts as its regulator. In March 2006 a new Chair was appointed for the statutory four-year term. Already a member of the Authority, he had been Chief Executive of the Welsh Language Board and 'was ordained a member of the *Gorsedd* at the 2004 Newport National Eisteddfod' (DCMS 2006), thus proving that in Wales, contra Billig, bards and bureaucrats can not only coexist but be the same person.

It is, of course, both necessary and natural that such an appointment would be made from within the Welsh-speaking administrative class, but this association with the 'Tafia' is one of the channel's contemporary problems. Since the mid-1990s S4C's audience, however measured, has fallen even more steeply than has been general in the new multichannel environment. In a forensic examination of the causes, Thomas and Lewis (2006) conclude that the principal reason is that, after the first flush of viewing as a patriotic cultural duty, the bedrock of S4C's audience has been those for whom Welsh is a first language – a section of the population that is not being replenished. The increase in self-declared Welsh-speakers between the 1991 and 2001 Censuses consisted, Thomas and Lewis suggest, mainly of residents for whom it was a second language which they did not use routinely at home and in which they might not be so proficient as to want to consume Welsh-language media.

Beside the barrier of uncertain language skills, the channel has acquired a reputation for being old-fashioned and parochial in its content. Even its most popular programme, the BBC-produced soap opera *Pobol y Cym* (People of the Valley) has lost ground. Add to this the 'Tafia' problem – a widespread popular belief that S4C, like the rest of Welsh media, is dominated by 'over-paid "Welshies"'(Thomas and Lewis 2006: 23) – and an actually ageing audience, and clearly the channel has several linked problems. First, advertisers will be discouraged. Even if this revenue stream is relatively unimportant in cash terms, it is a necessary symbol of the channel's viability. Second, and worse, as the definition of 'public purposes' moves inexorably from the public interest to what the public declares itself interested in when surveyed, how is the grant-in-aid to be legitimized? Much of S4C's output is addressed to a minority of a minority, for example, coverage of the National Eisteddfod. Undoubtedly important as a cultural event, the National Eisteddfod cannot be said to have the same kind of quasi-constitutional status that justifies the BBC's spending public money on broadcasting the state opening of (the UK) parliament or Trooping the Colour, also viewed only by a small minority.

To ensure its future, Thomas and Lewis suggest (2006: 33) that it may be time for a multilingual S4C, built around a mix of higher quality and more popular programming combined with nimble scheduling, for example, making strategic use of the ever-popular *Y Clyb Rygbi*. A channel, in other words, for and about Wales, but based on a more 'civic' and less 'essentialist' 'definition of Welshness that recognizes that 'only three-quarters of the people in Wales were born in Wales' (Thomas and Lewis 2006: 37). The proposal has manifest advantages: it is admirably inclusive and would not necessarily be opposed by nationalists – Barlow et al. (2005: 151) point out that Plaid Cymru have supported an English-language service for Wales – and might well boost advertising revenue. What, however, would be the political argument for hundreds of millions of pounds of public money, given that the vital Welsh language content would be not much more likely to cover its costs than it was in 1982? In a social environment where market-based performance criteria pass increasingly unchallenged, the 'space' for successful publicly funded public service broadcasting is squeezed constantly. Reach only a small audience and value for money will be questioned; compete successfully with the commercial sector and howls of outrage about unfair competition will follow. The adverse response of commercial broadcasters to S4C's increasing its popular appeal and thus its audience share would surely be even more determined and noisy than that already directed at the BBC's public support through the licence fee.

Being British for all Britons: the BBC and the nations

During the period running up to the 2007 BBC Charter renewal, its role in relation to the 'nations and regions' was considered sufficiently important to the corporation's self-defence to be the subject of a separate submission document (BBC 2004b). Much of the material therein passed, without major modification, into the final position statement *Building Public Value* (BBC 2004c) and thence to the government's Green (consultative) Paper (DCMS 2005b) and final White (pre-legislation policy) Paper, where 'reflecting the UK Nations, regions and communities' emerges as one of the future 'six public purposes' for the BBC (Cm 6763 2006: paras 3.1.4 and 3.5). As we have already seen with its regional policies and outreach work, the BBC is in a very delicate position in relation to the nations. The corporation is a powerful symbol of a unified UK *and* a highly successful worldwide brand *and* is required to show itself businesslike in financial (even if not in governance) terms. How much can or should such an organization devolve its resources or decision-making? Individual citizens of the UK can deal with the 'Moreno question' (Bryant 2006: 5) about the balance between their sense of being British and/or Scottish or Welsh or Irish (or Bangladeshi or Polish) in any way they wish. The BBC must somehow balance both – and at a time when, as have seen, increasing demands are being made for it to deal with the important, legitimate but potentially very resource-hungry claims of, for example, not only the speakers of the indigenous languages of the UK other than English, but expanding non-indigenous language communities.

As was suggested earlier, an important element of the BBC's response to the distinctiveness of the UK nations is expressed symbolically through its governance. The nations have specific representation on the BBC Trust, indicating that they are more than mere 'regions', a status semiotically reinforced by the nations' having direct links on the BBC's homepage. Many of those active in the public life of the countries concerned ask where the real devolution of decision is but, as Hannan writes (1999: 138), the renaming of the BBC Welsh Region of the BBC as BBC Wales in 1964 'at least suggested a more independent existence'.

Radio is often said to be the forgotten medium but in the nations it is a quantum more important than television for the BBC's distinctive service to them. When the BBC finally ventured into local radio – with some hesitation, as we saw in Chapter 4 – the nations were treated as single localities. Here again we see the cultural and political subtleties of administrative arrangements. 'The BBC and You' web pages for Northern Ireland state flatly 'Radio Ulster commenced in January 1975 and Radio Foyle in September 1979': two parallel stations for this 'uniquely divided audience' (BBC 2004b: 41).

These BBC Northern Ireland (BBCNI) pages also inform us that in 2004–05 the corporation produced 5.21 hours of television in the Irish language, but 260 hours of radio; and 1.67 hours of television as against 10 hours of radio in Ulster Scots. The fiftyfold difference in Irish language output might be partly explained by the audience's potential access to television broadcasts from the Republic of Ireland. A sixfold difference in Ulster

Scots production, however, when there is no such alternative, suggests that cost continues to be a decisive consideration, as it always has been in the BBC's internal debates. Should the regions' main task be producing programmes for their own consumption or for national networking? (see, for example, Briggs 1995: 652.) Radio is relatively cheap, the first of the two linked reasons why radio broadcasting is so important to the BBC's provision for the UK nations. The second reason is its capacity to respond to politically large but numerically small and scattered indigenous language communities. The government's White Paper on the renewal of the BBC Charter declares 'The BBC is in a unique position to be able to contribute to the development of content that serves the UK's nations and communities'; 'The BBC has been broadcasting in Gaelic for over 80 years, has been committed to Welsh since its pioneering broadcasts in the 1920s and has broadcast in Irish . . . for nearly 25 years' (Cm 6763 2006: paras 3.5.7 and 3.5.8).

'The arrival, in November 1978, of Radio Wales . . . was the institutionalisation of the idea of a separate, English-speaking Wales' writes Hannan (1999: 142–3) because 'if Radio Wales exists, then Wales must exist too.' He goes on to call this an 'illusion', by which he means that the community thereby created is a construct arising from, for example, the choice and interpretive framing of news and other content. Hannan is writing with the amused scepticism of a very experienced journalist from 'the posh part of Aberaman', but is clearly aware that sociologically speaking such illusions are, as WI Thomas put it, 'real in their consequences'. Such consequences can be unexpected, given the complex class and cultural politics of nationalism. The BBC radio in Wales is actually Radio Wales/Radio Cymru, two parallel services which for the last decade have broadcast almost the same number of hours, 18 per day in the case of Radio Cymru (Barlow et al. 2005: 110). It might be assumed that Radio Cymru owes its existence to the station addressed to the majority, English-speaking population. Hannan (1999:143) persuasively argues that the reverse is true: that Radio Wales would not have been launched if there had not been concerns about the 'persistent resentment at the privileged treatment handed out to the language, particularly . . . among those who think it's denied them jobs'. At issue is, of course, are the rival historic, linguistic and class-based definitions of what it is to be Welsh.

Grudges against the 'Tafia', also alluded to by Thomas and Lewis (2006), are even recognized in a coded way by the BBC in a reference to the 'traditional perception of the BBC as remote and paternalistic' in the course of a specific discussion of its provision in Wales. Part of the corporation's response has been to try to reach a younger audience, with some success. In 2003 Radio Cymru had a greater, and rising proportion of younger listeners than Radio Wales. Thomas and Lewis (2006) suggest that this may be because Welsh language radio is more easily consumed by the 'new' speakers who have come to Welsh through the education system and thus may be the only person in the household who is reasonably fluent.

The 'imagined community' becomes virtually real: the Internet

Radio's ability to reach minority audiences, and particularly language communities, at a reasonable cost to both producer and consumer used to be unrivalled. It could even claim to have been the first medium to become modestly interactive. Now the Internet offers the same possibilities on an incomparably larger scale. Where Anderson ([1983] 1991) called the community created by shared media consumption 'imaginary' because its members could not communicate with one other, now they can. The potential for the economy, social structure and culture of small nations is obvious: for providing and exchanging information; for using and promoting the indigenous language; for enhancing a sense of identity both regionally and locally; for reaching the diaspora; and for 'its rôle as a forum for mediated public debate' (Barlow et al. 2005: 155). All these have been seized on with enthusiasm by the National Assembly for Wales which has produced, with all-party support, a policy for 'A Better Wales Online' with a 'firm emphasis on its participative and regenerative functions' as Barlow et al. (2005: 158) summarize it. Their discussion, though accepting of the possible advantages, concludes that the NAfW analysis is over-optimistic – and their commentary on Wales clearly applies to Northern Ireland and Scotland too.

According to Ofcom's comprehensive review of access to and use of communications technology, by 2005 in England 59 per cent of the population had home access (of any kind) to the Internet. For Scotland it was 51 per cent, for Wales 49 per cent, and for Northern Ireland 48 per cent. Effective use of the Internet now requires a high-speed broadband service. Rural communities used to be disadvantaged because cable companies had concentrated their installation in areas of high population density. This problem was solved by the broadband enabling of British Telecom's near-universal network of telephone landlines. But, as Ofcom's report reminds us, usable download speed depends on a household or business being within 5 km or, better, 2 km of the exchange. In Northern Ireland, for example, a quarter of the population fall outside the 5 km boundary (Ofcom 2006: 38) which partly explains why, although Internet usage in the UK is higher in rural areas, the proportion of the population with a broadband connection is below the national average. This barrier to broadband access might, in turn, have been solved by the introduction of long-distance wireless broadband. In 2003, however, when the licences for this service were auctioned, the regulator 'could have stipulated support for rural areas but didn't' (Bradbury 2006). By 2006 the service was only available in parts of west London and the Thames Valley, in socio-economic terms almost as far from deprived or isolated areas as it is possible to be.

Technical problems can be overcome, with sufficient investment, but even in an environment where the cost of computer hardware and of connection and service charges are falling, people on low incomes are at a severe disadvantage. A key cause of limited access is limited cash (Ofcom 2006: para. 6.6 and s. 4). This is particularly perverse when, as for the NAfW, redistribution is a key policy aim. In Scotland 72 per cent of social class ABC1 had access to the Internet, compared with 31 per cent of class CDE homes. For Northern Ireland the respective figures are 68 per cent and 30 per cent and in Wales 64 per cent and 34 per cent (Ofcom 2006: 70). At the sub-national level, Internet access varies not only by income, but age. In both the most remote rural areas of north Wales and the most impoverished of the south Wales valleys, write Thomas and Lewis (2006), there was a *fall* in home access between 2002 and 2005 and a *rise* in those between 16 and 24 years not accessing the Internet.

Being on the wrong side of the 'digital divide' now bars you from many of the taken-for-granted experiences and opportunities of everyday life. Services to consumers, for instance arranging all aspects of travel, are migrating to the web – and often on more advantageous terms. In relation to active citizenship and an effective public sphere, however, it is the increasing richness of the informational and educational content of the web which sharpens the problem of this divide. The BBC 'Where I Live' (hereafter WIL) pages, for example, contain much more than news. In England these are organized on a county basis; in Scotland into six geographical areas and for Wales into five. Northern Ireland is treated as a single area and although there is abundant information about events and activities, there is a complete lack of more fine-grained community news, presumably because sectarian divisions are geographically inscribed. By contrast, the Welsh WIL pages include detailed information for 31 towns. This content is more akin to 'features' than 'news', dealing with, for example, famous people born in the town: Laura Ashley the fabric and fashion designer in Merthyr Tydfil; Sara Siddons the eighteenth-century actress in Brecon. In providing this, the BBC is addressing both the identity enhancement potential of the Internet and the popularity of very local news in Wales revealed by Ofcom social survey (Ofcom 2005g).

These sites also make an explicit appeal to tourists (which aligns with NAfW's hopes for economic development) and to the expatriate community. The latter is an aspect of local sites that is not lost on commercial media. *The Western Mail* has an 'Expats Club' with, as at June 2006, a pop-up link to Ancestry UK.

More importantly for the politics of media in the nations, the BBC provides extensive – but nuanced – minority language provision on these web pages. Like the BBC News pages, WIL in Wales is available in an alternative Welsh-language version: *Cymru'r Byd* (Wales in the World). Opportunities to learn Welsh at a variety of levels and for all ages are available. BBC Scotland, however, only offers a pared-down version of the WIL site in Gaelic, and the language learning is aimed at children. BBCNI, no doubt because using the Irish language still carries an excess of meaning, restricts itself to assistance with General Certificate of Secondary Education (GCSE) revision, thus positioning itself alongside the formal educational system.

Access to minority language content is also available at no cost on the Internet from other for-profit and non-profit media: for example, the online version of the Irish language newspaper *Lá Nua* and the proposed Welsh daily paper *Y Byd*. S4C's web site offers courses for language learners at several levels and the possibility of viewing the channel's programmes in very high-quality sound and vision. Wherever you are, you can commune via the Youth National Eisteddfod. Provided, of course, that you have broadband.

7 Working in local media: from smoke-filled rooms to sweatshops

At the heart of the craft; at the heart of the community

Local media, whether print or broadcast, are often overlooked by both the public and academic commentators. Yet they are at the heart of the occupational culture of news journalism and for many years were a key element in its institutional structures.

The impetus for the setting up of an industry-wide training scheme was provided by the 1947–49 Royal Commission on the Press (Cmd. 7700 1949). In the early 1950s the National Council for the Training of Journalists (NCTJ) was established by agreement between the proprietors, the National Union of Journalists (NUJ) and (later) the Institute of Journalists (IoJ) to validate courses and to assess and certificate entry-level technical skills. Local and regional newspapers were the major stakeholders in the system in two senses: they funded it by a levy variable according to the number of their staff and, as a fragmented industry with many more small and medium-sized businesses than today, they relied on externally provided basic training.

From the late 1960s until the mid-1980s the NUJ had an agreement with nearly all the national newspapers that they would not hire journalists unless they had worked in the regional press either for three years if non-graduate, or two years, if a graduate (Cole 2006b: 79–81). Even the larger newspaper conglomerates which ran their own training schemes, for example the Mirror group and the Thomson Organisation (in those days owner of *The Times* and *The Sunday Times*), started trainees at their regional titles. The only exceptions were those recruited into the BBC's own trainee scheme or as high-flying specialists by the national broadsheets. Both mechanisms were, at that time, notoriously skewed towards young men from elite universities and lubricated by patronage. Neither commercial television (which started in 1955) nor commercial radio (first licensed in

1972) provided journalism training, instead employing journalists who were already qualified. For most would-be news journalists, therefore, a stint in the regions was unavoidable, even if their career goal was to work in national print or broadcast news.

Histories of journalism as an occupation (Carr-Saunders and Wilson 1933; Tunstall 1971, 1996; Christian 1980; Aldridge and Evetts 2003) all draw attention to its self-identification as a craft, rather than a profession. For many journalists this was a practical reality: they were apprentices, legally tied to their employer. 'In my very first job . . . my father had to come to the place and we signed these indentures and they put a seal on it . . . and he had to put his thumb on it and say "by this my deed and word"' (permanent freelance with city evening paper, personal communication). Such was the control over apprentices that Michael Buerk writes of his gratitude to his first employer who was willing to be flexible. 'I was still legally indentured to the [Bromsgrove] *Messenger* and weekly papers were famous for treating their reporter apprentices like galley slaves, chained to their task until their very last day' (Buerk 2004: 66). Wanting to move onward and upward, Buerk managed to get a job offer from a big city evening paper, the Thomson-owned *South Wales Echo*. He approached the *Messenger* editor who

> wanted to persuade me, rather than force me to stay [but] I was desperate and it showed . . . The following week he said that the group management had agreed to let me go. He must have argued long and hard on my behalf because they had turned down everybody else who had tried to move in the past . . . I never did thank him enough.
>
> (Buerk 2004: 67)

Not all participants in the system were as generous. A woman who had started her career on a small town weekly in 1975 secured a job on the *Oxford Mail* because she was about to get married and move home, but her owner/editor

> decided that, in his words, he'd 'paid a lot of money to train me and no-one else was going to get the benefit of it'. So I resigned but because I had then broken my indentures . . . I was blacklisted and not allowed to take up the job at the *Oxford Mail* even though the NUJ at that stage was very sympathetic, they said 'well rules are rules', you've broken your indentures, that's it, you can't work here.
>
> (section editor/sub-editor, small town weekly,
> personal communication)

Consonant with the concept of the craft worker, news journalism's occupational value system has always exhibited a strong vocational dimension: that no amount of intellectual agility or formal training can substitute for innate 'news sense' (Aldridge 1998; Cole 2006b). Most of the further skills and knowledge that are needed can be acquired through on-job learning, the rest by intensive practical instruction in essential tools of the trade such as shorthand and the legal issues likely to arise day to day in relation to, for example, reporting the criminal and civil courts.

Describing the 'direct entry' route into newspaper journalism, the NCTJ web site (www.nctj.com, accessed 17 June 2006) says: 'The entry requirement for reporters is a minimum of five GCSE passes or equivalent – one of these must be in English'. Before the expansion of journalism as a degree subject in the early 1990s, a development discussed in greater detail later on, almost all the courses recognized by the NCTJ were at sub-degree level, requiring only these basic school-leaving qualifications, but 'In recent years it has become rare for a trainee to come into the industry at this level. Currently more than 60 per cent of recruits are university graduates' (www.nctj.com, accessed 17 June 2006). Graduating *in journalism* whether at first degree or taught MA level is, however, still a minority pattern. Most recognized qualifying courses, whether for graduates or non-graduates, are at certificate or diploma level.

Everyday experience does not, therefore, conflict with a central trope in journalism's habitual self-mythologizing: the 'self-made person' (Aldridge 1998). So powerful is this archetype that many well-known names tend to minimize any privilege in their background, emphasizing rather that they have learned the hard way by starting in a menial post at an insignificant title – inevitably a local weekly. For a long time the supertypical case was Kelvin MacKenzie, editor of *The Sun* (London) in its most triumphant period (Chippindale and Horrie 1990). Presenting himself very much in the 1980s market-trader-meets-City-trader mould, MacKenzie actually went to a well-known independent school, which he left with an O-level in English Literature (not woodwork as he later claimed). Both his parents were very hard-working local journalists, successful enough to move to a 'large comfortable house in leafy Dulwich' (Chippendale and Horrie 1990: 94, 75). Presumably to offset this, once working in Fleet Street Kelvin 'hammed up his rasping south ("sarff") London accent' (Chippindale and Horrie 1990: 79). MacKenzie's first job was with the weekly *South-East London Mercury*. Elements of this pattern can also be seen in Piers (Pughe-)Morgan, protégé of MacKenzie and later editor of the *Daily Mirror* (1995–2004), direct rival to *The Sun*. His 'two-year stint on local London papers' (Morgan 2005: vii) followed a spell with the Lloyd's of London insurance market.

The nostalgic construction of journalist-as-outlaw is embellished by accounts of work in the local media as sometimes archaic and often chaotic, but always colourful and collegial. Kate Adie remembers Radio Bristol: 'Our workload was ludicrous, but we were all having a good deal of fun', and goes on to describe 14-hour days enlivened by drinking and non-standard uses of the Unattended Studio. 'I could compose scripts just seconds before the red light came on' (Adie 2003: 74–5). At the *Bromsgrove Messenger* the editor 'seemed to have come barrelling into the 1960s from another era' while 'the Bromsgrove it described, the social order it endorsed, and the attitudes it reflected were already rapidly fading into the past . . . The type-writers were all pre-war and no more than half were ever working' (Buerk 2004: 54–5). Things were different on the *South Wales Echo*: 'Few things are as exciting as being in a big breaking news story, and most of them are illegal . . . before mobile phones and computers, the main thing was to secure contact with the office to send the story back' writes Buerk (2004: 73–5), before describing the various methods employed to sabotage public telephones against their use by rival media.

Richard Stott started his career at the weekly *Bucks* [Buckinghamshire] *Herald* where the junior staff worked in a 'steamy, smoke-ridden little room' managed by a senior reporter who 'didn't drive – he went everywhere on his bike – and smoked roll-up Old Holborns'. He was 'A local newspaper-man to his fingertips, who could have made it to Fleet Street without any bother. But he loved Aylesbury and he knew it inside out . . . all the coun-cillors and the cops at his beck and call, the holder of 1000 borough secrets' (Stott 2002: 90–1). Eventually Stott moved to a London news agency having had 'the best possible grounding in the journalist's trade' from this man and his deputy 'neither of whom wanted to go anywhere else . . . They were the guardians of its future as well as custodians of its past' (Stott 2002: 103).

Nor is this classic amalgam of vocation and local rootedness restricted to the small town weekly paper. The *Manchester Evening News* is the third-biggest selling regional daily in the UK. When Paul Horrocks was appointed editor in 1997 his career had 'never taken him out of his Greater Manchester home ground'. This was the job he had wanted since he started with his father's news agency after he left school (Marks 1997c). So too Barrie Williams, who edited regional newspapers for nearly 30 years. From the age of 11 he had wanted to be a journalist, inspired by the tales of his next door neighbour's working life, but was apprenticed to *The Shrewsbury Chronicle* because the newspaper in his native Oswestry regarded him as looking too much like a Teddy Boy. Like many in regional media, Williams actively rejected moving to the national press: 'I decided I wanted to be a big fish in a small pond' (Slattery 2005).

Forty years later this sense of being part of a community, of having direct contact with readers and the potential to 'make a difference', is still a powerful source of satisfaction for at least some of those who stay in, rather than pass through local media. 'In the regionals you have to live

among the people that you're writing about. I think that leads to the opportunities to get more satisfaction out of the job . . . because when you do
things for the good . . . it's immensely satisfying, it's got to be one of the
biggest buzzes around' (senior journalist/manager, city evening paper – personal communication). Most of the [Hexham, Northumbria] *Courant*'s staff
live on the patch . . . we are not afraid to be controversial but it is vital that
we get our facts right and that the stories are properly balanced. Our rivals
to a major story do not have to live with the consequences, (Fuller 1999:
39). At a more personal level 'I like walking down the street and seeing
people talking about things I have written' (trainee reporter, small town
weekly, personal communication).

A career in national newspapers is sometimes rejected on overtly moral
grounds: 'I'm ashamed that these people are in the same industry as me . . .
I do firmly believe that the public have a right to know what affects them
and I'm driven by that . . . its my job to tell fairly and accurately what's happening and how things around them are likely to or will affect them'
(deputy news editor, small town evening paper, personal communication).
Editors too, share this sense that regional newspapers operate on a different
and preferable moral plane. As explained in Chapter 3, campaigning is
regarded as an essential editorial strategy, particularly among daily titles.
Commercial realism does not, however, prevent editors finding it intrinsi-
cally rewarding. 'The *Grimsby Telegraph* has an historic bond with its readers
. . . it gives real satisfaction and pleasure to effect real change . . . that makes
a difference to the lives of the people in the community we serve'.
According to the editor of the Sunderland *Sunday Sun* 'if no-one of sound
mind ever entered our business in search of wealth, a great many chose this
path so that they might help change the world. And change the world they
do' (Lagan 2005a). This distrust of national newspaper values and operating
methods was highlighted by the resentment expressed when Northcliffe
imposed 'former Fleet street executives' as editors of two West Country
titles (Morgan 2001). Barrie Williams, quoted earlier, edited newspapers in
Kent, Nottingham and Plymouth. All far from his Welsh borders home
town, yet he does not seem to have been treated as an outsider, precisely
because he came from within the same moral universe.

For local commercial radio, encouraging the 'imagined community'
through direct contact with the public is imperative, so claims of embed-
dedness in the community must be treated with a little caution. As Fleming
(2002: 79) reports, however, presenters can enjoy their work so much that
for six weeks in 1999 a Radio Trent joint breakfast presenter 'presented his
part of the show from his home via an ISDN line while he was recovering
from a leg operation'. Regional newspaper staff regularly refer to their
answerability to readers: 'People did get terribly upset if you got their names
even slightly wrong' (Buerk 2004: 58) but the greater quasi-intimacy of

radio presenters' relationship with the public can be commensurately more trying. 'The hardest part for me is when people walk up to me and say "You're crap" – it's just rude' (Fleming 2002: 79).

Given the much greater news and actuality content of BBC local radio output, staff could be expected to see themselves in a public role more akin to that of regional newspaper journalists. For one of the BBC Radio Nottingham presenters, also interviewed by Fleming, 'the best programmes are those that actually make a difference to the lives of those listening, as happened in November 2000 when his programme was extended . . . every night for a week to keep people up to date with flood news' (Fleming 2002: 83). Nevertheless, the affective dimension of the 'imagined community' is also prominent in the station's publicity, and to a greater extent than that of their commercial rival. Despite its intensely personalized broadcasting style (see Fleming 2002: ch. 4), 96 TrentFM (www.trentfm.musicradio.com) provides very little biographical detail about presenters. There is no information at all about Jo, of their highly publicized and very professionally successful breakfast-time 'Jo and Twiggy'. The exception is Twiggy, whose detailed biography positions him as Everyman, specifically not a journalist or career broadcaster.

In contrast, as at March 2006 Radio Nottingham (www.bbc.co.uk/nottingham) listed 20 presenters, 13 of whose biographical details emphasized some combination of local origins, being a local by adoption, or their long service at the station. For instance, John Holmes, 'first broadcast on BBC Radio Nottingham in 1970', having come to the city as a student and met his future wife in a well-known local pub. An invitation to email presenters is prominent on the web site. In John Holmes's case the appellation is even more direct: a series of photos and a blog showed the effect on his appearance of preventative treatment for skin cancer. Clearly the intention behind making a private problem into a public spectacle is serious and entirely appropriate to the BBC's public service role. The imagined personal relationships characteristic of local radio are being harnessed to an important health education message.

One might expect, given the problematic scale of the television regions, that this level of intended audience involvement would not be attempted. Not so: the web site for BBC1's *East Midlands Today* (www.bbc.co.uk/england/eastmidlandstoday/profiles, accessed 15 December 2005) includes life stories for both reporters and presenters. Among the presenters most (five of seven) also have a journalism background, but the tension between news and entertainment, so much a feature of regional news (see Cottle 1993; and Chapter 5) is vividly illustrated. Unlike those of the reporters, their biographies including a 'Top Ten List' of, for example, favourite/worst food, best song ever, best place in England. Local origins are less prominent than in the accounts provided by their BBC radio colleagues, perhaps because a greater proportion appear to have pursued a more formally structured and thus peripatetic pathway into regional broadcast news. In one notable respect, however, their self-presentation mirrors the genre: in the absence of common experience of the locality, present and past, the universals of family life are invoked. Six of the seven presenters and five of the six reporters mention either their family of origin, their own children or their domestic circumstances.

Central News East (www.itvregions.com/Central/About) provides very little information about their main presenters, reflecting ITV1's ambiguous relationship with the sub-region, already alluded to in Chapters 2 and 3. For *Central News West*, however, we are invited to 'Meet the Team', who provide detailed biographies.

Regional journalists: too middle class and too white?

The regional media of the 1960s and 1970s about which Adie, Buerk and Stott (and many others – journalists' autobiography is an extensive literature) reminisce was dominated by white men of uncertain mid-age. By the late 1990s, in many newspapers little had changed. At one big city evening daily title men continued to 'hold all the positions of authority' (sub-editor/page designer – personal communication). This had not come about by chance, even if it was not deliberate discrimination: 'basically . . . there is a tendency for them to promote other men' (feature writer at the same paper, personal communication). At that time the editor of another paper in the same group predicted that sexism in the bigger regional papers was going to be 'very hard to change . . . there's an awful lot of people . . . that have been here 25 to 35 years . . . there's a real bottleneck at middle-management level'.

In the event, a shift in the demographics of regional newspaper journalism has been much more rapid than this respondent expected, accelerated by the repeated rounds of 'rationalization' reported in Chapter 2 which have affected jobs at every level of seniority, including editor. At entry level many recruits are now women, who now form the majority in journalism training – not that this guarantees their inevitable progression into middle and senior management, as we shall see later on. While the gender profile of the workforce has become more representative of the readership and the wider public, that is not the case in relation to ethnic origin or social class. The managements of many city daily titles are increasingly troubled by their lack of success in recruiting journalists from the ethnic communities and by the falling number of entrants from 'ordinary' local backgrounds. The regional workforce is remaining, as is that of national newspapers, stubbornly white. It is also becoming increasingly middle class,

the outcome of two parallel processes: the graduate takeover and deteriorated pay and conditions. Journalism has both become an occupation
'which people "pay to enter"' (Journalism Training Forum 2002: 25) and
one in which paying off any debts incurred in so doing has become very
difficult.

In the 1990s the coincidence of a phase of employer indifference and
the funding regime in UK education produced near chaos in the institutional arrangements for professional journalism training. As in other industries, many media employers responded to the recession of the late
1980s/early 1990s by reducing their spending on training. They withdrew
both 'in-house' programmes and their support for trainee staff attending
college-based courses part time, the 'post-entry' route into journalism. In its
weakened state the NUJ could not block this trend.

Until 2006, UK residents studying for a first degree in the UK had most
or all of their fees paid and were eligible for low-interest loans to cover
living costs. (From 2006 a greater proportion of the real cost of the fee
became payable, but repayment of that and the loan was deferred.) Despite
the debts that most students accumulated, it was much easier to finance
undergraduate than non-graduate or postgraduate study. This financial
logic ensured demand for university courses in media studies, further
fuelled by the popularity of the media as a hoped-for career. On the supply
side there was a rapid and totally unplanned expansion in the number of
such courses, driven by the higher education funding regime. For all higher
education institutions, government payments based on UK student
numbers are their core funding; for those granted university status after
1992 this income stream is even more vital. In this quasi-market, courses
with large numbers of applicants have inevitably expanded at the expense
of those less heavily subscribed.

Only some of these new courses were recognized by the NCTJ and its
broadcast equivalent, the Broadcast Journalism Training Council (BJTC).
Many of the students graduating from them must, therefore, like those
coming from other subjects, undertake additional study to acquire a basic
professional qualification, the National Certificate Examination from the
NCTJ or an award from a BJTC-recognized provider. One option is to gain
the college-based part of the qualification 'pre-entry'. Some of these courses
are organized by further education (FE) colleges for both graduates and
non-graduates. Other courses are run by FE colleges and universities for
graduates only. Both routes impose high costs on students, as nearly all
must find their living expenses and pay their fees. In the case of postgraduate courses with a high reputation, the fees alone are several thousand
pounds a year. Now that most entrants have a first degree (Journalism
Training Forum 2002; www.nctj.com; Sutton Trust 2006) these costs are in
addition to the debts they will have incurred as an undergraduate.

On top of these direct payments come potentially large hidden costs. Most employers demand evidence of aptitude and commitment through having worked in journalism. Increasingly the only way to acquire such experience is through work 'placements', that is to say, working without pay. This kind of exploitation is less entrenched in news journalism than in magazines and independent television production companies (*Press Gazette* 21 November 2003; Sarler 2005; Silver 2005a; White 2006). Nevertheless, it is a free gift to employers only feasible for people without dependants and with alternative sources of income, whether in the form of savings or support from their family. Hardly surprisingly then, by the end of the 1990s 'New entrants . . .[were] being drawn overwhelmingly from families headed by individuals working in professional or other high level, middle class occupations' (Journalism Training Forum 2002: 8). Worse, it further entrenches patronage in an industry long notorious for recruiting on the basis of personal contact rather than open competition (see, for instance, examples in Sutton Trust 2006).

Like Delano and Henningham (1995) before them, the authors of the Journalism Training Forum report *Journalists at Work* remark on the difficulty of assembling labour force data. Neither in print nor broadcast are news-gatherers and news-processors distinguished from the many other occupational groups in the media industry (Journalism Training Forum 2002: ch. 2). Membership of the NUJ, once almost universal, can no longer be used as the basis for drawing a sample. Nor do media employers readily cooperate, seeming to set their threshold of what is 'commercially sensitive' information very low and being, ironically, very resistant to social research – that is, responding to questions (Sutton Trust 2006). Attempts to capture the demography of journalism are thus sporadic, which is particularly problematic in an industry with high 'churn'. One consequence of this is that assertions about the labour force are essentially a mix of anecdote and prejudice, and are probably out of date, but they quickly acquire a patina of facticity through repetition because of the intensely reflexive nature of journalism.

Despite problems with sampling and the low overall rate of return of the questionnaires (Journalism Training Forum 2002: 11–12), *Journalists at Work* provides useful evidence to set alongside the anecdotes. It carefully pulls apart the idea that journalism is becoming a middle-class occupation because of the higher educational attainment of recruits from the question of those recruits' social background. The conclusion is 'quite clear: new entrants to the journalism profession are much more likely to have a parent from one of the highest occupational orders than would be the case given the distribution of all employment in the economy' (Journalism Training Forum 2002: 25). Elsewhere in the report it is suggested that the age profile of the different media sectors 'accords with the image of regional newspapers and radio being "entry-points" for the industry' (Journalism Training Forum 2002: 22).

So regional journalism is indeed becoming more 'middle class', but why should this matter to regional media, and particularly to newspapers? As is often the case in trade talk, nostalgia and sentimentality, moral principle and market imperatives are fused together. According to a respected former editor, credentialism has 'cut out the council house kids' but their lost opportunity to build success on a combination of natural talent and hard work is also a commercial problem. 'A lot of regional papers have lost touch with their readers. You have middle-class journalists writing for people who aren't on the same wavelength. They have lost the common touch' (Slattery 2005). For regional newspapers this 'common touch' is not a carefully constructed populist rhetorical style like *Sun*speak, but a grasp of local history, geography and culture. Where was the old Player's factory? Which is Crown (traffic) Island? Accuracy and authenticity are at a premium because, as we have seen, regional media make implicit – and sometimes explicit – moral claims to represent their readers which are easily undermined by trivialities like misspelling a favourite local seaside resort. Or more dramatic errors like a Nottingham *Evening Post* front page splash including a word which readers in Newark, a traditional centre of Gypsy culture, would have known was obscene (*Press Gazette* 7 July 2006). Here social class and geographic mobility are being confused, but the central empirical fact remains. Once most aspiring journalists are graduates, even if from a working-class background, the likelihood of their undertaking professional training in their home area, as the cheerfully middle-class Michael Buerk and covertly middle-class Kelvin MacKenzie did (Chippindale and Horrie 1990; Buerk 2004), is considerably reduced.

But again, why should this matter? Surely the young and energetic reporter can quickly get to know an area and develop the contacts they need? Or used to need: if insiders like 'Pecke' (2004) are to be believed, this kind of 'leg-work' away from the office is now exceptional rather than the core activity. What is being expressed is the essentialism which forms a central part of journalism's occupational ideology: like must speak to like to achieve the commercially vital audience identification. Sliding sales in all newspaper sectors have led to the appointment of women – even women editors in the case of the national press – in the belief that this will ensure success with this hitherto neglected sector of the audience. Within regional newspapers the same kind of reasoning, coupled with the financial necessity of appealing to as high a proportion of the local population as possible, underpins the belief that a significant section of the workforce should not just be local but from an 'ordinary' background.

Journalists at Work reported that 4 per cent of their respondents classified themselves as other than 'white' as against 6 per cent of the general population, but that to be truly representative the proportion should be higher because

> journalists are predominantly employed in London and the South East and in other urban areas . . . London's black and ethnic minority population is currently estimated as being 24 per cent . . . and most journalists are young, again it would be expected to find a higher proportion of ethnic minorities in younger age groups.
>
> (Journalism Training Forum 2002: 21)

Moreover, the survey included broadcast journalism, a sector in which formal policies on equal opportunities exist, as explained below. When data from the 2001 Census (www.statistics.gov.uk/cc1) were published they showed that the non-white population of the UK was actually 7.9 per cent, indicating an even poorer level of ethnic diversity among journalists. For regional newspapers, it later emerged that the situation was worse still. In the absence of official statistics or systematic monitoring by employers, the Society of Editors undertook a case-study approach, selecting titles 'in areas of significant ethnic minority population' (Society of Editors 2004: 8). The closest 'fit' with the composition of the audience was at the Stoke *Sentinel* with five (5.4 per cent) staff from ethnic minorities in an area where they comprised 7 per cent of the population. In Leicester, with 38 per cent ethnic minority population, there were four (3.3 per cent) non-white staff (Society of Editors 2004; Cole 2006a: 66).

Rather than relying on morality, or even the importance of social cohesion, those trying to organize a constructive response to this issue of social justice rely on business-based arguments. As well as the collective belief about 'address' and the practical matter of having the contacts to develop and stand up stories, why should people buy a paper that 'had nothing to say to them' (Society of Editors 2004: 7) or fails to employ people from their community? According to one campaigner, in commercial terms this is 'the new reality of Britain'; 'Why has the newspaper industry lagged behind the broadcasters?' he asks. The question is slightly disingenuous because, while he is no doubt personally 'passionate about the minority ethnic employment issue' (Media Trust/Society of Editors 2005: 29) as the then managing director of ITV News, the speaker would know that for broadcasters morality is underpinned by statute. The Communications Act 2003 (s. 27, para 2(a)) requires Ofcom to 'promote equality of opportunity in relation to 'employment by those providing radio and television services'. The section goes on to specify that this means 'between men and women', 'different racial groups' and disability. Ofcom is simply carrying forward the responsibilities of its predecessors, the Independent Television Authority and the Radio Authority under Sections 38 and 108 respectively of the 1990

Communications Act. One practical outcome of this has been the production of a 'toolkit for broadcasters' (Ofcom 2005e). The BBC has its own targets and policies: see below and www.bbc.co.uk > Plans Policies and Reports > Diversity.

This fundamental difference in institutional arrangements is rarely referred to in trade talk. Typically of media occupational ideology, cause is attributed to outstanding individuals (see, for example, Society of Editors 2004: 37). Presumably all players are reluctant to acknowledge what the contrast with newspapers demonstrates: that external regulation has at least some effect and, by implication, is necessary and should be extended to other media sectors. Its absence has perpetuated the reluctance to recognize, let alone confront, exclusionary mechanisms. One of the most entrenched (for women too) has been arbitrary hiring and firing practices: 'Jobs continue to be sealed in pubs and bars on the back of a recommendation from a friend of a distant friend' (Francis 2003: 68). 'We receive many applications from young journalists working on local newspapers . . . The interview process is relatively informal' (Sutton Trust 2006: 10). Not just informal, probably illegal. At the very least, formal equal opportunities policies would put those who operate this way on the defensive.

Upstream of employment is training, for which recruiting from ethnic communities is such a well-established problem that a number of black-only courses were set up in the 1980s. Ainley (1998: 50–4) reports, however, that the majority of her black respondents were not enthusiastic. They saw them as only a short-term solution, despite the outright discrimination that many had faced when trying to obtain a training place. Since Ainley carried out her research, all sectors of education have become more considered in their selection practices, but as rapidly as that blockage has diminished, the whole 'pay to enter' cluster has taken its place. That this is a particular burden for students from ethnic minorities has been recognized by the launch of a Diversity Fund by the NCTJ (NCTJ 2005) to complement the NUJ's George Viner Fund (www.nuj.org.uk) and small-scale schemes offered by, for example, Trinity Mirror and the Scott Trust, owners of the *Manchester Evening News* (Society of Editors 2004: 14, 25).

The *Manchester Evening News* was also one of the papers working to offset another dimension of 'pay to enter': it has offered *paid* work experience. But despite its 'deliberate policy to increase the number of ethnic minority staff', like his colleagues at the *Birmingham Mail* and *Yorkshire Evening Post*, the editor had had few applications (Society of Editors 2004: 13, 20, 27). Why? Part of the explanation must be the 'graduate takeover' with its double hurdles of first qualifying for university and then taking on a burden of debt. On this, statistics from the Higher Education Statistics Agency (HESA) (www.hesa.ac.uk./holisdocs/pubinfo/ student/ethnic0405) provide a seemingly contradictory picture. In 2004–05 among first degree students 'of known ethnicity' the total for all ethnic minorities was 18 per cent. Asians and Asian-British of Indian, Pakistani or Bangladeshi background constituted 7.5 per cent, but 'Black or Black British Caribbean' accounted for only 1.4 per cent. This by itself probably explains the lack of regional journalists of Caribbean origin, but why do south Asian young people not come forward in numbers proportional to their presence in higher education? Many editors believe that two aspects of family and community opinion are the reason. First, that journalism is not a respectable profession, particularly for young women, because of its self-conscious posture of social marginality, and 'beer and pork pies' culture (editor, *Birmingham Mail*, personal communication; Society of Editors 2004: 15, 20, 27). Not only that but, as we shall see, junior jobs in regional journalism are poorly paid and less secure than they once were.

For many people in the south Asian communities, however, it is not just a matter of disdain but of outright rejection. Like many members of the public, they make no distinction between regional newspapers and the national press 'who they describe as Islamophobic. They are anti-media, particularly the *Daily Express*, which they see as hostile with all its asylum coverage' (Society of Editors 2004: 17). Quite, to the extent that some of its own journalists tried, without success, to report their own paper to the Press Complaints Commission (Donovan 2004; see also Francis 2003; Greenslade 2005b).

Ironically, newspaper journalism's problems with social status and respectability have been the driver of what some regard as an undesirable development in broadcast journalism: the influx of women into the workforce. One element of this, which passed with little comment at the time, was the opportunity offered by the relatively informal methods of recruitment into early commercial radio, then and now predominantly a locally based medium. Neither the 'boys' club' networking of the print media, nor the elaborate and elitist bureaucracy of the BBC operated – although the BBC also has a long history of taking people into local radio after they have spent time 'helping out'. While admirably egalitarian in that it focuses on competence, this raises all the familiar questions about patronage and access to alternative means of support. As Ofcom observes, 'The "who you know" method of filling jobs is very common in broadcasting' because it is thought to be cheap, quick and low-risk (Ofom 2005e: 10). And, as the Journalism Training Forum (2002: 8) points out, radio is a regular route into television.

At one stage in 2000 it seemed that the entire intake of (London) City University's high-prestige broadcast training course might be female, an extreme manifestation of the trend in applications nationwide (Richardson 2000). Several interconnecting explanations were applied to this startling situation. One was the literal visibility of female role models on national television, even if their presence was partly decorative and based as much on the pull of competition between channels as the push of equal opportunities policies. Another was what Professor Brian Winston described as the 'Samantha syndrome': the high costs of entry to a supposedly respectable and glamorous form of employment skewing applications towards those from relatively affluent backgrounds. Commenting on this, a former BBC senior editor argued that the rate at which, even then, both ITN and the BBC News Directorate were recruiting women was raising a new diversity problem: 'Broadcast news should fairly reflect the society in which it operates. It was wrong when it was dominated by men; it would be just as wrong if it ended up being dominated by women' (Richardson 2000).

It appears, however, that other forms of diversity have come to preoccupy broadcasters. The Cultural Diversity Network, a consortium of British television broadcasters, was founded in 2000 and is quoted extensively in the Society of Editors' advice to the regional press (Society of Editors 2004; Media Trust/Society of Editors 2005). Its web site (www.cdnetwork.org.uk) speaks of 'new or neglected minority groups' but appears to focus primarily on the portrayal and employment of ethnic minorities. Ofcom's 'toolkit' takes its remit from the Communications Act 2003 but, no doubt reflecting the new labour force realities and developments in legislation, much of its practical advice is also directed towards matters of ethnicity and disability. For example under the heading 'Where and how to look' for employees (Ofcom 2005e: 7) there are ten bullet points: four relate to disability, one to ethnicity, while the rest are unspecific but refer to 'under-represented groups'.

In terms of formal equal opportunities policies, the BBC is regarded as an 'exemplary employer' (Browne 2004). Born writes that in the early 1990s the corporation had a dedicated department that was 'proactive, well funded and independent . . . under a dynamic leader' and was notably successful in setting and meeting targets on the employment and advancement of women. As financial pressures intensified, however, 'The corporate focus became narrowly legalistic . . . as opposed to the former concern with positively furthering equality' (Born 2004: 201–2). And in what Born describes as 'a very nervy organization' attacks on so-called 'political correctness' by right-wing commentators increased defensiveness about equality policies. The result, according to an informant, was that 'the clubbishness that was such a problem at the BBC is now [in the early 2000s] reasserting itself with a vengeance. The BBC tradition of the old boy network has become the culture of the whizz-kid, equally elitist and exclusionary' (Born 2004: 207).

In its statement on equal opportunities the BBC (www.bbc.co.uk/info/policies/diversity) takes a broad definition, including age, class and sexual orientation but, as at August 2006, seemed to be most active in the area of disability.

Despite high profile legislation in the form of the Disability Discrimination Act 1995, the issue of disability has not yet attracted any attention in the regional press, either in terms of portrayal or employment policies.

Middle class origin; proletarian experience

In terms of corporate rhetoric, if not of daily experience, the gender 'problem' is treated as solved. In Ofcom's 'toolkit', the most substantial consideration of gender appears in exhortations about flexible, family-friendly working (Ofcom 2005e: 13). The reality is that most media sectors are not family-friendly and are becoming less so. 'Flexibility' is usually an employer demand, not the offer of more congenial working conditions. In an industry characterized by what Tunstall (1996) called 'supercompetition', the hours of work, security of employment, and levels of pay have deteriorated at the same time that the work has intensified. Nor has there been effective collective resistance to these developments.

Journalists in regional newspapers were once highly unionized. In the mid-1980s many employers took advantage of changes in employment legislation to abandon their 'house agreements' (Gall 2002). They no longer negotiated pay and conditions with the NUJ as the collective representative of its members – and in effect the small number of non-members as well – based on national agreements. Instead, employees were dealt with individually which, in many cases, meant being offered contractual terms specific to them. Belonging to a union was still legal, but inevitably fewer employees saw the point of it (until they were in real trouble and needed expert advice and support) or were afraid of being seen as a union member. In some workplaces the NUJ managed to retain a presence by acting as an 'illegitimate agent representing members through individual services (advice, legal representation, training)' (Gall 2004: 34), a risky strategy for those working for the most aggressively anti-union employers.

Since 1997 employment legislation has required union recognition where sufficient of the eligible workforce demand it. By 2004 in the regional press '44 agreements, covering some 3000 journalists [had] been regained' (Gall 2004: 35) but the union faces a much-changed industrial landscape: a new generation with no memory of union organization; technologies and working practices that allow managements the possibility of producing some kind of paper themselves if a strike is threatened; and the very real threat of redundancies as corporate owners 'rationalize'. 'The moment [Northcliffe] realise we are recruiting or we get near to claiming recognition, editors hold one-to-one meetings with all editorial staff. They make it clear that there is no point in joining the union and that it could lead to disinvestment' (Chamberlain and Cookson 2006).

Journalists in regional television and radio are also represented by the NUJ. While relations with the BBC and the Channel 3 licence-holders are frequently tense, de-recognition of either it or the Broadcasting, Entertainment, Cinematograph and Theatre Union (BECTU), which represents those involved in production, has not arisen.

In regional newspapers low pay has emerged as an issue not only for the employees themselves but for local managements, concerned about retention in the short term and the calibre of recruits in the longer term. Once retired they can be more frank: 'You felt terrible for the people who wanted to stay and were loyal to you because that loyalty was repaid by keeping them on very, very low money' recalled a former editor of three major regional papers in *Press Gazette* (6 February 2004). Reversing the trend will be difficult. The relative deterioration of salary levels has been a gradual process coinciding with union derecognition and the growing domination of a small number of large corporations. Originally they were attracted by the pre-Internet monopoly of local advertising and the potential for rationalizing assets, including of course by cutting staff costs in a highly labour-intensive industry. Now they face a shareholder and financial market expectation of very high rates of profit, (see Chapter 2).

In late 2005 the starting salary for trainees in regional newspapers could be as low as £10,000–£12,000; the minimum for senior reporters (that is, those who have done three years and passed the National Certificate Examination) was £17,000 (Silver 2005b); and 'half of journalists in the UK earn[ed] less than the national average wage of £27,000' *Press Gazette* 9 September 2005). A broadside from the Campaign for Press and Broadcasting Freedom (Barter 2005) alleged that graduate trainees with Johnston Press – the most rapidly expanding group – 'routinely start on less than £13,000' and that some employed by Newsquest were claiming Family Tax Credit, a state benefit for the low paid. Hardly surprising that some have second jobs or that, as a senior reporter at a Trinity Mirror newspaper put it: 'The only reason that I stick it out is because I love it so much. I know I would be better off as a teacher, but would I be as interested in my work?' (*Press Gazette* 22 February 2004). The NUJ believes that, as at mid-2006, achievable minimum salary levels should be £16,000 for a trainee and £30,000 for a senior qualified journalist (David Ayrton, personal communication).

Many do, indeed, give up and move on just as they have developed the all-important local knowledge. One of the dimensions of Winston's 'Samantha Syndrome' was access to continuing financial assistance, even when employed, because of entry-level pay rates. Regional newspaper journalism is remaining white and becoming middle class not just because of the graduate takeover, but because 'Once accepted into the bosom of a local rag . . . you are often expected to run a car. All on a salary of £12,000–£14,000. Soon it won't be possible for local boys to work at their local paper. Unless you have rich parents, or like me you get left something in a family member's will you're knackered', according to a young reporter (Silver 2005b). In London and the South East of England the higher cost of living means that for graduate trainees 'Their wages just about pay their rent and service their debt . . . they can't afford bus and tube fares' according to the group news editor and father-of-the-chapel (union branch) at a south London series of weekly titles (Silver 2005b; see also Sutton Trust 2006).

In regional newspapers the pay may be poor but most of the workforce is still employed on permanent rather than time-limited contracts, unlike independent television production where short contracts and systematic reliance on freelance, unpaid or below-subsidence paid 'work experience' have become the norm – to the extent that the sector is now a byword for ruthless exploitation (Silver 2005a; see also Paterson 2001; Ursell 2003). Born's ethnographic study of the BBC describes the shift towards the use of freelance workers in television: peaking at 54 per cent in 1994, but falling back to around 45 per cent by the early 2000s. At the BBC a deliberate cutback in freelance working reduced it to around 35 per cent by 2001 (Born 2004: 181); it is not clear whether radio was included in this figure. Employment in television *news*, however, has not been transformed to the same extent: Ursell (2003: 37) quotes a Skillset total of only 17 per cent being freelancers across the UK in 2001. Her explanation for this 'protection' is the 'the idiosyncratic knowledge of journalists and residual public service broadcasting requirements'. In fact BBC news staffing was growing, to accommodate the then new BBC News 24 (Born 2004: 181). As we saw in Chapter 4, the BBC is continuing to expand its local news services on the web, both in text and the experimental 'ultra-local' television services. Presumably this will generate jobs, even if those in post find their work further intensified.

Meanwhile, regional programming on Channel 3 is being reduced to the minimum allowed by Ofcom and the rationalization of ITV plc's regional news organization (see Chapter 4) has continued. With sharing stories or even complete bulletins between regions under discussion, employees face not only intensification and indifferent pay but job insecurity (Azeez 2004; Tomlin 2004a; P. McLaughlin 2006; Upshon 2006).

At most commercial radio stations, in-house news production is vestigial, to the extent that Ofcom has, as we saw in Chapter 4, felt compelled to be uncharacteristically interventive (Ofcom 2005d).

Regional press journalism may not have been casualized, but it has certainly become much less secure. After the rationalizations designed to achieve economies of scale, described in Chapter 2, during the mid-2000s the major owning groups entered a new round of cost-cutting, partly in order to compete with each other over their already remarkable profit levels, and partly as a defensive move against the perceived threat from Internet-based advertising. An 'estimate that more than 1000 jobs [had] been lost in the last six months' led to a meeting between a junior minister in the Department of Trade and Industry and the NUJ parliamentary group of MPs (*Press Gazette* 10 March 2006).

There is, of course, a distinction between making workers compulsorily redundant, offering workers voluntary redundancy and making posts redundant. Few of the job losses were the 'clear your desk in ten minutes' exit inflicted on the deputy editor of the Bristol *Evening Post* (*Press Gazette* 8 July 2005), but even if achieved through agreement, a shrinkage of editorial staff of 22 per cent, as announced by the *Manchester Evening News* in February 2006 (*Press Gazette* 17 March 2006), can have only one outcome: yet more intensified working for those that remain.

'Multi-skilling' is a persuasively attractive term, suggesting that individuals will develop more competencies and, naturally, will be more fulfilled. In some respects new technology has indeed been liberating, as Ursell writes (2003: 38). Mobile phones and laptop computers allow copy to be filed easily and promptly without the romantic but essentially time-wasting scramble for public telephones, described by Buerk (2004) above. In television the process was even more clunking: reports from outside the studio required a full film crew, then the film had to be physically transported back for processing and editing. Today's 'video-journalist' can undertake the whole process him or herself from originating the story to sending the package back for broadcast. Any satisfactions gained from this increased creative autonomy are, however, likely to be offset by increased throughput of work. Journalists are now expected to produce not only more stories per day, but more versions of them for the multiplying news outlets. At the BBC this includes working 'bi-medially', that is, for both television and radio (Ursell 2003: 39–42). Inevitably, less time is available for originating stories, leading to a further increased reliance on source-led and on-diary stories.

In radio, too, carrying out tasks that used to be done by specialists does not always increase job satisfaction. 'Desktopping' is 'where broadcast news items are sourced, edited, scripted and sent to air by one person using a networked desktop computer' and while it has broken up the old gender-based monopolies of skill, it is also 'a form of disempowerment for both men and women since the journalist is forced to become a . . . Jill of all trades and mistress of none, so her work may appear mediocre' (Haworth 2000: 261, 253).

For regional newspaper journalists, electronic technologies for entering copy and then editing it to fit the pages are now relatively long established.

(See Gall 2002 for a full account.) Early predictions that reporters would not only collect and file content but take over the sub-editing function of adjusting the length, the language and expression, and adding the headline have not come about. Instead the sub-editor's role has tended to expand to the designing of whole pages. It is an article of faith in newspapers that 'more pages is good', based on the assumption that greater volume is more attractive to readers, and is an implied message of success to advertisers. On top of this, many regional titles, notably the *Birmingham Mail* (see Chapter 3 case study) have tried to establish their relevance to an increasingly diverse audience by producing more distinct area-based editions. Thus for both news-gatherers and news-processors the throughput of work has increased as a diminished workforce attempts to sustain or even increase the volume of content. 'Whereas before you could always go out and interview people in person, now you do it on the telephone ... The pressures are much greater to turn the stuff over, churn it out, rather than really refine it, re-hone it, spend time on it' (experienced reporter, regional morning daily, personal communication).

Producing output for any news medium has never been a job with conventional – or, for many, predictable – hours. Broadcast news has long been the most demanding. Its crucial 'selling proposition' is its capacity to react quickly to breaking news. Even before the emergence of 24-hour 'rolling news' channels like BBC News 24 and Sky News, all terrestrial television channels were producing several bulletins on a daily cycle starting at breakfast and finishing late in the evening. What is often argued to be the most influential of all broadcast news programmes starts at 6.00 a.m. – *Today* on BBC Radio 4. In this situation, both the journalists on duty and studio-based staff are tied to unsocial hours. For regional broadcasters the 'newsday' is shorter, and the likelihood of dealing with vital late-breaking news considerably less. Nevertheless, broadcast reporters cannot reliably predict the end of their working day. Television coverage, in particular, requires travel to locations – and both the BBC and Channel 3 regions cover several counties.

This kind of unpredictability is clearly not 'family-friendly' in terms of sustaining it alongside having primary responsibility for the care of dependants. The only solution is open-ended alternative arrangements, which essentially means a partner with entirely flexible commitments, or buying live-in care. In 1990 the now defunct trade publication *Journalists' Week* calculated that this kind of provision required a minimum salary of £25,000; the equivalent figure at 2005 is £38,067 (Officer 2001). Salaries in that range are earned by middle and senior management, not frontline staff. Hardly surprising, then, that being a regional journalist is today constructed as a 'young person's job': they are assumed to have more energy and ambition, but also are less likely to have family commitments – if, of course, they could afford to contemplate acquiring them.

Unsocial and unpredictable hours have always been a feature of regional newspapers, whether on a six-day or weekly production cycle. Even journalists on a weekday title can face Sunday working: 'we work on average one in every two' writes a reporter on *The Birmingham Post* in a diary of six consecutive working days (*Press Gazette* 6 June 2005). In passing he jokes that 8.00 am is 'the middle of the night', a reminder that morning titles require working into the evening. 'Your ordinary day shift is 10.00 am until 6.00 pm which makes it very difficult to do extra-curricular activities' (trainee reporter, regional morning daily, personal communication), but shifts of 12.00 p.m. until 8.00 p.m., and 6.00 p.m. until 1.00 a.m. were also a possibility, with only a week's notice. Production staff must work evening-to-night, offsetting one of the key advantages of sub-editing over reporting – its predictable hours. According to a reporter at the same paper, 'I love subbing, if the hours weren't so awful I'd really want to sub . . . but they come in about 5.00 p.m. and they're here until 1.00 a.m. or more'.

The production cycle of daily evening (these days often effectively afternoon) newspapers creates a different pattern of unsocial hours. Again being a sub-editor is potentially more compatible with managing home and family responsibilities: 'I go in today at 11.00 am and know by 9.00 pm tonight, unless the third world war breaks out I should be back [home]'. Nevertheless, shift rotas were announced at such short notice that, for example, arranging to meet friends becomes either logistically difficult or potentially exhausting. 'I've got some friends coming for supper . . . so I put in "not late shift". . . so I get 6.45 in the morning which means getting up at 5.45 am, so it's going to be a hellishly long day' (experienced sub-editor, big city evening paper, personal communication).

At a daily evening title this kind of early start applies to everyone involved in the collecting and editing of news, as opposed to less time-sensitive content such as features and comment. The pivot is the news editor, a senior and very demanding post which often leads to the editor's chair because it combines production skills with news-gathering expertise. Few women have held this position in a big city regional daily. One who has remembered how 'I had to be in the office for 6.15 every morning and if I was ever so, ever so lucky I was away just after 7.00 pm . . . and then once I got home the phone would start ringing and you'd get the security men at [location of paper] ringing you at 3.00 am . . . I don't know how I did it.' Nevertheless she did, with extensive family support, and then went to be deputy editor of a weekly title where she was 'sort of being groomed for an editorship' first of a weekly, but then 'hopefully moving on to a [daily] evening'. At that stage, however, she decided that the home–work conflict was so great that she moved sideways into a middle-management role in an evening title nearer her home. Her experience goes a long way to answering Reeves's (2000) question: 'Why aren't more women editing regional dailies?' At that time seven were, less than 10 per cent of the total. By mid-2006 the situation had not improved. Only one (5 per cent) of the editors of the 19 paid-for regional morning titles listed on the Newspaper Society's database (www.newspapersoc.org.uk > Newspaper Search) was a woman. For the 77 newspapers classified as evening dailies the number was still seven, or 9 per cent – and falling, if the newly appointed male editor of *thelondonpaper* was added in.

Nor is work on one of the small number of regional Sunday papers necessarily any more family-compatible. 'Any Sunday hack will tell you that working a very long Saturday leaves you fairly shattered the following day – and that's the end of the weekend for you – and your family' (Hastings 2004b).

Paid-for weekly newspapers are lower down the newspaper prestige hierarchy, as the career history above illustrates, but this does not make working conditions any more leisurely – rather the reverse. A district reporter on a big city evening daily recalled: 'once a week we would have to get a paper out and we would have to fill X amount of space and if it wasn't done you just had to sit there until it was done . . . I have worked from nine in the morning to ten or eleven at night'. Small town weeklies market themselves by the sheer volume of local news, but the number of reporting staff collecting and entering the copy can be tiny. Sometimes they are under still more time pressure because this kind of title is now more likely to send a reporter to a local political or other meeting than a city daily. 'There's two reporters here, just two people, and it's a 48-page newspaper, which obviously aren't all news pages, but there's still a lot of space' (trainee reporter, small town weekly, personal communication). As a result, she said, 'it cuts down severely the amount of time [we] can be out getting really good news stories' particularly given that, with a press day of Wednesday for Thursday publication, real 'news' is effectively events that happen on Monday and Tuesday. The weekend is slow for news, and events occurring at the end of the previous week have become too stale. Still in her early 20s, this new entrant to the profession said that between her job and her home life she did not 'get much time for a social life as such'.

Being an editor of a small town weekly may not be glamorous or high status in the trade, but it brings its own problems. To lack of time and staff is often added the pressure of proximity to the readers. A high street shop front is much more accessible than the modern building on the periphery of town now increasingly common among the dailies:

There are the ladies from the WI on the cake stall photograph making sure you've spelled their names right . . . you're supposed to be making money . . . you're supposed to be keeping your staff happy bunnies. All of which can keep you awake and often does.

The hours are crushing, they really are . . . [Yet] there's a heck of a buzz putting the paper on the streets and there's even a buzz, masochistically, in waiting for the reaction . . . I think the day it stops being good fun is the day you quit.

(Editor, small town weekly, personal communication)

But they do not, and like their colleagues in big city titles, in radio and in regional television, they keep coming back for more.

8 What is the future for local media?

Local media: needed by democracy; wanted by the audience

Local media may lack glamour, but their importance is beyond doubt. The community of residence is, as Friedland so vividly expresses it in Habermasian terms, the 'seam' between the system and the lifeworld (2001: 374). Here institutional structures and processes become daily reality. For most people, most of the time, everyday needs are met and regular routines played out within familiar territory. In normal times only the unusually political active engage with, or protest against the mechanics of democracy at a national or international level. Most people do not belong to a political party or campaigning groups. Those that do on a long-term basis are likely to be working at a local level and from a local perspective, whether in their workplace trade union branch, or the local Women's Institute. And those who become involved because of a short-term issue are even more likely to be focused on the specifically local, for example organizing against the expansion plans of a big-name supermarket. Such protests are often dismissed as 'nimbyism', Not In My Backyard – back garden in UK English – and as local as it is possible to be. The locality, in short, is where democracy is enacted.

Ordinary citizens may not muse abstractly about the lifeworld but they demonstrate that news of the locality is valued both in their attitudes and by their behaviour. Sometimes, as we saw in Chapter 1, this is for very practical reasons. 'You want to know a local school will be good for your child' (white, over-35, upper-income group woman from Manchester) (Hargreaves and Thomas 2002: 65), or your work is locality-specific like those who buy the *News Letter*, Belfast, only on Saturdays for its farming supplement (Crummy 2006). Sometimes, as the Future Foundation (2000, 2003) and Sancho (2002) found, the attachment is much more diffuse and emotional. This appetite for relevant local news is often frustrated: 'Local news on TV is really boring – the people are really old' in the view of a young lower income group Asian man from Leicester (Hargreaves and Thomas 2002: 66). Nevertheless, in an environment of falling newspaper sales and multiplying channels and platforms for broadcast news, those that speak to particular nations, regions and localities continue to be relatively popular: a third of UK adults who read a regional paper do not read a national daily paper (www.newspapersoc.org.uk > Readership).

Even more startling for those preoccupied with the promise of an effective electronic global public sphere, the Newspaper Society also reports that 'over 14 million adults read a newspaper but do not use the internet'. Well yes, they would say that, but it is an important reminder of how easily scholarly concerns can part company from daily life, even of the scholars themselves, who may or may not want the new tram line to pass close to their house. If an inclusive democracy is to function it must have meaning; for it to have meaning we need *local* public spheres, however imperfect in terms of their accessibility, weddedness to the institutional order, and distortion by commercial rather than citizen considerations. At least for the time being, this means that the traditional media forms, daily and weekly newspapers, local radio and the main terrestrial television channels need to provide news that informs as well as engages and entertains, in breadth and in depth. What are the prospects?

This time a real crisis for local media?

Media histories, particularly of the press, contain a recurrent 'how wrong they were!' theme. Regional and local newspapers have triumphantly survived first terrestrial and then cable television; after a stuttering start both BBC and commercial local radio continue; and the regional news bulletins are among the most popular on the main terrestrial television channels. Now, however, the advertising-driven financial logic of commercial media is under threat. This time the problem is not just the normal fluctuations of the national and international economic cycle affecting employment and consumer spending; there are real changes in the ecology of the media landscape.

Regional newspapers are among the most profitable of *all* industrial sectors. As we saw in Chapter 2, this has been achieved in two ways. First, ever-larger owning groups have formed, attracted by the lucrative 'monopoly of local information', of which the Newspaper Society used to boast – in other words, the classified advertising, which still forms 80 per cent of regional newspaper revenue (Mintel 2005: exec. sum.). Conglomeration has enabled economies of scope and scale, and thus reduced costs. High rates of return naturally make the shares attractive, but also create an expectation that this exceptional situation will continue. Once surplus assets have been realized, for how long can the process of rationalizing first 'back office' and then editorial functions be continued before there is an obvious adverse impact on a product that is labour intensive (to say nothing of exploitative rates of pay: see Chapter 7)? Such 'efficiencies' may even work against one of the strategies being pursued by some very experienced editors when trying to arrest falling sales, particularly among the daily titles: increasing the volume of news and making it more neighbourhood-specific. (See Chapter 3 for a discussion of this in action in Birmingham.)

Influential regional editors have argued for a decade that their paper's unique selling proposition must be local exclusives and in-depth background, because broadcast media will always beat them to the breaking story. In 2006 the logic of this drove several titles, such as the *Coventry* (Evening) *Telegraph* to become morning papers, published and distributed overnight, thus inviting home delivery or casual purchase on the way *to* work, school or shopping. Putting the paper in direct competition with the London-based national press is a risky strategy, however, as the problems of most of the remaining English regional morning dailies demonstrate. Are people really buying regional dailies (as opposed to weeklies) principally for their rich local news content, or are the classified advertisements the attraction? If the latter, the panicky talk may be justified. Some of the most profitable categories of classified advertisements – those read by younger people with money to spend – such as employment, houses for sale, and motor vehicles are migrating to the Internet. As we have seen, the largest owning groups are responding by purchasing web sites but, down the line, would they happily use these to cross-subsidize their newspaper holdings? Similarly, would those groups, for example Archant, who have responded to falling sales among weekly papers by becoming 'frees' (*Press Gazette* 21 October 2005; and see Chapter 2 for a fuller explanation of the rationale) be willing to sustain their spending on editorial content?

In commercial television, a vortex is created when under-investment in appealing content and the consequent erosion of share audience results in a loss of current advertising revenue, dire predictions about future revenues and, inexorably, a collapse in shareholder confidence. Thus ITV plc started down the metaphoric corporate plughole in mid-2006. As we saw in Chapter 4, the company, which holds 12 of the 15 Channel 3 licences, had pursued economies of scale in much the same way as the major regional newspaper publishers. Further 'savings' were achieved by persuading Ofcom to reduce the annual payments for the broadcasting franchises and also by Ofcom's relaxation of Channel 3's public service broadcasting requirements. Despite all this, ITV plc was marked down as a poor investment, given the wider context of multiplying commercial television channels, all fighting for advertising between themselves and with other media.

Although news was specifically left out of Ofcom's reduction of Channel 3 PSB commitments, how much resource is likely to be put into this expensive activity, despite its popularity and importance to the channels' 'brand'? As the stalled 'Tartan 10.30' project shows (see Chapter 6), from a business point of view the balance sheet is more pressing than public service. That said, in mid-2006, uniquely among the ITV1 regions, the Meridian (south of England) web site (www.itvlocal/tv) included video news clips relating to 12 towns and more substantial news and feature material for three (Brighton, Hastings and Bournemouth). Curiously, what appeared to be a low-key experiment in ultra-local television passed without public comment from the Newspaper Society, in contrast to its vigorous campaign (Newspaper Society 2006) against that put in place by the BBC (see Chapters 4 and 5). Yet the Meridian site offered free classified advertising: the challenge to regional newspapers could not be more direct.

The new advertising landscape is also a serious problem for **commercial radio** where, as we have seen, typically news programming is minimal and, in nearly all cases, selected to appeal to its target audience rather than to provide broadly based news of the locality.

Suddenly the combination of technical change and the opening up of the broadcasting market has pitched commercial broadcasters into the kind of ruthlessly competitive arena familiar to UK newspapers. In such an environment the potential profitability of all genres of content is critical. Regional news is a guaranteed net cost, yet the regulator's touchstone citizen/consumers demand it. Ofcom's solution to this conundrum has effectively been to unload the principal responsibility for this – and other socially important but financially disastrous activities – on to **the BBC**. As we saw in Chapter 6, this clash between profits and the wider public interest emerges most dramatically in media for the nations of the UK. So, too, do the contortions that Ofcom can get into about 'plurality'. Having acceded to a situation where the BBC could be the only 'voice' in some broadcast genres, for instance minority language provision, and despite its core principle of minimal market intervention, Ofcom seems dedicated to developing intricate quasi-market mechanisms to keep what is anyway 'a very nervy organization' (Born 2004) on edge. It is, in other words, preventing the logic of the market working itself out.

Loss of alternative voices and perspectives to the BBC's is undoubtedly a negative development but offset by the scale and scope of the corporation's news organization. As Chapter 4 indicated, radio is potentially one of the most effective of local media. It is cheap, flexible and can operate on a geographic basis which maps on to the lives of listeners. BBC local radio provides strong local news coverage because it can draw on its multimedia news infrastructure. It has though, with the interesting exception of Radio Cymru (see Chapter 6), tacitly settled for an older 'at home' audience able to give the necessary attention to speech radio. Now that it can be heard online and on demand, surely it is time to use the resources of the corporation to address a younger audience as well – not just as the future consumers so loved of commercial media, but as current citizens?

Of course, proposals like this typify the BBC's problem. It is a vast and complex organization, but so are its commitments. Not only the level, but the very existence of the licence fee is constantly contested by politicians and, especially, by rival media organizations. (The Newspaper Society campaign, mentioned earlier, is at least overt. Much of the sniping comes in the form of supposedly detached 'news' and comment in, for example, the *Daily Mail* and *The Times*.) The BBC is, therefore, under constant pressure to justify its activities and priorities. News of localities must compete with service to other types of 'community' in a multicultural, multi-faith society. Serving the 'nations and regions', whether in locality-specific programming, educational outreach work, or contemplating (again) the shifting of jobs away from London, is always in competition with the BBC's fundamental justification: that it serves and symbolizes the nation as a whole. All the signifiers of this status, from owning the rights to major sports events with mass appeal to appropriately extensive coverage of a state funeral, are enormously expensive.

The sheer size of the analogue television regions is a technical problem which will be solved by digitalization, although smaller regions imply greater expenditure as well as organizational change. In the medium term, however, the existing regions bring, as we saw in Chapter 3, consequences for the textualization of regional news. Keeping the audience engaged requires a lack of specificity which in turn privileges the subjective and descriptive over the analytical. A tendency towards a cosily consensual interpretive frame is then further reinforced by the reassuring narrative structures customarily employed when addressing the early evening family audience.

Another dilemma facing the BBC is its key role in advancing technology. The worldwide reputation of its web site is probably the most dramatic example, and is an important element in its provision of local news. 'Where I Live' operates at a scale similar to that of the corporation's local radio stations and is thus much more fine-grained than its terrestrial television bulletins, which are now re-broadcast on the web site, alongside local news in text and still photo format. These pages were also the platform for the 'ultra-local' experiment, also available on Freeview digital television – another initiative in which the BBC has played a leading role. The corporation has seized the technical opportunities but can it produce the content to match? Not all those in regional newspapers share their trade body's antagonism to this additional news service, predicting instead that the BBC will have to form alliances with local papers if their news provision is have more substance as well as more platforms. Visits to the ultra-local television sites during the experimental period suggested that while the geographic area of coverage was smaller, the choice of items combined the human interest style of the terrestrial bulletins with the tendency of the Where I Live pages to lean heavily on material from institutional sources.

Like all contemporary media, the BBC is soliciting audience input as a partial solution to the content problem: 'If you capture an unfolding event on camera or mobile phone . . . please send it to BBC News'. Unlike some of its rivals, the BBC credits such contributions, does not try to claim intellectual property rights and continues *'Please do not endanger yourself or others, take any risks or infringe any laws'* (www.bbc.co.uk > News > Have Your Say > Help US Make the News; original emphasis). For all news organizations this exponential development of the old-fashioned 'tip-off' is invaluable in the struggle to break news first and to acquire dramatic actuality, preferably exclusively. For the BBC, whose stature has undoubtedly encouraged members of the public to approach it first, there is the additional benefit of making its notoriously closed world a little more open to the public that pays for it.

Those at such 'unfolding events' do not just turn to national media. Many local people sent images of the Buncefield oil depot fire of December 2005 to the local paper, the *Hemel Hempstead Gazette* (Ward 2006).

'Citizen journalism', the blogosphere, community media: how should we interpret the potential of this sudden access of ordinary people to mass communications media? More specifically, could it provide the depth, detail and robust debate missing from all forms of local and regional news? Or is it a free source of exploitable content that will just encourage a picture-driven, human interest-dominated news frame, while undermining journalism employment?

Shock! New media – same old problems

Nobody likes the term 'citizen journalism'. Working journalists argue that it devalues their skills and does not provide any real benefit to citizens. The only gainers are the media big beasts: 'highway robbery' was the NUJ's view of the *Daily Telegraph*'s invitation to readers to 'snap and send' while expecting them to indemnify the paper against legal claims (*Press Gazette* 2 December 2005; see also Stabe 2006a). Nor, applying the same analysis but for different motives, do advocates of truly alternative or independent media. True 'native reporting' (Atton and Wickenden 2005: 349) dissolves the distinction between producer and consumer, enabling ordinary people to 'become reporters of their own experiences, struggles and lives'. New communications technologies have generated great excitement about their ability to do this, but the old problem remains: generating content *of value to the public at large*. On this basis most blogs simply do not count because 'Only occasionally does "me media" become "we media"', as a professional journalist quoted by Stabe (2006b) put it. 'The tools of the internet have been put to individual rather than collective use . . . the dialogue is little different from the chatter overheard in most public places'; 'the frequency with which only a handful of examples are trotted out tends to suggest the blogosphere's counter-hegemonic activities are novel because they are so rare' (Bolton 2006).

Alternative newspapers have an honourable history of allowing the community to speak for itself (see, for example, Harcup 2003) but even independent media, whether trying to represent a locality or a particular social movement, are not relaying reality unmediated. They, too, have to source and edit their content. As Atton and Wickenden (2005: 351, 353) point out, 'Low capital funding, poorly paid or voluntary staff and organisational pressures might all affect the ability to access a wide range of sources'. The outcome, they argue, is 'a hierarchy of credibility emerging which, whilst it might be considered an inversion of the dominant media model, maintains the status of its sources through a mechanism of legitimacy and credibility just as powerful as that of its mainstream counterparts'.

Nor are not-for-profit community media free of commercial pressures. In the UK community radio and television are expanding under Restricted Service Licences (RSLs) issued by Ofcom. (It should be noted that 'community' in this context can mean cultural, rather than local.) While they are required to be motivated by 'social good rather than profit' and usually rely on volunteer labour, they still consume substantial funds. For radio, the average annual cost is £100,000 (Smith 2006). Inevitably this means looking for sponsorship or advertising, as a visit to most of the radio and television sites linked to the Community Media Association (www.commedia.org/about-community-media/) quickly reveals. However altruistic the principles driving such media ventures, dependence on advertising is dependence on advertisers. The implications for the choice of news and the views expressed in the editorial matter can be little different from those for commercial media.

For the same reason what seemed to be the liberating effect of the 'publish then filter' (Stabe 2006a, quoting Bowman and Willis 2003) ethos of the Internet is being displaced by commercially-driven aggregators. Search engines are a wonderful facility, but how many users fully appreciate that some of the most used give 'premium placement in search lists in return for premium payments' (Bolton 2006)? This is not Habermas' 'ideal speech' producing social consensus; this is commodification.

One of the most celebrated aggregators is OhmyNews, the South Korean news site which sources 'the bulk of its material from its 42,000 citizen reporters' and is among those, like the Craigstlist free advertising site, 'wreaking terror in the boardrooms of traditional journalism companies' (Stabe and Reeves 2006). Yet its founder is quite clear: 'We are a news organisation: the facts are important; credibility is very important.' Even more tellingly, OhmyNews employs 60 reporters: 'staff journalists are responsible for editing and fact-checking stories, occasionally going to the scene of events and supplementing citizen reporters' first-hand accounts . . . do in-depth reporting . . .and *initiate much of the site's reporting on major social and political issues, largely to overcome problems of access* (Stabe and Reeves 2006; emphasis added). Moreover, the site is 'funded by advertisers interested in its millions of young readers'.

To reiterate: news is not a discrete and self-evident category of social reality, it is a process of selection, and this process of editing always embodies a point of view. There are no 'facts', only accounts. Gathering up and presenting these accounts always costs money, whether through an employment relationship or through the opportunity cost of a volunteer's time. Very few individuals or organizations have the resources to pursue the collection of information, background and explanation beyond their direct experience.

Essentially what mass access to communications media has done is to expose the question of the provenance of information to proper scrutiny: who says? Who is paying? Before, if not actively concealed, these were rendered mysterious by the complexity of the media production process and the veil of authority shielding institutional sources. Viewed optimistically this must be at the heart of the 'discursive formation of opinion and will' argued by Habermas (for instance 1992: 446) to be the precondition of true deliberative democracy.

Do traditional local media forms and conventional journalism have any useful place in this supposed new world where eager participation and profound scepticism meet? One compelling reason why they must is that new media technologies are not socially inclusive, even in the relatively wealthy UK. We saw in Chapter 6 that access to broadband is least likely in those regions which need it most. Mobile phones capable of processing still or moving images are expensive. Above all, the majority of these new media products are jostling for youngish, securely employed consumers. For all their limitations, at least regional newspapers have a commercial reason to attempt to address everyone, and public service broadcasting requires radio and television, however imperfectly, to do the same.

Commentators within news media are starting to argue that if the industry is to continue to claim the right to edit reality for the rest of us, it must build trust. Here two groups among the traditional media are at an advantage. Regional newspapers and television, especially the BBC, always come near the top of the list when the public is surveyed (*Press Gazette* 24

September 2004, 21 January 2005, 5 May 2006.). This is not a haphazard outcome. As we saw in Chapter 7, a degree of access by the audience is a practical reality in regional newspapers – even big city dailies – and a deliberate policy on the part of local radio. Such local media cannot hide behind the debased interpretation of 'objectivity' in news work: that it is the morally neutral collecting and processing of 'facts'. Recognizing that what is at stake is rival accounts necessitates a reasonable even-handedness in sourcing and reporting news.

Put another way this is the 'impartiality' required of all UK broadcasters' news output. For these more remote organizations, the regulatory framework of public service broadcasting represents the public interest where the public as individuals cannot stamp into reception and demand to talk to the editor. For how long commercially funded broadcasters will have to deliver this trustworthy service is an interesting question.

The great advantage of publicly funded media is that we can demand that they earn our trust. When the BBC's news-gathering practices are questioned, its response is semi-public self-scrutiny – too much and too readily, one might argue – not a disingenuous elision of the public interest with what interests the public. For all its imperfections, the unique relationship between the BBC and the British public is a demonstration that trust is indeed the key to containing the provenance problem. We should cherish the right to pay for it and hope that commercial regional media, especially newspapers, continue to see the advantage of working practices which generate the same kind of social capital.

References

Unless another date of visit is indicated, web addressed **included in the text** were correct as at 31 August 2006. Web addressed **listed in the references** were correct as at 1 December 2006.

Ackerman, S. (2006) Why a local station had to hand back its licence, *The Guardian*, 9 October.

Adie, K. (2003) *The Kindness of Strangers*. London: Hodder Headline.

Ainley, B. (1998) *Black Journalists, White Media*. Stoke-on-Trent: Trentham Books.

Aldridge, M. (1998) The tentative hell-raisers: identity and mythology in contemporary UK press journalism, *Media, Culture & Society*, 20(1): 109–28.

Aldridge, M. (2001a) Confessional culture, masculinity and emotional work, *Journalism: Theory, Practice and Criticism*, 2(1): 91–108.

Aldridge, M. (2001b) 'Lost expectations? Women journalists and the fall-out from the "Toronto Newspaper War"', *Media, Culture and Society*, 23(5): 607–24.

Aldridge, M. (2003) The ties that divide: regional press campaigns, community and populism, *Media, Culture & Society*, 25(4): 491–509.

Aldridge, M. (2004) Professionalism and the public interest: the uninspiring story of regulating the UK press, *Knowledge, Work and Society/Savoir, Travail et Société*, 2(3): 39–56.

Aldridge, M. and Dingwall, R. (2003) Teleology on television? Implicit models of evolution in broadcast wildlife and nature programmes, *European Journal of Communication*, 18(4): 435–53.

Aldridge, M. and Evetts, J. (2003) Rethinking the concept of professionalism: the case of journalism, *British Journal of Sociology*, 54(4): 547–64.

Anderson, B. ([1983] 1991) *Imagined Communities: Reflections on the Origins and Spread of Nationalism*. London: Verso.

Andrews, L. (2005) Wales and the UK's communications legislation 2002–3, *Cyfrwng*, 2: 32–48.

Atkinson, R. and Kintrea, K. (2004) 'Opportunities and despair, it's all in there'. Practitioner experiences and explanations of area effects and life chances, *Sociology*, 38(3): 437–55.

Atton, C. and Wickenden, E. (2005) Sourcing routines and representation in alternative journalism: a case study approach, *Journalism Studies*, 6(3): 347–59.

Azeez, W. (2003) Regional TV news? Eat my shorts, *Press Gazette*, 19 September.

Azeez, W. (2004) 'I want to liberate journalists not tie them down', *Press Gazette*, 23 January.

Barlow, D.M., Mitchell, P. and O'Malley, T. (2005) *The Media in Wales: Voices of a Small Nation*. Cardiff: University of Wales Press.

Barnett, S., Seymour, E. and Gaber, I. (2000) *From Callaghan to Kosovo: Trends in British Television News 1975–1999*. Harrow: University of Westminster.

Barter, M. (2005) It's money that matters, *Campaign for Press and Broadcasting Freedom*, http://keywords.dsvr.co.uk/freepress/body.phtml?category=&id=1099 (15 August).

BBC (2004a) *The BBC's Audiences. Submission to the Independent Panel on Charter Review*, http://bbc.co.uk > Future of the BBC > Links and Documents

BBC (2004b) *The BBC's Role in Representing the Nations and Regions. Submission to the Independent Panel on Charter Review*, http://bbc.co.uk > Future of the BBC > Links and Documents

BBC (2004c) *Building Public Value; Renewing the BBC for a Digital World*, http://bbc.co.uk > Future of the BBC > Links and Documents

Billig, M. (1995) *Banal Nationalism*. London: Sage.

Birks, J. (2006) 'Voice of the people'. How the local and regional press campaign on public policy. Paper delivered to the British Sociology Association Annual Conference, Harrogate, April.

Blackhurst, R. (2005) The freeloading generation, *British Journalism Review*, 16(3): 53–9.

Boden, S. (2003) People's champion, *Press Gazette*, 9 May.

Bolton, T. (2006) News on the net: a critical analysis of the potential of online alternative journalism to challenge the dominance of mainstream news media, *Scan*, 3(1), http://scan.net.au/scan/journal/

Born, G. (2004) *Uncertain Vision: Birt, Dyke and the Reinvention of the BBC*. London: Secker and Warburg.

Bourke, D. (2003) The charge of the frees, *Press Gazette*, 28 February.

Bowman, S. and Willis, C. (2003) We media. How audiences are shaping the future of news and information, www.hypergene.net/wemedia/weblog.php

Bradbury, D. (2006) Rural users lack aerial view, *The Guardian*, 20 July.

Braithwaite, B. (1995) *Women's Magazines; The First Three Hundred Years*. London: Peter Owen.

Briggs, A. (1995) *The History of Broadcasting in the United Kingdom Vol. 5*. Oxford: Oxford University Press.

Brown, M. (2005) Why Ofcom's on the right wavelength, *The Guardian*, 3 January.

Browne, J. (2004) Resolving gender pay inequality? Rationales, enforcement and policy, *Journal of Social Policy*, 33(4): 553–71.

Brunsdon, C. and Morley, D. (1978) *Everyday Television: 'Nationwide'*. London: British Film Institute.

Bryant, C.G.A. (2006) *The Nations of Britain*. Oxford: Oxford University Press.

Buerk, M. (2004) *The Road Taken*. London: Hutchinson.

Carr-Saunders, A.M and Wilson, P.A. (1933) *The Professions*. Oxford: Clarendon Press.

Carter, M. (2003) *Independent Radio: The First 30 Years*. London: The Radio Authority. Also available at www.ofcom.org.uk > Legacy Regulators

Chamberlain, P. and Cookson, R. (2006) An unfair fight, *The Guardian*, 12 March.

Charon, J.-M. (2003) *Les médias en France*. Paris: Éditions la Découverte.

Chinn, C. and Dyson, S. (2000) *We Ain't Going Away! The Struggle for Longbridge*. Studley: Brewin Books.

Chippindale, P. and Horrie, C. (1990) *Stick It Up Your Punter: The Rise and Fall of The Sun*. London: Hutchinson.

Christian, H. (1980) Journalists' occupational ideology and press commercialisation, in H. Christian (ed.), *The Sociology of Journalism and the Press*, Sociological Review Monograph 29. Keele: University of Keele.

Clother, H. (2001) Law and disorder: covering the courts, in R. Keeble (ed.). *The Newspapers Handbook*, 3rd edn. London: Routledge.

Cm 6075 (2003) *Broadcasting* (Amendment to 1996 Charter). London: Department of Culture, Media and Sport. Also available at http://bbc.co.uk/info/policies/charter/pdf/agreement_amend.pdf

Cm 6763 (2006) *A Public Service for All: the BBC in the Digital Age* (White Paper on the BBC). London: Department for Culture, Media and Sport. Also available at www.bbccharterreview.org.uk/have_your_say/white_paper/bbc_whitepaper_march06.pdf

Cmd. 7700 (1949) *Royal Commission on the Press 1947–49 – Report*. London: HMSO.

Cmnd 1753 (1962) *Report of the Committee on Broadcasting 1960* (Pilkington Committee). London: HMSO.

Cmnd 9824 (1986) *Report of the Committee on Financing the BBC* (Peacock Report). London: HMSO. Extracted in B. Franklin (ed.) (2001) *British Television Policy: A Reader*. London: Routledge.

Cole, P. (2006a) Mixed communities: mixed newsrooms, in E. Pool and J.E. Richardson (eds), *Muslims and the News Media*. London: I.B. Tauris.

Cole, P. (2006b) Educating and training local journalists, in B. Franklin (ed.), *Local Journalism and Local Media: Making the Local News*. London: Routledge.

Communications Act (2003) www.opsi.gov.uk/acts/acts2003/20030021.htm

Competition Commission (2002) *Johnston Press plc and Trinity Mirror plc: A Report on the Proposed Merger*, www.competition-commission.org.uk/rep_pub/reports/2002/463johnston

Cottle, S. (1993) *TV News, Urban Conflict and the Inner City*. Leicester: Leicester University Press/Pinter.

Cox, W. and Morgan, D. (1973) *City Politics and the Press: Journalists and the Governing of Merseyside*. Cambridge: Cambridge University Press.

Crisell, A. (1997) *An Introductory History of British Broadcasting*. London: Routledge.

Crisell, A. (1998) Local radio: attuned to the times or filling time with tunes? in B. Franklin and D. Murphy (eds), *Making the Local News: Local Journalism in Context*. London: Routledge.

Crisell, A. and Starkey, G. (2006) News on local radio, in B. Franklin (ed.), *Local Journalism and Local Media: Making the Local News*. London: Routledge.

Cross, S. and Lockyer, S. (2006) Dynamics of partisan journalism: journalist-source relationships in the context of a local newspaper's anti-paedophile housing agenda, *Journalism Studies*, 7(2): 274–91.

Crow, G. (2002) Community studies: fifty years of theorization, *Sociological Research Online*, www.socresonline.org.uk/7/3/crow.html

Crow, G., Allan, G. and Summers, M. (2001) Changing perspectives on the insider/outsider distinction in community sociology, *Community, Work and Family*, 4(1): 29–48.

Crow, G., Allan, G. and Summers, M. (2002) Neither busybodies nor nobodies: managing proximity and distance in neighbourly relations, *Sociology*, 36(1): 127–45.

Crummy, C. (2006) The calm after the storm? *Press Gazette*, 12 May.

Culture, Media and Sport Committee (2003) *Privacy and Media Intrusion, Vol. 1 – Report HC458-1*, www.publications.parliament.uk/pa/cm200203/cmselect/cmcumeds/458/458.pdf

Curran, J. (2002) *Media and Power*. London: Routledge.

Curran, J. and Seaton, J. (2003) *Power Without Responsibility; The Press, Broadcasting and New Media in Britain* 6th edn. London: Routledge.

Dahlgren, P. (2000) Media, citizenship and civic culture, in J. Curran and M. Gurevitch (eds), *Mass Media and Society* 3rd edn. London: Arnold.

Darnton, R. (1975) 'Making news and telling stories', *Daedalus*, Spring: 175–93.

Davies, I. (2004) Regional papers want the BBC to get its tanks off their lawn, *The Guardian*, 10 May.

Davies, J. (1994) *Broadcasting and the BBC in Wales*. Cardiff: University of Wales Press.

Day, G. and Murdoch, J. (1993) Locality and community: coming to terms with place, *The Sociological Review*, 38: 82–110.

Dayan, D. and Katz, E. (1992) *Media Events: The Live Broadcasting of History*. Cambridge MA: Harvard University Press.

Delano, A. and Henningham, J. (1995) *The News Breed: A Report on British Journalists in the 1990s*. London: London Institute.

Department of Culture, Media and Sport (DCMS) (2004) *Independent Review of BBC Online* (Graf Report), http://culture.gov.uk/NR/rdonlyres/45F9953F-CE61-4325-BEA6-400DF9722494/0BBC_Online_Review.pdf

Department of Culture, Media and Sport (DCMS) (2005a) *Coverage of Sport on Television*, www.culture.gov.uk/NR/rdonlyres/E4039BD6-FF27-49F2-9ECF-907518C4BDDF/0/SportLeafletrevmarch05.pdf

Department of Culture, Media and Sport (DCMS) (2005b) *Review of the BBC's Royal Charter; A Strong BBC, Independent of Government* (Green Paper on the BBC), www.bbccharterreview.org.uk/have_your_say/green_paper/bbc_cr_greenpaper.pdf

Department of Culture, Media and Sport (DCMS) (2006) Appointment of new Sianel Pedwar Cymru (S4C) Chair, www.culture.gov.uk > Press notices > Archive 2006 > 24 March

Department of Trade and Industry (DTI) (2004) *Guidance Document, May 2004: Enterprise Act 2002: Public Interest Intervention in Media Mergers*, www.dti.gov.uk/ccp/topics2/guide/ukdmediaguide.pdf

Devine, F., Britton, N.J., Mellor, R. and Halfpenny, P. (2003) Mobility and the middle classes: a case study of Manchester and the North West, *International Journal of Urban and Regional Research*, 27(3): 495–509.

Donovan, P. (2004) Perpetuating a myth, *Press Gazette*, 2 April.

Doyle, G. (2002) *Understanding Media Economics*. London: Sage.

Engel, M. (1996) *Tickle the Public; One Hundred Years of the Popular Press*. London: Victor Gollancz.

Ferguson, M. (1994) Television, identity and diversity in the United States and Europe, in M. Aldridge, and N. Hewitt (eds), *Controlling Broadcasting: Access Policy in Britain and North America*. Manchester: Manchester University Press.

Fleming, C. (2002) *The Radio Handbook*, (2nd edn). London: Routledge.

Francis, P. (2001) Secrecy creeps back in, *Press Gazette*, 9 February.

Francis, J. (2003) White culture, black mark, *British Journalism Review*, 14(3): 67–73.

Franklin, B. (ed.) (2001) *British Television Policy: A Reader*. London: Routledge.

Franklin, B. (2006) A right free for all! Competition, soundbite journalism and the local free press, in B. Franklin (ed.), *Local Journalism and Local Media: Making the Local News*. London: Routledge.

Fraser, N. (1992) Rethinking the public sphere: a contribution to the critique of actually existing democracy, in C. Calhoun (ed.), *Habermas and the Public Sphere*. Boston, MA: MIT Press.

Friedland, L.A. (2001) Communication, community and democracy; toward a theory of the communicatively integrated community, *Communication Research*, 28(4): 358–91.

Frost, C. (2006) Ethics for local journalism, in B. Franklin (ed.), *Local Journalism and Local Media: Making the Local News*. London: Routledge.

Fuller, E. (1999) Portrait of a local weekly, *British Journalism Review*, 10(3): 34–40.

Future Foundation (2000) *The Renaissance of Regional Nations; Local and Regional Identity in a Global World*. London: The Newspaper Society.

Future Foundation (2003) *My UK – Redefining Regions: Exploring Regional and Local Identity*. London: The Newspaper Society.

Gall, G. (2002) The return of the National Union of Journalists to the provincial newspaper industry in Britain?, *Media, Culture & Society*, 24(5): 673–92.

Gall, G. (2004) State of the union, *British Journalism Review*, 15(3): 34–9.

Galtung, J. and Ruge M. (1965) The structure of foreign news: the presentation of the Congo, Cuba and Cyprus in four foreign newspapers, *International Journal of Peace Research*, 1: 64–90.

Garnham, N. ([1986] 1990) The media and the public sphere, in N. Garnham, *Capitalism and Communication; Global Culture and the Economics of Information*. London: Sage.

Gibson, O. and Day, J. (2006) Radio gaga, *The Guardian*, 12 June.

Graham, V. (2003) The Borrell brief, *Press Gazette*, 24 January.

Gransby, A. (2002) Biggest? Yes. Best? No way, *Press Gazette*, 15 November.

Greenslade, R. (2004a) The Standard bearer, *The Guardian*, 7 June.

Greenslade, R. (2004b) Have the regional takeovers run out of steam?, *The Guardian*, 29 November.

Greenslade, R. (2005a) Forget the free CDs and expect a knock at your door, *The Guardian*, 16 May.

Greenslade, R. (2005b) Scapegoat for every ill in society, *The Guardian*, 30 May.

Griffee, A. (2005) BBC – we are not an 'ultra local' threat to newspapers, *Press Gazette*, 23 September.

Gripsrud, J. (1992) The aesthetics and politics of melodrama, in J. Dahlgren and C. Sparks (eds), *Journalism and Popular Culture*, London: Sage.

Grundy, E., Murphy, M. and Sheldon, N. (1999) Looking beyond the household: intergenerational perspectives on living kin contacts in Great

Britain, in *Population Trends 97 Autumn*. London: Office for National Statistics.

Habermas, J. ([1962] 1989) *The Structural Transformation of the Public Sphere*. Cambridge: Polity.

Habermas, J. ([1981] 1986) *The Theory of Communicative Action Vol. 1 – Reason and the Rationalization of Society*. Cambridge: Polity.

Habermas, J. ([1981] 1987) *The Theory of Communicative Action Vol. 2 – Lifeworld and System: A Critique of Functionalist Reason*. Cambridge, Polity Press.

Habermas, J. (1992) Further reflections on the public sphere, in C. Calhoun (ed.), *Habermas and the Public Sphere*. Boston, MA: MIT Press.

Habermas, J. ([1992] 1996) *Between Facts and Norms: Contributions to a Discourse Theory of Law and Democracy*. Cambridge MA: MIT Press.

Hall, S., Critcher, C., Jefferson, T., Clarke, J. and Roberts, B. (1978) *Policing the Crisis: Mugging, the State and Law and Order*. London: Macmillan.

Hannan, P. (1999) *The Welsh Illusion*. Bridgend: Seren.

Harcup, T. (2003) 'The unspoken – said', *Journalism*, 4(3): 356–76.

Hargreaves, I. and Thomas, J. (2002) *New News, Old News*. London: Broadcasting Standards Commission/Independent Television Commission. (Downloadable from http://www.ofcom.org.uk/static/archive/bsc/pdfs/research/news.pdf)

Harris, C.C. (1987) *Redundancy and Recession in South Wales*. Oxford: Basil Blackwell.

Harris, Z. (2003) Mad Cows and Journalists: How Media Production Practices Influence Risk Communication in News Reports of Food Scares. Unpublished PhD thesis, University of Nottingham.

Harrison, J. (2000) *Terrestrial Television News in Britain*. Manchester: Manchester University Press.

Harvey, S. and Robins, K. (1994) Voices and places: the BBC and regional policy, *The Political Quarterly*, 65(1): 39–54.

Hastilow, N. (2000) As easy as ABC, *Press Gazette*, 29 September.

Hastings, A. (2003) Where will the axe fall?, *Press Gazette*, 12 September.

Hastings, A. (2004a) Don't devalue the sub's art, *Press Gazette*, 13 February.

Hastings, A. (2004b) The ex-editors mystery, *Press Gazette*, 8 October.

Haworth, J. (2000) Women in radio news: making a difference? in C. Mitchell (ed.), *Women and Radio: Airing Differences*. London: Routledge.

Herman, E.S. and McChesney, R.W. (1997) *The Global Media; The New Missionaries of Global Capitalism*. London: Cassell.

Higgins, M. (2006) Substantiating a political public sphere in the Scottish press, *Journalism*, 7(1): 25–44.

Hobsbawm, E. (1983) 'Introduction: inventing traditions', in E. Hobsbawm and T. Ranger (eds), *The Invention of Tradition*. Cambridge: Cambridge University Press.

Jackson, I. (1971) *The Provincial Press and the Community*. Manchester: Manchester University Press.

Jones, B.A. (1981) *The Story of Halfords*. Privately published.

Journalism Training Forum (2002) *Journalists at Work: Their Views on Training, Recruitment and Conditions*. London: Publishing NTO/Skillset.

Keane, J. (1998) *Civil Society – Old Images, New Visions*. Cambridge: Polity Press.

Kitzinger, J. (1999) The ultimate 'neighbour from hell?' in B. Franklin (ed.), *Social Policy, the Media and Misrepresentation*. London: Routledge.

Lagan, S. (2004) County's free kick, *Press Gazette*, 30 July.

Lagan, S. (2005a) Editors have regions to be cheerful, *Press Gazette*, 20 May.

Lagan, S. (2005b) Ultra-local TV puts papers in the line of fire, *Press Gazette*, 9 September.

Langer, J. (1998) *Tabloid Television; Popular Journalism and the 'Other News'*. London: Routledge.

Law, A. (2001) Near and far: banal national identity and the press in Scotland, *Media, Culture & Society*, 23(3): 299–317.

Lewis, P.M. and Booth, J. (1989) *The Invisible Medium; Public, Commercial and Community Radio*. Basingstoke: Macmillan.

Lowe, M. (2005) Confessions of a former editor, *Press Gazette*, 29 July.

MacWhirter, I. (2006) Scots on the rocks, *The Guardian*, 25 September.

Maguire, C. (2004) How to fight a winning battle, *Press Gazette*, 16 April.

Marcuse, P. (2002) Depoliticizing globalization: from neo-Marxism to the network society of Manuel Castells, in J. Eade and C. Mele (eds), *Understanding the City*. Oxford: Blackwell.

Marks, N. (1997a) Inside *Evening Chronicle*, Newcastle, *Press Gazette*, 9 May.

Marks, N. (1997b) Two hundred and fifty not out, *Press Gazette* 5 September.

Marks, N. (1997c) The home boy done good, *Press Gazette*, 17 October.

Marr, A. (2004) *My Trade*. London: Macmillan.

McCrone, D. (1999) *The Sociology of Nationalism: Tomorrow's Ancestors*. London: Routledge.

McGuigan, J. (2005) The cultural public sphere, *European Journal of Cultural Studies*, 8(4): 427–43.

McLachlan, S. and Golding, P. (1998) Tabloidization in the British press: a quantitative investigation into changes in British newspapers 1952–1997, in C. Sparks and J. Tulloch (eds), *Tabloid Tales: Global Debates Over Media Standards*. Lanham, Maryland: Rowman and Littlefield.

McLaughlin, G. (2006) Profits, politics and paramilitaries: the local news media, in Northern Ireland, in B. Franklin (ed.), *Local Journalism and Local Media: Making the Local News*. London: Routledge.

McLaughlin, L. (2004) Feminism and the political economy of transnational public space, in N. Crossley and J. M. Roberts (eds), *After Habermas*. Oxford: Blackwell.

McLaughlin, P. (2006) 'ITV would do well to listen to the concerns of staff', *Press Gazette*, 28 April.

McLuhan, M. (1962) *The Gutenberg Galaxy: the Making of Typographic Man*. Toronto: Toronto University Press.

McManus, J. (1994) *Market-driven Journalism: Let the Public Beware*. Thousand Oaks, CA: Sage.

McNair, B. (2000) *Journalism and Democracy; An Evaluation of the Political Public Sphere*. London: Routledge.

McNair, B. (2006) News from a small country: the media in Scotland, in B. Franklin (ed.), *Local Journalism and Local Media: Making the Local News*. London: Routledge.

Media Trust/Society of Editors (2005) *Reporting Diversity: How Journalists Can Contribute to Community Cohesion*. London: Media Trust/Society of Editors.

Melody, W.H. (1996) Communication policy in the global information economy: whither the public interest?, in M. Ferguson (ed.), *Public Communication; The New Imperatives*. London: Sage.

Mintel (2005) *Market Research Report – Regional Newspapers UK*, http://reports.mintel.com >Reports > By Category > Media > Regional

Morgan, J. (2001) So, you're not local?, *Press Gazette*, 7 December.

Morgan, P. (2005) *The Insider*. London: Ebury Press.

Morley, D. (1992) *Television Audiences and Cultural Studies*. London: Routledge.

Murphy, D. (1976) *The Silent Watchdog: the Press in Local Politics*. London: Constable.

National Assembly for Wales (2006) Culture, Welsh Language and Sport Committee – CWLS (2) 04-06 (Paper 3) Annex, *Newspapers in Wales*, wales.gov.ukkeypubassemcultwelsport/index.htm > Agendas, Papers and Transcripts, March

National Council for the Training of Journalists (NCTJ) (2005) *Annual Report*. Harlow: Essex: NCTJ.

New Towns Committee (1946) *Final Report* (Cmnd 6876). London: HMSO.

Newspaper Society (2004) *Consumer's Choice V: The Pocket Book*. London: The Newspaper Society.

Newspaper Society (2005a) News release 18 July – Regional press warns BBC: stay off our patch, www.newspapersoc.org.uk > News Releases

Newspaper Society (2005b) News release 1 September – Regionals lead way in transparent daily reporting and focus on base sale, www.newspapersoc.org.uk > News Releases

Newspaper Society (2005c) News release 1 September – Regional press broadens reach through innovative use of media, www.newspapersoc.org.uk > News Releases

Newspaper Society (2006) News release 25 May – National coverage for NS campaign against BBC ultra local services, www.newspapersoc.org.uk > News Releases

Nicoll, R. (2005) Blood on the tartan carpet, *The Guardian*, 21 November.

Ofcom (2004a) *Reshaping Television for the UK's Nations, Regions and Localities*, www.ofcom.org.uk/consult/condocs/psb2/psb2/nations/?a=87101

Ofcom (2004b) *Proposed Merger of Capital Radio plc and GWR Group plc: Ofcom's Statutory Assessments*, www.ofcom.org.uk/radio/radio-archive/213987/capgwr.pdf

Ofcom (2005a) *Ofcom Review of Public Service Television Broadcasting; Phase 3 Competition for Quality* (final report), www.ofcom.org.uk/ consult/cndocs/psb3/

Ofcom (2005b) Ofcom accepts commercial public broadcasters' proposals on Tier 3 obligations (news release), www.ofcom.org.uk/media/news/2005/02/nr_20050225

Ofcom (2005c) *Radio – Preparing for the Future. Appendix A: Results of Audience Research*, www.ofcom.org.uk/consult/condocs/radio_reviewp2/appendix_a.pdf

Ofcom (2005d) *Radio – Preparing for the Future. Phase 2: Implementing the Framework*, www.ofcom.org.uk/consult/condocs/radio_reviewp2/p2.pdf

Ofcom (2005e) *Equal Opportunities: a Toolkit for Broadcasters*, www.ofcom.org.uk/tv/ifi/guidance/eo-toolkit/eo-toolkit-web.pdf

Ofcom (2005f) *Statement on Programming for the Nations and Regions*, www.ofcom.org.uk/consult/condocs/psb3/statement/#content

Ofcom (2005g) *Views in the Nations: A Summary of the Qualitative and Quantitative Audience Research Carried out for Phase 3 of the PSB Review*, www.ofcom.org.uk/consult/condocs/psb3/views_in_the_nations.pdf

Ofcom (2006) *The Communications Market: Nations and Regions*, www.ofcom.org.uk/research/cm/nations/nations_regions/nations_regions.pdf

Officer, L.H. (2001) *Comparing the Purchasing Power of Money in Great Britain from any Year from 1264 to the Present*, www.eh.net/hmit/ppoweruk/

OFT (Office of Fair Trading) (2006) *Associated Newspapers Limited*, www.oft.gov.uk/Business/Competition+Act/Decisions/ANL.htm

Pahl, R. (1984) *Divisions of Labour*. Oxford: Basil Blackwell.

Paterson, R. (2001) Work histories in television, *Media, Culture & Society*, 23(4): 495: 520.

'Pecke, S.' (2004) Local heroes, *British Journalism Review*, 15(2): 26–30.

Pike, C. (2006) A radio station with a passion for news, news and more news, *Press Gazette*, 23 March.

Pinker, R. (2006) Regulating the local press, in B. Franklin (ed.), *Local Journalism and Local Media: Making the Local News*. London: Routledge.

Plunkett, J. (2004) Mixing it with the big boys, *The Guardian*, 5 April.

Ponsford, D. (2003) Winning the weekly war, *Press Gazette*, 18 July.

Ponsford, D. (2004a) Global paper promotes a free for all, *Press Gazette*, 12 March.

Ponsford, D. (2004b) Nationals race to re-press, *Press Gazette*, 10 December.

Powell, R. (2005) Ultra-local: BBC aims to really target TV audiences, *Press Gazette*, 18 February.

Reeves, I. (2000) Few are chosen, *Press Gazette*, 7 July.

Reeves, I. and Blyth, J. (1999) Back over here, *Press Gazette*, 2 July.

Richardson, I. (2000) Women's hour, *Press Gazette*, 13 October.

Richardson, J. (2007) *Analysing Newspapers: an Approach from Critical Discourse Analysis*. Basingstoke, Hants: Palgrave Macmillan.

Robson, W. (1935) The BBC as an institution, *The Political Quarterly*, 6(4): 468–88.

Robinson, P. (2005) Why a regional FM licence has caused such big waves, *The Guardian*, 19 September.

Rosie, M., MacInnes, J., Petersoo, P., Condor, S. and Kennedy, J. (2004) Nation speaking unto nation? Newspapers and national identity in the devolved UK, *The Sociological Review*, 52(4): 437–58.

Royal Commission on the Press (1947) *Memoranda of Evidence 3*. London: HMSO.

Sampson, A. (1996) The crisis at the heart of our media, *British Journalism Review*, 7(3): 43–51.

Sancho, J. (2002) *Pride of Place: What Viewers Want from Regional Television*. London: Broadcasting Standards Commission/Independent Television Commission. Available at www.ofcom.org.uk/static/archive/bsc/pdfs/research/pride.pdf

Sarler, C. (2005) Mix the ladies with the tramps, *Press Gazette*, 12 August.

Saunders, P. (1980) *Urban Politics: A Sociological Interpretation*. Harmondsworth: Penguin Books.

Shaw, C. (2005) Local news is a source of profit for ITV, not subsidy, *Press Gazette*, 15 July.

Silver, J. (2005a) Exploitation is wider than ever, *The Guardian*, 11 April.

Silver, J. (2005b) Pressed for cash, *The Guardian*, 10 October.

Slattery, J. (2000) Frankly speaking, *Press Gazette*, 11 February.

Slattery, J. (2002) 'Being the best is what counts', *Press Gazette*, 31 May.

Slattery, J. (2005) 'Don't mention profits in front of the Colonel', *Press Gazette*, 30 September.

Smith, L. (2006) Community challenge to commercial radio, *The Guardian*, 11 April.

Society of Editors (2004) *Diversity in the Newsroom: Employment of Minority Ethnic Journalists in Newspapers*. Cambridge: Society of Editors. Also available at www.societyofeditors.co.uk

Society of Editors (2005) *Reporting Diversity: How journalists can contribute to community cohesion*. London: The Media Trust. Also available at www.societyofeditors.co.uk

Stabe, M. (2006a) 'Citizen journalism' – it's still a case of them and us, *Press Gazette*, 12 May.

Stabe, M. (2006b) The four critiques of 'citizen journalism', *Press Gazette*, 9 June.

Stabe, M. and Reeves, I. (2006) Saviours or saboteurs?, *Press Gazette*, 2 June.

Stacey, M. (1969) The myth of community studies, *British Journal of Sociology*, 20(2): 134–47.

Stott, R. (2002) *Dogs and Lampposts*. London: Metro.

Sutton Trust (2006) *The Educational Background of Leading Journalists*. London: Sutton Trust. Also available at www.suttontrust.com/reports/Journalists-backgrounds-final-report.pdf

Tacchi, J. (2001) Who listens to radio. The role of industrial audience research, in M. Bromley (ed.), *No News is Bad News: Radio, Television and the Public*. Harlow: Pearson Education.

Temple, M. (2005) Carry on campaigning: the case of 'dumbing down' in the fight against local electoral apathy, *Local Government Studies*, 31(4): 415–31.

Thomas, J. (2006a) The Regional and Local Media in Wales, National Assembly for Wales Culture, Welsh Language and Sport Committee – CWLS (2) 03-06 (Paper 3), http://wales.gov.uk/keypubassemcultwelsport/content/tor-e.htm > Submissions to Committee

Thomas, J. (2006b) A note on Scottish newspapers and update to the Welsh newspaper market, unpublished supplement to J. Thomas (2006a).

Thomas, J. (2006c) The regional and local media in Wales, in B. Franklin (ed.), *Local Journalism and Local Media: Making the Local News*. London: Routledge.

Thomas, J. and Lewis, J. (2006) Coming out of a mid-life crisis? The past, present and future audiences for Welsh language broadcasting, *Cyfrwng*, 3: 7–40.

Thomas, L. (2006) Streets of London paved with frees, *Press Gazette*, 8 August.

Thompson, J.B. (1995) *The Media and Modernity. A Social Theory of the Media*. Cambridge: Polity.

Tomlin, J. (2004a) Regional champion, *Press Gazette*, 14 April.

Tomlin, J. (2004b) Brand new thinking, *Press Gazette*, 17 September.

Tunstall, J. (1971) *Journalists at Work*. London: Constable.

Tunstall, J. (1996) *Newspaper Power: The New National Press in Britain*. Oxford: Clarendon Press.

Turner, J. (2006) Powerful information. Reporting national and local government, in R. Keeble (ed.), *The Newspapers Handbook*, 4th edn. London: Routledge.

Upshon, L. (2006) The real threat that should worry journalists at ITV, *Press Gazette*, 21 April.

Urry, J. (1990) Conclusion: places and policies, in M. Harloe, C. Pickvance and J. Urry (eds), *Place, Policy and Politics*. London: Unwin Hyman.

Ursell, G. (2003) Creating value and valuing creation in contemporary UK television: or 'dumbing down' the workforce, *Journalism Studies*, 4(1): 31–46.

Vipond, M. (1989) *The Mass Media in Canada*. Toronto: James Lorimer.

Ward, M. (2006) Finding a role in the realm of the bloggers, *Press Gazette*, 24 March.

Welsh, T., Greenwood, W. and Banks, D. (2005) *McNae's Essential Law for Journalists* 18th edn. Oxford: Oxford University Press.

Wernick, A. (1991) *Promotional Culture*. London: Sage.

White, G. (2006) Life at the bottom, *Broadcast*, 3 March.

Williams, G.A. (1991) *When Was Wales? A History of the Welsh*. London: Penguin.

Williams, K. (1995) *The Western Mail's* Wales, *Planet: The Welsh Internationalist* 113: 6–10.

Williams, K. (2003) What's happening at *The Western Mail?*, *Planet: The Welsh Internationalist*, 157: 32–6.

Index